SAMUEL JOHNSON

A Layman's Religion

PORTRAIT OF JOHNSON BY JAMES BARRY
By permission of the National Portrait Gallery, London

SAMUEL JOHNSON

A Layman's Religion

Maurice J. Quinlan

The University of Wisconsin Press
MADISON, 1964

820.81
J6938

FV

ACKNOWLEDGMENTS

In producing this book, I wish to acknowledge the help I have received from various scholars, though merely to mention their names is an inadequate token of my gratitude for their interest and kindness. Professor Joseph P. Maguire has contributed by supplying translations of several of Johnson's Latin poems. Dr. L. F. Powell and Mr. J. D. Fleeman have directed me to sources I might otherwise have missed. Several others have read my manuscript, either in whole or in part, and have given me the benefit of their timely advice and perceptive criticism. They are Mr. John Hardy, Professors Jean Hagstrum, James Gray, William K. Wimsatt, Jr., and, most notably, James L. Clifford and Edward L. Hirsh.

For assistance that enabled me to study in England I am indebted to a Faculty Fellowship awarded by Boston College and to a grant from the Penrose Fund of the American Philosophical Society.

M.J.Q.

Chestnut Hill, Massachusetts
June, 1963

CONTENTS

INTRODUCTION

S amuel Johnson once wrote, "The heart cannot be completely known; but the nearest approach which can be made is by opportunities of examining the thoughts when they operate in secret, without the influence of auditors and beholders."[1] This statement is pertinent to a study of Johnson's religion. We can discover much about the nature of his beliefs, especially from his private prayers and meditations, but for the most part we see only the outward reflections of his inner spiritual life. To write definitively about his religion, therefore, would appear to be impossible. My purpose is a more modest one. His biographers have emphasized his piety, and numerous articles have dealt with such matters as his fear of death. What I attempt is an examination of the broader aspects of his faith.

Although Johnson occasionally gave a special emphasis or an unusual interpretation to certain doctrines, on the whole he was an orthodox member of the Church of England. What most struck his contemporaries was not the nature of his convictions but rather his deep religious fervor. This seemed remarkable, partly because it contrasted with the attitude of his associates and with the prevailing secularism. His piety would have appeared less strange at an earlier period of English history.

It is also true that his religious intensity was related to the complex personality of the man. "His whole life," Sir John Hawkins wrote, "was a conflict with his passions and humors."[2] In the area of religion, Johnson's scrupulosity, his strict Lenten observance, and his fear of death often provoked astonishment. Some regarded these manifestations, like his rigid veracity, as evidence of his piety. Others viewed them as evidence of weakness—or even abnormality. Such was the analysis of Jeremy Bentham, the political philosopher and reformer, who as a young man had been a member of Johnson's City Club. Like so many others who knew Johnson, Bentham expressed great admiration for his "Herculean mind." Nevertheless, he thought one part of Johnson's intellect was so palsied that he "had lost the faculty of reasoning on certain topics connected with religion."[3]

Bentham was obviously wrong. The eighteenth century produced its share of fanatics and persons with strange religious delusions, but Johnson was neither a crank nor a madman. In religion, as in other matters, he constantly exercised his remarkable reasoning powers, and his spiritual concern was that of a devout and learned Christian.

Although Johnson had certain religious conflicts, his chief conflict was not between faith and doubt. It was a struggle, common enough in deeply pious persons, between a dedication to spiritual values and the attractions of the world. Johnson's religious tension, especially as seen in his prayers and diaries, has frequently been misinterpreted. Many if not most of his devotional exercises were composed during periods when he was engaged in an examination of his conscience. An account book of this kind differs from the commercial ledger in that only one's trespasses and debits are stressed. Under the circumstances, no one but the traditional Pharisee would be likely to record his virtues or his moral conquests. Yet, because Johnson commonly expressed dissatisfaction with his spiritual progress, it is sometimes said he found no joy in religion. To be sure, there is little evidence that he ever experienced the blissful state known to many devout individuals. But to reason on the record of his penitential exercises that religion brought him no comfort seems misguided. One might better argue that the very act of writing down his shortcomings had a therapeutic value.

In the following pages, although I am chiefly concerned with what Johnson believed, I shall sometimes suggest motives for his attitudes and behavior. Any thorough psychological study of the man must, in my opinion, be based on fuller knowledge of his childhood than we now possess. But an understanding of his religion can also provide important insights into his conduct and especially his values. Indeed, without such an understanding no psychological estimate of his character can be of much worth. For example, let us briefly consider his attitude on church attendance. Both Boswell and Hawkins mention that for one of such notable piety he was surprisingly lax in this matter. Johnson himself confessed he sometimes felt a reluctance about attending services, and his private diaries indicate he experienced a degree of guilt about his irregularity, though on the whole his deficiency in this respect troubled him less than certain other lapses.

Various explanations might be offered as to why he failed to attend church more frequently, but let us confine our discussion to four:

1. It was a habit developed in childhood, as the result of a traumatic experience. Such a theory might be erected on the fact that in 1716, while Easter services were being conducted at his parish church in Lichfield, stones began to fall from the spire. At this, alarmed members of the congregation, fearing the steeple would come crashing down, rushed to the windows and pushed through them.[4] Presuming that young Sam Johnson was present, one might argue in a modern manner that this experience left him with a subconscious fear that any church he entered thereafter might come tumbling down on his head.

2. Because of Johnson's deafness, he could not hear well in church. In connection with this point, there is clear evidence that Johnson was deaf, and more than once after coming from services he mentioned that he had had difficulty hearing what was said.

3. Johnson believed public worship to be less important than private worship. In support of this statement, it can be shown that he placed a high value on private devotions. He may have been influenced on this subject, as he was on other religious matters, by William Law's *Serious Call*. In this book,

though Law constantly emphasizes the necessity of private worship, he attaches less significance to public worship. He writes: "It is very observable, that there is not one command in all the Gospel for public worship; and perhaps it is a duty that is least insisted upon in Scripture of any other."[5]

4. Most pulpit oratory either bored or distracted Johnson. In his private diaries he admits that sermons sometimes made him restive. A prayer service was more to his liking. He attended church more often, he remarked, when there were prayers only, than when a sermon formed part of the service. By doing so, he explained, he set a needed example, since most people are better able to fix their attention on a sermon than on prayer.[6] According to George Steevens, he once said: "I am convinced I ought to be present at divine service more frequently than I am; but the provocations given by ignorant and affected preachers too often disturb the mental calm which otherwise would succeed to prayer. I am apt to whisper to myself on such occasions—How can this illiterate fellow dream of fixing attention, after we have been listening to the sublimest truths, conveyed in the most chaste and exalted language, throughout a Liturgy which must be regarded as the genuine offspring of piety impregnated by wisdom?"[7]

One might elaborate upon these explanations, adding, for example, the sensible though not very subtle suggestion that Johnson, like most of us, sometimes neglected duties because of laziness. Paradoxically, however, the chief reason for his not attending church more often seems to have been a religious one. As to the first hypothesis, to infer that Johnson had a lasting fear about entering a church seems ridiculous. The second explanation, dealing with his deafness, is logical enough and carries some weight when related to the fourth reason. The third may have some relevance; while William Law's views were probably not responsible for Johnson's failure to be a frequent church-goer, they may help to explain why he felt less guilt about absenting himself from church than he did about other lapses. The fourth explanation, in my opinion, comes nearest the truth. Coupled with the boredom he felt upon hearing a poor sermon was, perhaps, a slight degree of intellectual pride, for he wrote excellent sermons himself and could recognize how inferior were those of the "illiterate fellows" who occupied pulpits. But for a man of his piety, what was most objectionable was to be distracted, for it defeated his purpose in attending church—to worship and to receive spiritual comfort and inspiration. Consequently he preferred a simple prayer service. After being present at a sermon, he often came away dissatisfied with his failure to participate in public worship with the same devoutness that marked his private prayers and meditations.

In the above paragraphs, my purpose has been to show, rather sketchily, how an understanding of Johnson's religious position may explain his conduct, even in a situation that might at first suggest a weakness of religious motivation. Throughout the chapters which follow, the way Johnson's piety influenced his actions will be more fully discussed.

The materials bearing on Johnson's religion, when brought together, form a considerable collection. In the first place, there are the records of his contemporaries. No man before his time was the subject of so much written discussion. Because of the growing interest in biography, and because Johnson talked so well, Boswell was but one of many who recalled his observations. What Johnson is reported to have said, however, must be treated with a degree of caution. Even Boswell occasionally misjudged the tone of a remark. Furthermore, in the heat of controversy, Johnson himself sometimes failed to qualify his assertions with the care he generally exercised in his writing.

For this reason his own works serve as the most important source of information on his religion. His sermons, originally composed for John Taylor and other clergymen, provide the fullest insight into his theological views. His private prayers and meditations, the most personal of his writings, best reveal his spiritual side. But significant clues to his beliefs may be discovered in all his works, especially when they are studied in relation to each other. Johnson's *Dictionary,* for instance, proves constantly helpful in determining what his position was on particular questions.

Through his own works one is led to a consideration of various religious writers he mentions. I initially began this work because I was curious to learn what Johnson so much admired in the publications of two clergymen of his time. In this quest I have passed a month of Sundays, or so it seems in retrospect, with the forgotten sermons of Samuel Clarke. I have also examined, with greater interest, the too often neglected works of William Law. While I have not attempted to assimilate all the prodigious mass of religious literature that Johnson knew, I have consulted many books included in his personal library, as well as various authors mentioned in the *Dictionary* or elsewhere. In them I have sometimes found, if not a specific source for his views, a position similar to his own. At the same time, I have allowed caution to remind me that Johnson's religious beliefs, though generally derivative, were fused in the crucible of his own mind.

Because the story of Johnson's life has been told so often and so well, it does not seem necessary in a work especially devoted to a consideration of his religion to provide even an epitomized biography. While I try to establish, insofar as possible, the time when certain changes in his views appear to have occurred, the organization of this book is topical rather than chronological. The main subject of the first four chapters is Johnson's concern with salvation: separate chapters deal with his interest in William Law's counsels on the doctrine of perfection; his curious liking for the sermons of Samuel Clarke, whose teachings on salvation were in marked contrast with Law's; his conflicting interpretations of the Atonement; and the importance he attached to repentance.

In the latter part of the book, various other beliefs of Johnson are examined, especially in relation to his practice as a Christian. Thus Chapter V deals both with his sermon-writing activities and with certain theological views repeated in the sermons. The next chapter shows how his sense of charity was firmly based on orthodox Christian principles and how his devotion to these principles motivated and directed his practice of charity. The discussion that follows is concerned with the way Johnson's fear of death developed from his fear of God and with the relationship of his fear of God to the love of God. A penultimate chapter examines Johnson's position as an English Churchman, his loyalty to the Establishment, and his attitude towards other religious groups.

In a final chapter, which is chronological inasmuch as it describes Johnson's last two years of life, several topics are treated, such as the reports about his religious disposition at this time, his special preparations for death, the intensification of his piety, and his frame of mind at the end.

SAMUEL JOHNSON

A Layman's Religion

I · JOHNSON AND WILLIAM LAW

William Law "was not only a master of English prose, but also one of the most interesting thinkers of his period and one of the most endearingly saintly figures in the whole history of Anglicanism."

Aldous Huxley, The Perennial Philosophy

The stern-minded Evangelical William Wilberforce occasionally liked to engage in banter. He took particular pleasure in recalling a time when he had made James Boswell the butt of an innuendo. Long after the biographer was dead, Wilberforce remarked, "Poor Boswell! I once had some serious conversation with him; he was evidently low and depressed, and appeared to have many serious feelings. He told me that Johnson had assured him that he was never intimately acquainted with one religious clergyman. I was determined not to let him off; so I replied, 'That can only be because he never sought their acquaintance. They knew that he had about him such persons as they would not choose for companions.' "[1] Unfortunately Wilberforce failed to indicate how Boswell reacted to this pointed allusion to himself.

Johnson himself was probably more devout and certainly better informed on Christian doctrine than most clergymen of his time. He had a special interest in sermons. He read with discrimination, analyzing the style and comparing the views expressed. He observed who wrote best on evidence, on prayer, on free will and necessity. Furthermore, he could recall what writers on religion, as on other subjects, had said, years after he had read them. When Joshua Reynolds praised the sermons of Zachariah Mudge, he commented, "Mudge's sermons are good but not practical. He grasps more than he can hold. . . . I love Blair's sermons." He observed that Jeremy Taylor "gives

3

a very good advice: 'Never lie in your prayers; never confess more than you really believe.' " When asked about Richard Baxter's sermons, he replied, "Read any of them; they are all good." On the subject of prayer he favored Samuel Ogden as a preacher who "fought infidels with their own weapons." For style Johnson heartily recommended Atterbury, South, and Seed. He also considered Jortin's sermons "very elegant." But he would not advise a clergyman of his own day to imitate Tillotson's style, and when asked about Dodd's sermons, he dismissed them with the remark, "They were nothing, Sir."[2]

Although Johnson was especially well acquainted with the sermon writers, his reading embraced a great variety of religious literature, from the first centuries of Christianity down to his own age. Some indication of how widely he ranged, though by no means a complete record of his reading, is supplied by the list of books he owned at the time of his death. His personal library contained a rich assortment of philosophical, devotional, and theological works. Among them were a few rare items, like a 1491 edition of *De Consolatione Philosophiae* by Boethius. Many of the earlier volumes were printed in Latin, such as the *Opera* of St. Thomas Aquinas, and those of St. Anselm and of Erasmus, as well as the *De Legibus* of Suarez. The first centuries of Christianity were represented by Eusebius' *History of the Christian Church,* and the works of St. Ambrose, St. Athanasius, St. Augustine, and Justin the Martyr. Also on Johnson's bookshelves were volumes of such diverse nature and different dogmas as the *Roman Missal,* Sale's *Koran,* and the writings of Calvin. English authors were represented by works like Goodman's *Penitent Pardoned,* Pearce's *Commentary on the Evangelists,* and Fuller's *Church History.* There were also dozens of volumes of sermons by seventeenth- and eighteenth-century divines.[3]

Johnson read so many authors on religion that it would be impossible to trace, in every instance, the source of the particular views he expressed in his works and in his recorded conversation. Furthermore, he arrived at his own convictions, not simply by comparing writers, but by testing what they said against his own observations and by engaging in long hours of reflection. On religion, as on other subjects, he was a man of independent mind, and, as we shall see, his opinions upon certain points changed during the course of his life. Nevertheless, it is significant that among the scores of authors he had read on Christianity, he himself singled out two as having most contributed to his spiritual outlook. One of these was William Law; the other was Samuel Clarke.

The influence of William Law upon the youthful Johnson is attested in a well-known passage in Boswell's *Life*. "When at Oxford," Johnson remarked, "I took up 'Law's Serious Call to a Holy Life', expecting to find it a dull book, (as such books generally are,) and perhaps to laugh at it. But I found Law quite an overmatch for me; and this was the first occasion of my thinking in earnest of religion, after I became capable of rational inquiry." Henceforth, Boswell adds, religion was to become the principal subject of Johnson's reflections.[4]

Mrs. Thrale also believed that *A Serious Call* made a lasting impression on Johnson, but the most specific evidence of Law's influence has been provided by a contemporary scholar. In two recent articles, Katharine C. Balderston has shown that in the revised fourth edition of his *Dictionary,* published in 1773, Johnson quotes the clergyman no fewer than 196 times. Some of the quotations reveal the lexicographer's admiration for Law's clear and vivid diction, but many are "precepts of piety and prudence."[5]

In this chapter we shall examine Law's religious views with the purpose of comparing them with Johnson's. The point of view of these two men on many questions is so similar that, in my opinion, one conclusion is inescapable. Law, more than any other single writer, gave the temper to Johnson's religion. Nevertheless, Law was but one of several authors who helped to shape his beliefs. Our purpose in this chapter, then, is not simply to engage in a source-hunting safari, but to compare and contrast the religious dispositions of the two men, with the object of showing to what extent Johnson followed or departed from the religious spirit of a writer he greatly admired but who, as Johnson would have been the first to admit, was a more consistently devout and more deeply dedicated Christian than he himself.

William Law (1686–1761) was born in King's Cliffe, Northhamptonshire. He attended Emmanuel College, Cambridge, and in 1711 became a fellow of his college and received holy orders. Because he strongly favored the Stuarts, he refused to take the oaths of allegiance to George I and was debarred from church appointments. For several years he lived in the household of Edward Gibbon, grandfather of the famous historian, as a tutor and a friend of the family. In 1740 he retired to King's Cliffe, where he passed the remainder of his life, occupied with his writing, serving as spiritual director to two pious ladies, supervising a school he had founded, and dispensing charity to the poor.

Law occupies an unusual position in the eighteenth century. Although a Nonjuror, he was never closely associated with the Nonjuring group. His *Practical Treatise Upon Christian Perfection* (1726) and still more *A Serious Call to a Devout and Holy Life* (1728) had an important influence on Wesley, Whitefield, and other Evangelicals, but Law himself was never an Evangelical. He was still further removed from the clergymen of the Establishment who, as apostles of reason, argued the credibility of Christianity. Law assumed his readers were Christians; his efforts were devoted to awakening them to the profound implications of their faith. The term "mystic," often associated with him, is appropriate to his later period, but the key to Law throughout his whole writing career is that he believed in, practiced, and preached the doctrine of Christian perfection.

This traditional doctrine, stated in its simplest terms, asserts that the object of existence is a dedication of oneself to an imitation of Christ. Like the perfectionists of earlier centuries, Law recognized that it is impossible for man to achieve the absolute perfection of Christ. Human perfection, because of human limitations, must always be of a different order. What mattered most was for the individual to set a high ideal of holiness and to strive constantly towards that goal. Indeed, as Law viewed the subject, salvation depends not so much on the attainment of perfection in this life as on the unremitting effort of the Christian to achieve it. In his *Practical Treatise Upon Christian Perfection* he writes: "For though it may be true that people will be admitted to happiness, and different degrees of happiness, though they have not *attained* to all that perfection to which they were called; yet it does not follow that any people will be saved who did not *endeavour* after that perfection. For surely it is a very different case to *fall* short of our perfection after our best endeavours, and to stop short of it, by not endeavouring to arrive at it. The one practise may carry men to a high reward in heaven, and the other casts them with the unprofitable servant into outer darkness."[6]

Besides *A Serious Call* and *An Appeal to All That Doubt,*[7] Johnson probably knew Law's *Treatise Upon Christian Perfection* and the other earlier works. He may never have read the later mystical writings, but even if his familiarity with Law had been confined to the *Serious Call,* from that book alone he would have grasped the fundamentally ascetic point of view of the clergyman. For this work contains a comprehensive and urgent discussion of how the Christian must live in order to approach perfection. First of all, said Law, he must renounce the world, no matter what his walk in life; secondly, he must, by a severe regimen of self-discipline and by engaging in various devotions, dedicate himself to a spiritual existence.

Critics have argued whether Law's appeal was directed essentially to the heart or to the head. In the earlier works, where he relies much on logic, Law was certainly addressing the mind with the ultimate object of arousing the hearts of men. Johnson, with his ability to find the right adjective, succinctly described the tone of *A Serious Call* when he termed it "the finest piece of hortatory theology in any language."[8] The following passage, in which Law achieves remarkable emphasis by the repeated use of infinitive phrases, will serve to illustrate his style. It is also an excellent summary of what he meant by renunciation of the world:

Our Blessed Saviour and his Apostles are wholly taken up in doctrines that relate to common life. They call us to renounce the world, and differ in every temper and way of life, from the spirit and way of the world: to renounce all its goods, to fear none of its evils, to reject its joys, and have no value for happiness; to be as new born babes, that are born into a new state of things; to live as pilgrims in spiritual watching, in holy fear, and heavenly aspiring after another life; to take up our daily cross, to deny ourselves, to profess the blessedness of mourning, to seek the blessedness of poverty of spirit; to forsake the pride and vanity of riches, to take no thought for the morrow, to live in the profoundest state of humility, to rejoice in worldly sufferings; to reject the lust of the flesh, the lust of the eyes, and the pride of life; to bear injuries, to forgive and bless our enemies, and to love mankind as God loveth them: to give up our whole hearts and affections to God, and strive to enter through the strait gate into a life of eternal glory.[9]

It has sometimes been observed that Law did not understand human frailty. Yet his own practice might have served as a model of what he recommended. Living in retirement, where, to be sure, he was supported by private means, he proved that it is not impossible to follow the devout and unworldly pattern of existence that he urged others to adopt. No doubt it was partly his own sanctity that led him to believe that everyone, no matter what his calling and no matter how much engaged in sublunary affairs, could, even while living in the world, achieve a spiritual state divorced from the corruptions of the world. Although he frequently says that man is a weak creature, he nevertheless assumes that, with the help of proper devotional aids, man has the will to free himself from the snares of earthly pleasures and to live piously. From his point of view the chief difficulty is not that the spirit is willing and the flesh weak. He believed rather that man has the power to fortify himself against sin, provided his spirit, so often deaf to the message and blind to the example of Christ, is once aroused to the importance of setting perfection as a goal.

Having renounced the world, the Christian was to devote himself to the cultivation of true piety. To do so, he must rigidly discipline himself. The great enemy to a devout life, says Law—and he writes at length on this subject—is sloth. By sloth he meant chiefly late sleeping. This he considered a positive evil because it disorders one's existence, makes one a "slave to bodily appetites," and gradually "wears away the spirit of religion and sinks the soul into a state of dullness and sensuality." Here, as he so frequently does, Law introduces an analogy to practical life to impress upon readers the logic of his contention. A businessman who lies abed when he should be up tending his shop, he comments, strikes one with contempt, and it is difficult to believe any good of such an indolent person. Let this example teach us, he adds, "to conceive how odious we must appear in the sight of heaven if we are in bed, shut up in sleep and darkness, when we should be praising God, and are such slaves to drowsiness as to neglect our devotions for it."[10]

The positive way to advance towards the goal of perfection, according to Law, is through meditation, self-examination, religious reading, and, above all, prayer. One should imitate the example of the early Christians, he urges, and begin the morning with prayer. Then for the remainder of the day, one should follow a time schedule, similar to the plan of the canonical hours, in order to establish frequency and regularity in devotions. In recommending the contemplative life and in prescribing practical measures to enable one to lead it, Law never confuses means with ends; that is, he never loses sight of the fact that perfection itself is no more than an immediate goal to serve as a stepping stone to the ultimate goal of salvation.

Johnson frequently gives evidence of his thorough understanding of what is meant by the doctrine of perfection. In his
Dictionary, where he defines "perfection" as "the state of being perfect," he illustrates the meaning by a quotation from
Law: "The question is not, whether gospel *perfection* can be
fully attained; but whether you come as near it as a sincere
conscience, and careful diligence can carry you." There is also
an allusion to perfection in *Rambler* 7. Here he explains the
importance of withdrawing from society to meditate, to
"weaken the temptations of the world," and to "reinstate religion in its just authority." He adds: "This is that conquest of
the world and of ourselves, which has been always considered
as the perfection of human nature; and this is only to be obtained by fervent prayer, steady resolutions, and frequent retirement from folly and vanity, from the cares of avarice, and
the joys of intemperance, from the lulling sounds of deceitful
flattery, and the tempting sight of prosperous wickedness."

A more extended discussion of perfection appears in his
famous reply to Soame Jenyns. In his *Free Enquiry into the
Nature and Origin of Evil,* Jenyns had asserted that man's imperfections are in accord with his place in the scale of being,
and that if "he became perfect, he must cease to be a man."
Johnson sternly reprimands him for this opinion. While he
grants that man could not achieve absolute perfection, he nevertheless observes, "The perfection which man once had, may
be so easily conceived that, without any unusual strain of imagination, we can figure its revival. All the duties to God or man,
that are neglected, we may fancy performed; all the crimes,
that were committed, we can conceive forborne. Man will then
be restored to his moral perfections."[11]

In his private diaries there is evidence that Johnson tried,
in some measure, to follow the counsels on perfection. In July,
1755, after accusing himself of failing to accord proper attention to religious duties, especially on the Sabbath, he resolved

to "once more form a scheme of life for that day such as alas I have often vainly formed which when my mind is capable of settled practice I hope to follow." He then lists the steps he intends to take. He will rise early, read the Bible, as well as other religious works, and perform special devotions in the morning. He resolves also "to wear off by meditation any worldly soil contracted in the week," and, following another of Law's stipulations, he determines "to examine the tenour of my life & particularly the last week & mark my advances in religion or recession from it."[12]

The most interesting proof of Johnson's concern with the doctrine of perfection is his Latin poem "Christianus Perfectus." This work, which was first published after Johnson's death, gives an excellent summary of the doctrine. All the main points are stressed—the importance of renouncing the world and its pleasures, of living in holiness with every thought directed towards God, of subduing all rebellious feelings, and of striving always to imitate Christ. Because this poem seldom appears in translation, a fairly close English version of it is provided here.[13]

Whoever desires to be numbered among the Holy under Christ's urging should wash away the stain of the world, renouncing the joys of the flesh and the swellings of pride, and fix his mind always on the afterlife, plucking the barbs of fear from his heart, until at last he may look up to the Father, kind in his divine majesty.

He should also have a reverent love of creation, despising no race or creed, that he may ever delight in helping the wretched and, limited by no narrow bounds of righteousness, forgive the trespasses of all men and find joy in his Godliness. Let a holy fire burn in his heart, so that, if the occasion require, he may be able to give up his life to truth.

Let his first and his last care be to please God; let his desire be to preserve, unbroken, the tenor of a holy life. Though the fool and the sinner offend him hourly, let him hold safe in his breast all that is right. Let him not waver, choosing now this and now that role, or doubt whom he should call master, but, always dedicated to one, and, despising mortal things, let him devote himself faithfully to Christ.

But let him always fear and take special pains lest, like the unthinking crowd, he should presumptuously decide which laws he is willing to keep, which laws he lightly sets aside, thus evading his full task, and, by his own choice infatuated, fit his neck to soft yokes. God, who has given all to you, wishes nothing of the sum to be wanting, but demands all in return.

Finally he strives with ceaseless efforts towards the heights and, with the help of God, proceeds now with peaceful mind and feels he is led by a gentle authority. Little by little he remakes his habits, his spirit, his very life, and he dons the likeness of God, insofar as he will be able to observe it, and, transcending earthly things, tastes the joys of heaven.

This poem, not as well known as it deserves to be, gives clear and persuasive evidence of Johnson's concern with the doctrine of perfection. It might be highly revealing to know when and under what conditions he wrote it, but unfortunately we do not know the circumstances of its composition.

Because Johnson had read so widely in religious literature, it would be presumptuous to assume that William Law was the sole source of his knowledge about the meaning of perfection. He might, for instance, have learned about this dedicated mode of existence from St. Augustine or St. Thomas Aquinas, whose works he owned, or from Thomas à Kempis, whose *Imitation of Christ* he greatly admired. But *A Serious Call* seems to have been the first book to arouse him to the full implications of Christian perfection.

It is also clear that Johnson never renounced the world and never followed the counsels on perfection to the extent or in just the same manner that Law had urged. Far from renouncing the world, he passed much time in society. Although he meditated and prayed, he seldom, it would appear, pursued a regular course of daily devotions. He read many religious works, but read them, not systematically, but as they came to hand. Religion often occupied his thoughts, sometimes because he consciously turned his mind to it, but as frequently, perhaps, because fears and scruples forced his attention. Nevertheless, Boswell makes a telling observation when, after describing Johnson's first introduction to *A Serious Call,* he writes: "From this time forward, religion was the predominant object of his thoughts; though, with the just sentiments of a conscientious christian, he lamented that his practice of its duties fell far short of what it ought to be."[14]

Boswell here intimates that Law had a dual influence on Johnson. In the first place, *A Serious Call* awakened in him a lively and lasting sense of the importance of religion. In the second place, the acknowledged hortatory message of this work compelled him thereafter to engage in frequent comparisons between the high ideal that Law had set before him and his own shortcomings. The inevitable result was an intensification of his native fears and scruples.

One subject on which he felt a particular sense of guilt was sloth. Throughout his adult life, Johnson was constantly resolving to rise early, constantly accusing himself of indolence, constantly blaming himself for breaking his resolutions to reform. It is significant that he began keeping a diary of his prayers and meditations in 1729, the year he first encountered *A Serious Call;* and, in view of the extended discussion of the evils of sloth in that book, it is perhaps doubly significant that Johnson's first notation is a Latin sentence translated as "I bid farewell to Sloth, being resolved henceforth not to listen to her syren strains."[15]

Such good resolutions, accompanied by accusations of his previous failure to live up to them, appear in his private diaries until almost the end of his life. To say that Law's exhortations were the sole source of his scruples on sloth would oversimplify a complex matter. His scruples on this subject, as on other matters, were of deep-seated origin, and much too complex psychologically to be explained completely by his encounter with one book. Yet somewhere in his early reading he must have been deeply impressed by a discussion of the dangers of lying abed until midmorning. Others, like John Wesley, wrote on this topic, but we cannot be sure that Johnson was familiar with his warnings. We can be certain of Johnson's early and thorough knowledge of *A Serious Call* and of the profound impact that work as a whole had on him.

Because Law was the first religious writer to make a deep impression on him, it seems probable that this clergyman contributed to the shaping of his High Church position. During Queen Anne's reign there had been a distinct High Church party that stood for autonomous church authority in spiritual matters, an emphasis on the sacramental aspects of faith, respect for the patristic writers, and for religious practices in keeping with the long tradition of Christianity. After the accession of George I, Whigs were generally appointed as bishops, the authority of the High Church party declined, and its political influence dwindled so much it came to be known as the "High and Dry Party."[16] Nevertheless, there remained many High Church clergymen, like Thomas Wilson, Bishop of Sodor and Mann, and Daniel Waterland, whose individual influence in maintaining traditional principles has too often been neglected.

Law's High Church position was manifested by his refusal to swear allegiance to George I as head of Church and State, by his theological views, and by such practices as self-denial and fasting. "No Christian that knows anything of the Gospel," he writes, "can doubt whether fasting be a common duty of Christianity, since our Saviour has placed it along with secret alms and private prayers."[17] Johnson similarly believed in imposing austerities on himself. Mrs. Thrale remarks that he "kept fast in Lent, particularly the holy week, with a rigour very dangerous to his general health." And when he began to abstain from wine, she thought it was "for religious motives."[18]

William Law especially demonstrated his High Church position in stressing the importance of the Sacrament of the Lord's Supper. In his answer to Bishop Benjamin Hoadly's argument that the Sacrament is chiefly a commemorative rite, he refutes this position and maintains, on the contrary, that the Eucharist is the means by which one puts on the Christ, who is truly present in the Sacrament.[19] As we shall see, Johnson may not have subscribed to a belief in the Real Presence in the sense that various High Churchmen did. Nevertheless, he regarded the Sacrament as much more than a commemorative rite. To him, as to Law, it was an indispensable means of grace that strengthened the believer against the temptations of sin.

So far we have been concerned with certain areas in which there exists a general similarity in Law's and Johnson's views. A more specific correspondence appears in their thinking on two doctrinal matters. One of these is the Atonement, about which more will be said later; the other is prayer.

Because he believed the seeker of perfection must rely upon prayer above everything else, Law devoted several chapters to this subject. His main position was that the Christian "prays *without ceasing;* that he prays *always;* and that he cries to God *night and day;* for these are essential qualifications of prayer, and expressly required in Scripture." He assumed that professed Christians would recite formal prayers at church, and upon regular occasions, such as at meals. But he believed an established pattern of prayer, while important, constituted only a small share of true devoutness. He urged, especially, the necessity of frequent, spontaneous prayer. "The repeating of a creed at certain times is an act of faith," he says, "but that faith which *overcometh* the world, stays neither for times nor seasons, but is a living principle of the soul, that is always believing, trusting, and depending upon God." A particular advantage of spontaneous prayer, he observes, is that one can adapt the language to external conditions, such as one's state of sickness or health, pains, losses, or disappointments; or shape it to correspond to the condition of the heart, "as of love, joy, peace, tranquillity." Because individual prayer also allows the Christian to intercede for those who are dead, Law adds, it not only benefits others but increases one's sense of charity, for "he that daily prays to God that all men may be happy in heaven takes the likeliest way to make him wish for and delight in their happiness on earth."[20]

Law constantly warns against the danger of regarding prayer as a mere formality. In order to prevent its becoming perfunctory, he says, "persons careful of the greatest benefit of prayer ought to have a great share in the forming and composing their own devotions." In other words, devout Christians should compile a private manual of prayer, wherein they would record the deep religious stirrings of the heart, spontaneous expressions of praise, and thanks and petitions for pardon and peace. To assist in the composition of such a manual, Christians should read such works as the Bible, books of devotion, and the lives of the saints, and select arresting phrases or passages to employ as "proper fuel for the flame of their own devotion." Thus, in a personal manual, one's own petitions would be combined with notable expressions of praise, confession, or thanksgiving, taken from various works of piety.[21]

Johnson similarly emphasizes the importance of prayer. In his third sermon he sums up much of Law's thinking on the subject when he remarks, "The great efficient of union between the soul and its Creator, is prayer; of which the necessity is such, that St. Paul directs us, to pray without ceasing; that is, to preserve in the mind such a constant dependence upon God, and such a constant desire of his assistance, as may be equivalent to constant prayer."

The similarity to Law is even more striking when we compare the spirit and method of the prayers Johnson composed with Law's exhortations on this topic. Johnson, as we noted, began keeping a record of his prayers and meditations in 1729, the same year he first read *A Serious Call,* and both the substance and the tone of his private manual of devotions are in keeping with Law's advice. Many of the petitions were composed, as Law suggested, for specific occasions. Some were written at the beginning of the year, a time when Johnson periodically reviewed his past life; some upon undertaking a new venture, such as the writing of the *Rambler* essays; and still others at Easter, particularly in preparation for receiving the Sacrament. Johnson also incorporated in his prayers phrases from other religious works, especially from the Book of Common Prayer, and, like Law, he believed in the efficacy of praying for deceased relatives and friends.

In one notable respect Johnson did not follow Law's advice. *A Serious Call* particularly urges that petitions be addressed to Christ. For example, one may commence with such a salutation as "O Saviour of the world, God of God, Light of Light, Thou that art the Brightness of Thy Father's glory, and the express image of His person."[22] Johnson never begins a prayer in this manner. Indeed, except for the liturgical formula at the end, usually expressed by such a phrase as "for the sake of Jesus Christ, Our Lord," he has relatively few allusions to the Second Person of the Trinity in his earlier prayers. As we shall see, references to Christ do become more frequent in prayers he composed late in life.

Although invocations of Christ are surprisingly rare, Johnson's prayers have a remarkably large number of pious allusions to the Third Person of the Trinity. Most of his prayers contain some expression such as: "Grant me the help of thy Holy Spirit, that I may do thy will with diligence," "Grant me by the assistance of the Holy Spirit, I may so pass through life that I may obtain life everlasting," or "Take not, O Lord, thy Holy Spirit from me."[23] To refer to the Holy Ghost in Christian prayer is by no means unusual. Petitions and references to the Third Person of the Trinity appear throughout the Book of Common Prayer. Nevertheless, the regularity with which Johnson petitions for the help of the Holy Spirit is significant, for it shows he did much more than merely give tacit assent to the doctrine of the Trinity. Despite his rational bent, he wholeheartedly believed in this great Christian mystery and fervently embraced the opportunity to implore the assistance of the Holy Spirit, who is perhaps the least comprehensible member of the Trinity.

Because Johnson's special reverence for the Holy Ghost is based on traditional doctrines of faith, there is no difficulty in understanding in what sense and with what purpose he so often alludes to the Spirit in his prayers. In the first place, he regards the Third Person of the Trinity as the source of wisdom. Thus when he was about to begin the *Rambler* essays, he composed the following petition: "Almighty God, the giver of all good things, without whose help all Labour is ineffectual, and without whose grace all wisdom is folly, grant, I beseech thee, that in this my undertaking thy Holy Spirit may not be withheld from me, but that I may promote thy glory, and the Salvation both of myself and others."[24]

For the most part, however, he implores the assistance of the Holy Spirit to strengthen him against sin and to inspire him to lead a truly spiritual existence. That is because he reveres the Third Person of the Trinity as the Sanctifier, or as the indwelling force that operates to fill men's souls with grace, and unites them with God by quickening in them the spark of divinity. Thus we find Johnson asking for His aid to help him shun sloth, to withhold from his mind idle and dangerous thoughts, and to advance him in godliness. Sometimes he refers to the Spirit as "the Comforter," the term used in the Gospel of St. John (14:16–17), as well as in the *Te Deum* of the Anglican service. In Sermon IX, where he writes on the importance of the Sacrament, Johnson says, "To refuse the means of grace, is to place our confidence in our own strength, and to neglect the assistance of that Comforter, who came down from heaven according to the most true promise of our blessed Saviour." But no matter what term he uses, these petitions for assistance reveal his firm belief in the doctrine of grace—a belief reflected throughout the period during which he recorded his prayers. On his birthday in 1738 he writes, "And O Lord, enable me by thy Grace to use all diligence in redeeming the time which I have spent in Sloth, Vanity and Wickedness." On March 24, 1759, he implores, "Grant me the grace of thy Holy Spirit, that the course which I am now beginning may proceed according to thy laws, and end in the enjoyment of thy favour." And in 1782, he petitions, "Grant me the help of thy Holy Spirit, that I may do thy will with Diligence, and suffer it with humble Patience."

The origin of the belief in the efficacy of the Holy Spirit is the Bible, but the emphasis Johnson gave this doctrine was presumably the result of further reading. Because he was impressed relatively early by the mystical role of the Third Person of the Trinity, a possible source of his information was William Law, who discusses the subject at length in his *Practical Treatise Upon Christian Perfection*. He comments. "The invisible operation and assistance of God's Holy Spirit, by which we are disposed towards that which is good, and made able to perform it, is a confessed doctrine of Christianity." Linking the divine function of the Holy Ghost to his own doctrine of perfection, Law says that man is called from a mere animal life and from worldly distractions to "be born again of the Holy Ghost and to be made a member of the Kingdom of God." The work of the Spirit in the hearts of men, he writes, is "to give us a new understanding, a new judgment, temper, taste, and relish, new desires and new hopes and fears. So far, therefore, as we prepare ourselves by self-denial for this change of heart and mind, so far we invite the assistance, and concur with the inspirations of the Holy Ghost; and so far as we nourish any foolish passion, indulge any vanity of mind, or corruption of the heart, so far we resist the graces of God's Holy Spirit, and render ourselves indisposed to relish and improve his secret inspiration."[25] Because Johnson's own views are similar, they may have been inspired either by Law or by reading other writers who similarly stressed the doctrine of grace.

One characteristic of Johnson's prayers needs special emphasis. When they were first published, in the year following his death, they caused considerable consternation among readers. Many were disturbed by his petitions for the dead and by other Papist practices, but what troubled his admirers still more was the frank admission of broken resolutions and the frequent confessions of guilt. The allusions to his sinfulness, even more evident now that we have the unexpurgated text of his manuscript reproduced in the Yale edition of the *Works,* can be best understood if one observes that they appear chiefly in those prayers in which Johnson is making a periodic examination of conscience. In them Johnson charges himself with sins of omission and commission, asks forgiveness, and either resolves to amend his life or, more frequently, petitions for strength to do so. Some of the prayers were composed at the beginning of a new year, others on his birthday. Both occasions he regarded as especially appropriate for a review of his past life. But his examination of conscience took place most consistently at Easter, in preparation for receiving the Sacrament.

In spirit these petitions conform to the penitential exercises listed in the Book of Common Prayer, in the section entitled "The Order of the Administration of the Lord's Supper." The closest single pattern is the prayer of general confession, recited by members of the congregation about to receive the Sacrament. It reads as follows:

Almighty God, Father of Our Lord Jesus Christ, Maker of all things, Judge of all men; We acknowledge and bewail our manifold sins and wickedness, Which we, from time to time, most grievously have committed, By thought, word, and deed, Against thy Divine Majesty, Provoking most justly thy wrath and indignation against us. We do earnestly repent, And are heartily sorry for these our misdoings; The remembrance of them is grievous unto us; The burden of them is intolerable. Have mercy upon us, Have mercy upon us, most merciful Father; For thy Son our Lord Jesus Christ's sake, Forgive us all that is past; and grant that we may ever hereafter Serve and please thee In newness of life, To the honour and glory of thy Name; Through Jesus Christ our Lord, Amen.

Johnson's penitential prayers, while corresponding to this model, differ in that they are confessions composed by an individual. As such, they frequently name particular sins; often, as we have indicated, they implore the assistance of the Holy Spirit; and, in general, they contain reflections on his present state, or allusions to his failure to keep past resolutions. Furthermore, they were either composed at home before receiving the Sacrament in church, or composed at other seasons when he engaged in spiritual stock-taking.

To make an examination of one's conscience before Communion is a regular procedure in the Church of England, as in other churches. Various writers of religious manuals, such as Jeremy Taylor and Robert Nelson, had also recommended a spiritual self-examination at other periods as well,[26] but it was characteristic of Law's piety to urge a regular and systematic review of one's conscience at the end of each day. Chapter XXIII of *A Serious Call* is particularly concerned with prayers appropriate to evening. There Law writes: "As the labour and action of every state of life is generally over at this hour, so this is the proper time for everyone to call himself to account and review all his behaviour from the first action of the day. The necessity of this examination is founded upon the necessity of Repentance." The regularity of this exercise, Law adds, provides the most efficacious method of amending and perfecting one's life. If, for instance, one is guilty of repeated sins, daily examination and repentance serve to fill one with "sorrow and a deep compunction," until by degrees one is "forced into amendment." One should particularly search the heart to discover those sins to which one is especially prone.

Because particular occupations expose men to particular temptations, "the tradesman to lying and unreasonable gains, the scholar to pride and vanity," the penitent should consider to what extent he has succumbed to evils associated with his own calling. Finally, because everyone striving for self-betterment will have made good resolutions, he should "examine how and to what degree he has observed them," and "reproach himself before God for every neglect of them."[27]

From an examination of conscience one should proceed to contrition. Law dwells at great length upon this subject, urging the penitent to meditate on the odiousness of sin and not to hesitate to charge himself with being the worst sinner he knows, in order to lacerate his heart with a deep sense of guilt. The importance of achieving profound sorrow for sin is so strongly emphasized that Law assumes, rather than specifically mentions, that the penitent will next proceed to the final step in repentance, namely, a sincere resolve to amend one's life. In short, what Law recommends is that the reader perform by himself various steps in the process of auricular confession: an examination of conscience, with a review of one's sins; meditation on their heinous nature; and a sense of profound sorrow for having offended God, accompanied by the desire for amendment.

Although there is no evidence that Johnson engaged regularly in such a daily examination of conscience, he did follow this practice at various times. After his wife's death in 1752, he customarily received the Sacrament at Easter, and this was the period when he most consistently undertook the process of self-examination. He also refers to this season in his final *Idler* essay as one particularly appropriate for a spiritual scrutiny of self. He writes: "As the last *Idler* is published in that solemn week which the Christian world has always set apart for the examination of the conscience, the review of life, the extinction of earthly desires, and the renovation of holy purposes; I hope my readers are already disposed to view every incident with seriousness and improve it by meditation."

Elsewhere Johnson emphasizes that self-examination and repentance are always necessary before receiving the Sacrament, no matter what the season of the year. Several paragraphs are devoted to this topic in Sermon XXII. One who partakes of the Lord's Supper without engaging in "long and fervent meditation" on its significance, he writes, "will be in danger of eating and drinking unworthily." The proper way "to prepare ourselves for the Sacrament is that of self-examination . . . repentance and reformation are supposed, with great reason, inseparable from it; for nothing is more evident, than that we are to inquire into the state of our souls, as into affairs of lesser importance, with a view to avoid danger, or to secure happiness." If we discover our faith is weak, he continues, we should fortify ourselves by reading Scripture and works of piety, and reflect on "our creation, our redemption, the means of grace and hope of glory." When self-examination reveals that sins have been committed, we must resolve to avoid further transgressions and to restrain ourselves "by watching and fasting, by a steady temperance and perpetual vigilance." Above all, it should be remembered that "by grace alone can we hope to resist the numberless temptations that perpetually surround us."

How closely Johnson followed these precepts may be seen both in his meditations and in those prayers that summarize the process of self-examination. The following, which is a fairly typical prayer, was composed in preparation for receiving the Sacrament on Easter Day, 1766.

Almighty and most merciful Father, before whom I now appear laden with the sins of another year, suffer me yet again to call upon thee for pardon and peace. O God, grant me repentance, grant me reformation. Grant that I may be no longer disturbed with doubts and harrassed with vain terrours. Grant that I may no more linger in perplexity, nor waste in idleness that life which thou hast given and preserved. Grant that I may serve thee with firm faith and diligent endeavour, and that I may discharge the duties of my calling with tranquillity and constancy. Take not

O Lord thy Holy Spirit from me, but grant that I may so direct my life by thy holy laws, as that when thou shalt call me hence, I may pass by a holy and happy death to a life of everlasting and unchangeable joy, for the Sake of Jesus Christ, our Lord. Amen.

In this prayer we see the various elements that both Law and Johnson describe as necessary in the process of self-examination and repentance. The whole prayer is a confession of sorrow for sin, based on an examination of conscience. There is a reference to a particular sin, in this instance, as so often with Johnson, idleness, as well as allusions to other transgressions. There is a supplication for grace when he petitions, "Take not O Lord thy Holy Spirit from me." He also prays that he may be found worthy at death, although Law had recommended that reflections on one's mortal state should follow rather than be a fundamental part of the penitential exercise. Included, too, is the phrase, "pardon and peace," from the Book of Common Prayer. The chief difference between Johnson and the typical penitent is that the latter would be likely to assert that he repents and that he resolves to amend his life. Johnson prays, ". . . grant me repentance, grant me reformation." Indeed, it is noteworthy that he uses the word "grant" six times in this one prayer. The repetition of this term should not be taken as a sign of infirmity of purpose or of weak faith. Its use here, as so often in his prayers, is rather an indication of his persistent scruples.

As we have remarked, Johnson's scruples were probably strengthened by his early acquaintance with the lofty ideal of Christian perfection described in *A Serious Call*. Occasionally even his phrasing suggests the direct influence of this book on him. For instance, there is a close correspondence between what Law says on the subject of guilt and a remark Johnson once made. Law writes: "You may fairly look upon yourself to be the greatest sinner that you know in the world. . . . First, Because you know more of the folly of your own heart than you do of other people's, and can charge yourself with various sins that you only know of yourself, and cannot be sure that other sinners are guilty of them. . . . Secondly, The greatness of our guilt arises chiefly from the greatness of God's goodness towards us, from the particular graces and blessings, the favours, lights, and instructions that we have received from him."[28] Johnson, too, believed that one's sins were to be judged in a relative sense, inasmuch as a person who received special gifts and graces and had resisted them was more guilty than one not so favored. On one occasion, as Sir John Hawkins shrewdly observed, Johnson used virtually the same language as Law during a discussion of the prospect of death. When Hawkins tried to quiet his fears by reminding him that he had done much good in the world by his example and his writings, Johnson replied "that he had written as a philosopher, but had not lived like one." Hawkins added: "In the estimation of his offences he reasoned thus—'Every man knows his own sins, and also, what grace he has resisted. But, to those of others, and the circumstances under which they were committed, he is a stranger: he is therefore to look on himself as the greatest sinner that he knows of.' "[29]

Much the same thought appears in Johnson's sixteenth sermon. He says that God alone "knows what temptations each man has resisted; how far the means of grace have been afforded him, and how he has improved or neglected them. . . . No man can say that he is better than another, because no man can tell how far the other was enabled to resist temptation, or what incidents might concur to overthrow his virtue." Because Johnson held this view, it was logical that he should be charitable about the failings of others and extremely rigorous about his own.

Johnson also judged himself severely with regard to his positive contributions as a Christian. "Every man," he writes (*Idler* 88), "is obliged by the Supreme Master of the Universe to improve all the opportunities of Good which are afforded him, and to keep in continual activity such Abilities as are bestowed upon him." The parable of the talents was likewise in his mind when he composed his elegy "On the Death of Dr. Levet." He praised his humble friend for having well employed his single talent, but what of himself? He knew he enjoyed many advantages denied to others. His superior intellect had been the gift of nature, but when he looked back on his career later in life, he must have felt that fortune, too, had smiled on the obscure bookseller's son who had risen to eminence, had been received privately by his king, and enjoyed a generous pension in recognition of his writings. But had he made the best use of the abilities and graces bestowed upon him? His frequent self-accusations indicate what his answer would have been. In his severe judgment of himself, he felt he had neither employed his talents to the fullest nor, by the standard of Christian perfection, sufficiently cultivated opportunities for spiritual improvement.[30]

William Law, then, seems to have had a dual influence on Johnson. In the first place, *A Serious Call* helped to develop his deep sense of religion. Both the habit of recording his prayers and his practice of self-examination may have resulted directly from his study of this work. A second influence, it would seem, was to increase the severity of his scruples and to contribute to his fear that he might not be saved. In his essay on Johnson, Arthur Murphy observes, "In his meditations we see him scrutinizing himself with severity, and aiming at perfection unattainable by man."[31] Few people, and Johnson was not among them, have ever reached the height of Christian perfection. But the importance of striving to live according to the counsels of perfection was early impressed on his mind, and he never forgot it. Consequently when he contrasted Law's ideal of what is expected of the Christian with his own inadequate performance, he may, indeed, have considered himself the greatest sinner he knew. If he did believe this, he was of course literally adopting one of Law's principles.

II · JOHNSON AND SAMUEL CLARKE

Dr. Clarke was a metaphysical clock. A proud priest. He thought he had all by demonstration; and he who thinks so is a madman.

Voltaire, quoted in Boswell on the Grand Tour

Among the books in Johnson's library were two sets of sermons by Samuel Clarke, one in eight and the other in ten volumes.[1] These works Johnson greatly esteemed. In his religious diaries he frequently mentions reading Clarke as part of his devotional exercises, and when he was dying, one of his last acts was to urge Dr. Brocklesby to study the sermons of this divine. Several other acquaintances, though puzzled by his regard for the unorthodox clergyman, attest to his strong admiration for him. William Seward, for instance, records that "A friend of Dr. Johnson asked him one day, whose sermons were the best in the English language. 'Why, Sir, bating a little heresy those of Dr. Samuel Clarke.' " Seward adds, "This great and excellent man had indeed good reason for thus highly praising them, as he told a relation of Dr. Clarke that they made him a Christian."[2]

This statement seems so extravagant that one might be sceptical that Johnson ever made it, were it not for further testimony. A similar though less well known comment was attributed to Johnson in the *Gentleman's Magazine* of May, 1788. The writer, who signed himself R. G. R., can be identified as the Reverend Richard George Robinson, who served as Chancellor's Vicar of Lichfield Cathedral for fifty-five years preceding his death in 1825.[3] From the context it appears that Robinson is reporting observations that Johnson made in October, 1784, during his last sojourn in the town of his birth.

Because this interesting item has never, I believe, been reproduced, the entire pertinent portion of it will be given here:

That Dr. Johnson once had his doubts and fears, respecting his own title to happiness hereafter, is very certain; but it would be absurdity in the extreme in any one who is the least conversant with his moral and religious essays, to suppose for a moment, that he could receive information from any man on the fundamental doctrines of our holy religion. About three months before his death, he declared to a lady of my acquaintance, that he would gladly undergo several severe fits of asthma, and other painful diseases which he mentioned, for a few more years of life, in order to perfect his repentance. The lady, expressing her surprise at such a declaration from *him,* who, she observed, had lived so good a life, and had served the cause of religion and morality so much by his writings, he replied, "Madam, no man can know the state of another man's soul so well as himself." He said also to a gentleman, a friend of mine, much about the same time, that, if he was saved, he should be "indebted for his salvation to the sermons of Dr. Clarke."[4]

What did Johnson find in the sermons of this clergyman that made such a strong appeal? And what did he mean when he said if he was saved, he would be indebted to Dr. Clarke? I believe there is an answer to these questions, but first let us see what kind of person and writer Clarke was.

Like William Law, Samuel Clarke (1675–1729) was an eighteenth-century divine. The similarity between the two ends there. One man was a mystic; the other, an extreme rationalist. Law belongs not so much to his age as to the small group who at all times have aspired to perfection. Clarke, who has been called a "Christian deist,"[5] was a cleric of a kind hardly to be encountered in any other era in church history. Well known as a preacher and writer, Clarke, unlike Law, was prominent in the public eye. He had initially attracted attention by defending for his D.D. thesis at Cambridge the proposition that "no article of the Christian faith is opposed to reason." His fame as a controversialist was established when in his Boyle lectures he attacked the ideas of Spinoza and

Hobbes on free will and necessity. Yet, despite his abilities, he never rose to a position higher than rector of St. James's, Westminster.

No one in church circles could forget the scandal Clarke had caused by expressing his views on the Trinity. Although he was never an avowed Socinian or Arian, a posture adopted by a number of others in the early eighteenth century, he took the position in his *Scripture Doctrine of the Trinity* that the Bible supported neither the Athanasian nor the Arian view. He concluded therefore that the Trinity was a subject open to question and one upon which a Christian might believe as he pleased.[6] This stand naturally shocked orthodox believers. Clarke further stirred the fire of controversy when he failed to include the celebration of Holy Communion in his church service on Trinity Sunday, 1713. He omitted this rite, it was thought, because he wished to avoid reciting the proper preface, a text on which he had stated reservations in his book on the Trinity. As a result he was censured by the Lower House of Convocation, and the bishops undertook an investigation of his position on the Trinity. He then made a somewhat ambiguous recantation and said he would refrain in the future from preaching on the topic.[7] Many years later, when Queen Caroline favored his promotion to a bishopric, Sir Robert Walpole tried to persuade him to subscribe again to the Thirty-nine Articles. Clarke, feeling that he could not in conscience do so, steadfastly refused. Although such a subscription was not necessary in order for a clergyman to be promoted to a bishopric, Clarke never received the miter and never advanced beyond the position of rector.[8]

Despite his reputation as an unsafe and even unorthodox clergyman, Clarke was generally regarded in his own day as a brilliant thinker. But his fame in that respect has faded. Leslie Stephen, who refers to him as "a second-rate advocate of other men's opinions," observes: "He adopts almost entirely the deist method, but applies it on behalf of the colourless doctrine which was in his mind identified with Christianity. More fitly than Tindal, who claimed the name for himself, he might be called a Christian deist. As such he might be considered as the chief intellectual light of what was called the Low Church Party."[9]

Like the Deists, Clarke affirmed that the basic evidence for believing in God was to be found in nature. He differed from many Deists in insisting there was no conflict between reason and revelation, and in asserting that Scripture confirms the existence of the God seen in nature. Such convictions were far from uncommon among clergymen of the Establishment. Mark Pattison, who had remarkable insight into the religious temper of the eighteenth century, rightly observes that the rationalism of that time was "a method rather than a doctrine, an unconscious assumption rather than a principle from which they reason. According to the assumption," he adds, "a man's religious belief is a result which issues at the end of an intellectual process. In arranging the steps of this process, they conceived natural religion to form the first stage of the journey. That stage theologians of all shades and parties travelled in company. It was only when they had reached the end of it that the Deist and the Christian apologist departed." In support of this contention Pattison cites various statements by such divines as Bishop Gibson, Humphrey Prideaux, Dean of Norwich, Archbishop Tillotson, and even Joseph Butler. All of these would have subscribed to the rule-of-thumb method of interpreting Scripture that Butler enunciated in the statement, ". . . if in revelation there be found any passages, the seeming meaning of which is contrary to natural religion, we may almost certainly conclude such seeming meaning not to be the real one."[10]

Clarke similarly stressed the prime importance of natural evidence. In a sermon entitled "Of Faith in God" he insists that "Natural religion is the best preparation for the reception of the Christian." He defines faith as "a rational persuasion and firm belief of His attributes discovered by nature, and of His promises made known in the Gospel, so as thereby to govern and direct our lives." The Bible, as he sees it, serves as a splendid commentary on what God commands and wishes, but the basic text that proves his existence is creation. Consequently, he says that the various arguments that prove the reality of God can be reduced to two: first, the existence of human beings shows there must have been a creator, and second, "the order and beauty of the world" indicates that there must have been a first cause.[11]

Clarke is so much the eighteenth-century rationalist that he has little respect for Christian tradition. He has still less confidence in a subjective basis of faith, whether it be called mysticism, the witness of the spirit, the inner light, or the gift of God. In his sermons he warns his readers equally against the dangers implicit in the superstitions of the Roman Church and the fanaticism of the dissenters. To him there is nothing mysterious in Christianity. It is all as clear and as demonstrable as a proposition in mathematics. We know that the Bible makes certain statements about a future life. We assume that Christ and the Apostles were honest. Therefore we must regard these statements as promises that will be kept, much as we would the terms of a properly executed civil contract. Clarke is such a rigid rationalist that he cannot accept the idea of religious mysteries. He believes there is not sufficient evidence in the Bible either to affirm or to deny the Trinity by a process of reason, and because of his rationalism, he cannot accept a mystery as something by its very nature inexplicable. A statement in the form of a paradox posed equal difficulties for him. Consequently when he deals with St. Paul's definition of faith as the evidence of things not seen, he qualifies it as, "Faith is that firm belief of things at present not seen; that conviction upon the mind of the truth of the promises and threatenings of God made known in the Gospel."[12]

Although Clarke had the reputation in his own day of being a great ethical philosopher, his claim to that title has also dwindled. Generally speaking, he is opposed to the self-interest principle of Hobbes and in sympathy with much of Shaftesbury's thinking. Clarke reasoned that there is a kind of absolute norm of what is true and good, or, to use his own terms, that there are in nature certain fitnesses and unfitnesses. These, perceived by the intellect of man, determine the rule of action or the law of nature, and by complying with this supreme law, man is enabled to pursue what is good. Not to comply, says Clarke, is to attempt "to destroy the order by which the universe subsists."[13]

As Basil Willey has observed, Clarke does not abandon Revelation, but it becomes secondary to reason. Similarly the law of nature, which is determined by the fitness or unfitness of things, does not conflict with the will of God, "but it is observable that 'the Will of God' takes second place here, as if its function were merely to ratify the enactments of the natural legislation."[14] Ideally, according to Clarke, man's reason should prompt him to conform to the rule of what is good and proper, but, inasmuch as circumstances may interfere with man's spontaneous orientation towards virtue, Clarke, like Shaftesbury, regards the traditional sanctions of rewards and penalties as aids to enforce compliance. These sanctions, however, are subordinate to the obligation imposed by the law of nature. On this subject he writes:

For the judgment and conscience of a man's own mind, concerning the reasonableness and fitness of the thing that his actions should be conformed to such or such a rule or law, is the truest and formallest obligation; even more properly and strictly so than any opinion whatsoever of the authority of the Giver of a law, or any regard he may have for its sanction by rewards and punishments. For whoever acts contrary to this sense and conscience of his own mind is necessarily self-condemned; and the greatest and strongest of all obligations is that which a man cannot break through without condemning himself. The dread of superior power and authority and the sanction of rewards and punishments, however indeed absolutely necessary to the government of frail and fallible creatures, and truly

the most effectual means of keeping them in their duty, is yet really
in itself only a secondary and additional obligation, or enforcement
of the first. The original obligation of all . . . is the eternal Reason
of things: that Reason which God himself, who has no superior
to direct him, and to whose happiness nothing can be added nor
anything diminished from it, yet constantly obliges himself to govern this world by.[15]

To Clarke the law of the natural fitnesses of things is an absolute. In the above passage and elsewhere God appears as a
kind of first agent whose task it is to help keep "the eternal
Reason of things" in operation. As Leslie Stephen has remarked: "Clarke does not shrink from maintaining that moral
obligation is antecedent even to the consideration of its being
the rule of God. . . . Nature, the true metaphysical deity of
Clarke and his school, is sometimes identified with God, and
sometimes appears to be in some sense a common superior of
man and his Creator. The law of nature thus becomes a code
of absolutely true and unalterable propositions, strictly analo-
gous to those of pure mathematics." Because of this kind of
reasoning, Stephen adds, Clarke may be placed in a middle
position between the Deists and the orthodox believers of his
own day. "Though not an originator of thought, he represented that modification of current opinions which commended itself to the most freethinking party within the bor-
ders of the Church."[16]

Clarke's sermons were widely read in an age with a special
liking for homiletics. By 1756 his collected sermons, usually
printed in sets of eight or ten volumes, had reached an eighth
edition. Nevertheless, there were those, like Joseph Butler and
Francis Hutcheson, who felt compelled to challenge him on
one point or another. Even his deistical opponents could recognize that his stand was often rather distant from orthodoxy.
Anthony Collins, for instance, observed that, "Nobody doubted
the existence of God until Dr. Clarke strove to prove it."[17] This
witty remark appears to have had more truth in it than one
might suspect. When David Hume was dying, he was visited by

James Boswell, who eagerly questioned him on his beliefs. During the conversation the sceptical philosopher remarked that as a young man he had been religious, but "He said he never had entertained any belief in Religion since he began to read Locke and Clarke."[18] Although Boswell frequently baited Dr. Johnson by reporting Hume's heterodox opinions, he apparently missed the opportunity to repeat this particular comment. One would like to know Johnson's reaction upon hearing that the clergyman who had "made him a Christian" had caused David Hume to become a sceptic.

Having observed some of the more general aspects of Clarke's religion, we must now address ourselves to a consideration of his influence on Johnson. What explains Johnson's admiration for this clergyman, despite the evidence that his own religious beliefs were in many instances different from Clarke's?

It should be made clear in the first place that Johnson's esteem for Clarke developed relatively late in life. Earlier he had felt an antipathy for the writings of the clergyman, as indicated in a letter of Dr. Adams, Master of Pembroke College. After Johnson's death Adams wrote to James Boswell: "The Doctor's prejudices were the strongest, and certainly in another sense the weakest, that ever possessed a sensible man. You know his extreme zeal for orthodoxy. But did you ever hear what he told me himself? That he had made it a rule not to admit Dr. Clarke's name in his Dictionary. This, however, wore off. At some distance of time he advised with me what books he should read in defence of the Christian Religion. I recommended 'Clarke's Evidences of Natural and Revealed Religion,' as the best of the kind; and I find in what is called his 'Prayers and Meditations,' that he was frequently employed in the latter part of his time in reading Clarke's Sermons."[19]

In addition to the exclusion of Clarke from his *Dictionary*, there seems to be further evidence that in middle life Johnson had a positive distaste for this rationalist clergyman. Although he was later to express admiration for his style, at one point in *Rasselas* he appears to satirize both Clarke's metaphysical ideas and his abstract language. In Chapter XXII the young prince encounters a philosopher who preaches, "The way to be happy is to live according to Nature, in obedience to that universal and unalterable law with which every heart is originally impressed; which is not written on it by precept, but engraven by destiny; not instilled by education but infused at our nativity." Rasselas, intensely interested, then asks the philosopher "what it is to live according to Nature." He replies, "To live according to Nature is to act always with due regard to the fitness arising from the relations and qualities of causes and effects; to concur with the great and unchangeable scheme of universal felicity; to co-operate with the general disposition and tendency of the present system of things." Johnson then gives the satiric thrust to this reasoning with the remark, "The prince soon found that this was one of the sages whom he should understand less, as he heard him longer."

Although certain writers have interpreted this section of *Rasselas* as a satire on Rousseau's teachings, this opinion seems erroneous. In the first place, neither in his *Dictionary* nor elsewhere does Johnson use "nature" as an equivalent for primitive life. When he alludes to this subject, he uses the term "savage life" or "state of nature." On the other hand, one of the definitions of nature in the *Dictionary* is: "An imaginary being supposed to preside over the material and animal world." The satiric import of this definition is made clear later when, in expanding upon his definitions of the word, he quotes from Boyle, "*Nature* is sometimes indeed commonly taken for a kind of semideity. In this sense it is best not to use it at all." In *Rasselas* Johnson himself employs the term in this sense chiefly to satirize writers like Shaftesbury, Richard Cumberland, and Samuel Clarke, who treat nature as a kind of animated force acting sometimes independently of, or even in the place of, God. When the sophist in *Rasselas* tells his listeners that "the way to be happy is to live according to nature, in obedience to that universal and unalterable law with which every heart is originally impressed," he echoes the sentiments of Richard Cumberland, who remarks, "The law of nature is a proposition proposed to the observation of, or impress'd upon, the mind, with sufficient clearness by the nature of things, from the will of the first cause, which points out that possible action of a rational agent which will chiefly promote the common good and by which only the entire happiness of particular persons can be obtained."[20] When the sophist attempts to answer the query of Rasselas, however, the language seems more like a travesty on the vague metaphysical reasoning of Clarke, especially because of the latter's frequent use of the terms "fitness" and "unfitness." What particularly annoyed Johnson, it would appear, was Clarke's abstruseness in passages such as the following: "That there are differences of things, and different relations, respects, or proportions of some things towards others; it is evident and undeniable. . . . That from these different relations of different things there necessarily arises an agreement or disagreement of some things with others, or a fitness or unfitness of the application of different things or different relations one to another, is likewise as plain as that there is any such thing as proportion or disproportion in geometry or arithmetic."[21]

If Johnson satirized Clarke's style, as he appears to have done, how do we explain his later statement, reported by William Seward, that "In his opinion Clarke was the most complete literary character that England ever produced"?[22] Possibly his idea of Clarke's style changed, but it is important to observe that when Johnson praised the clergyman in later life, he confined his admiration to the sermons. It is noteworthy that though the *Sale Catalogue* of his library shows he owned two sets of the sermons, it lists none of Clarke's other writings.

Furthermore, it seems clear that Johnson never expressed anything but disdain for Clarke's view that the universe is governed by an insuperable law of the natural fitness of things. "His profound adoration of the GREAT FIRST CAUSE," Boswell observes, "was such as to set him above that 'Philosophy and vain deceit' with which men of narrower conceptions have been infected. I have heard him strongly maintain that 'what is right is not so from any natural fitness, but because God wills it to be right.' "[23]

Johnson's esteem for Clarke was based on certain opinions the clergyman expressed in his sermons. In these the style is quite different. The prose is simpler and clearer, and the sermons are well organized. Clarke generally begins with a scriptural text that forms the theme of his discourse; he next introduces the subject, often by defining important terms; he then proceeds to discuss each point in logical sequence. Johnson, whose own sermons follow a similar pattern, undoubtedly admired this clear method of presentation. Nevertheless, it was not for style but for content that he read the sermons.

His special interest in them can be dated from 1766. On March 28 of that year he notes for the first time in his private diaries that he has read one of them. The sermons occupied his attention frequently thereafter, and his admiration for Clarke continued to increase until the very end of his life. But despite the esteem in which Johnson came to hold Clarke, he never lost sight of the fact that on the Trinity, at least, Clarke was an unsafe thinker. In a conversation that took place on April 7, 1778, he remarked, "I should recommend Dr. Clarke's sermons, were he orthodox. However, it is very well known *where* he was not orthodox, which was upon the doctrine of the Trinity, as to which he is a condemned heretick; so one is aware of it."[24]

Here, although Johnson indicates strong opposition to Clarke's interpretation of the Trinity, what surprises one is the implication that on other matters Clarke was sufficiently orthodox to pass uncensured. It is surprising because it could hardly have been true. Time and again Johnson must have encountered notions in Clarke which were strongly at variance with his own opinions and practices. For instance, there was a fundamental disagreement between their views on the function and importance of prayer. To Clarke, prayer is chiefly a duty to be performed in order to show one's submission to God. It should be employed, he comments, to ask forgiveness, to implore assistance in being obedient, and to petition for whatever is good for ourselves and others. Prayer is misused, he cautions, when employed to ask mercy for those already deceased.[25] In contrast to the clergyman's rationalistic explanation is the tone as well as the substance of Johnson's own prayers. With him, as with Law, prayer is a means of communication with the Deity, a form of spiritual exercise that serves as nourishment to the soul. Furthermore, despite Clarke's warnings on the subject, Johnson continued to pray for his deceased relatives and friends.

Throughout his adult years, Johnson petitioned that he might be endowed, especially through the agency of the Holy Ghost, with the power of grace. Clarke, instead of seeing grace as an important supernatural element in Christianity, regards it chiefly as a part of man's rational faculties. To him, it is a gift of God in the same sense that nature or reason is. He writes: "The efficacy of the grace of God can consist only in laying before men strong arguments for their conviction, and giving them sufficient helps and assistances to overcome whatever would hinder them from acting according to such conviction." Furthermore, "the grace of God must of necessity always be understood to have the nature of a moral assistance only, which does perfectly agree with men's free use of their faculties."[26] In short, grace operates very much like reason, from which it is scarcely distinguished.

The different views of the two men on the nature of grace

help to explain their fundamental disagreement on the purpose and effect of partaking of the Lord's Supper. Johnson
discusses this subject at length in two sermons (IX and XXII),
and Clarke in four related sermons.[27] In Sermon IX Johnson
several times compares the Lord's Supper with the sacrament
of Baptism. He observes: "If we consider this Sacrament as a
renewal of the vow of Baptism, and the means of reconciling
us to God, and restoring us to a participation of the merits of
Our Saviour, which we have forfeited by sin, we shall need no
persuasions to a frequent communion." Clarke, on the other
hand, stresses what he considers as the important difference
between the sacraments. In the second of his four sermons
entitled "The Nature, End, and Design of Holy Communion"
he writes: "The Sacrament of the Lord's Supper is not itself
like Baptism, a rite appointed for the remission of sins: but
'tis a commemoration only of that all-sufficient sacrifice which
was once offered for an eternal expiation. To imagine that the
Lord's Supper, which is to be repeated perpetually, has such a
promise annexed to it of taking away all past sins, as Baptism
had, which was to be administered but once, is a dangerous
and fatal error." Johnson, of course, does not affirm that
Communion by itself is a means of obtaining remission of sins,
but he believes it to be much more than a commemorative
rite. Unlike Clarke, he regards it as the means by which the
will is strengthened and by which the Christian in his desire
for amendment secures the co-operation of God through "the
supernatural and extraordinary influences of grace" (Sermon
IX).

In general Johnson regards the sacraments as integral and
necessary parts of Christianity. Clarke, because of his rationalism, treats them as little more than a form of ritual. This becomes particularly apparent in a sermon entitled "Of Receiving the Holy Ghost." Here he affirms "that the nature and
spirit of the Christian Religion is to lay as little stress as possible upon all *external* rites; and to have the greatest regard

that can be to the moral qualifications of men's minds." He grants that Baptism and Communion are among the more valid external rites; yet even these have little or no value in themselves, for "no rites or observations whatsoever are ever accepted in the stead of, or without the inward moral and virtuous disposition of heart and mind. Not Baptism itself; not the Sacrament of the Lord's Supper; not even the miraculous gifts and graces of the Holy Ghost are of any avail to an unrighteous person."

Clarke's notions of what constitutes Christianity are thrown into grotesque relief when contrasted with those of a High Churchman like William Law. As we have seen, Law is one of the great exponents of the doctrine of Christian perfection. Clarke, too, writes on this subject in a sermon entitled "Christians Ought to Endeavour to Attain Perfection." He indicates that he knows the proper terms when he remarks that the virtues Christians should strive for are holiness, purity of mind, and Christian charity, but he seems incapable of grasping what is really implied by Christian perfection. "By being Perfect," he writes, "is signified a man's having attained such a habit of doing righteousness, or of virtuous living, as that it becomes *easy* and *delightful* and, in a manner, natural to him." Such a statement is, of course, contrary to the whole spirit of Christian perfection. As Law constantly emphasizes, perfection is such a lofty endeavor that one must constantly struggle even to approach the goal. By its very nature it can never be easy.

Although Clarke was an excellent classical scholar, he generally refrains from incorporating classical allusions in his sermons and, for that matter, almost never quotes any work other than the Bible. Nevertheless, the concept of the golden mean sometimes appears in his religious works. Because all extremes are deemed contrary to reason, it is perhaps not surprising that Clarke's idea of Christian perfection conforms pretty much to a Homeric pattern of virtue and integrity. Nevertheless, to have a clergyman caution Christians against going to extremes in trying to achieve perfection seems highly ironical. He writes, in the sermon entitled "Christians Ought to Endeavour to Attain Perfection": " 'tis evident that the perfection recommended in Scripture does not consist in works of supererogation, as the Church of Rome has vainly imagined. It does not consist in will-worship and works of voluntary humility, works performed over and above the commandments of God, and beyond the obligation of our Christian duty." It would thus appear that perfection is not an ultimate stage but a sensible middle-of-the-road position. Certainly if Johnson read this sermon, he must have perceived that to urge this kind of restraint upon the seeker after Christian perfection is like advising the contender for an eternal crown not to tire himself by sprinting.

What, then, did attract Johnson to Clarke? It could scarcely have been the clergyman's interpretation of such matters as prayer, the sacraments, or grace. Obviously it was not his fervor, for the sermons have none of the hortatory appeal of William Law's works. One must conclude, I believe, that Clarke appealed to him for two reasons. In the first place, he had a kind of tranquilizing effect on Johnson's scruples; in the second place, he made an important contribution to his understanding of the Atonement.

As S. C. Roberts has pointed out, Johnson was seldom happy in his religion, but "the divine who gave him the most satisfaction was the heterodox Samuel Clarke."[28] One explanation is that during most of his life Johnson was sorely disturbed by religious scruples. These scruples, as we have indicated, were probably augmented by his reading of William Law, especially when he compared Law's ideal of Christian perfection with his own shortcomings. The road Law marked out as leading to salvation was a steep and thorny way. That same road, as described by Clarke, was much smoother, and the goal much easier of access. Although I believe Johnson would have been annoyed with Clarke's superficial reasoning on perfection, if he read through the sermon on this subject, he might have been comforted by the conclusion in which Clarke affirms: "What has been said concerning the true nature of Christian perfection may suffice to remove needless fears and scruples out of the minds of melancholy and pious persons, who when they read that they are commanded *to be perfect, even as their Father which is in heaven* is perfect, are apt to be dejected and look upon their duty as impossible. . . . from what has been already explained, 'tis evident that in that precept cannot be meant perfection of degrees but only a similitude or imitation in kind."

Throughout his sermons Clarke preaches that the chief requirements of the Christian are a degree of resignation, a sense of charity, and conformity to the commandments. Besides his numerous brief admonitions on the danger of zeal and scrupulosity, he has two sermons especially devoted to consoling those unduly concerned with their own unworthiness. In the first of these, entitled "Of Religious Melancholy," he examines various causes of apprehension. They are: (1) a bodily indisposition or lack of health, (2) a feeling that causes people to think that in spite of their conformity to religious duties they have not improved, (3) a belief that some special decree has excluded them from mercy, (4) a fear of having committed the unpardonable sin, and (5) a fear that past sins have not been pardoned. Melancholy caused by any of these reasons, Clarke affirms, is usually evidence of unwarranted scrupulosity. In another sermon, "Of the Sin Against the Holy Ghost," Clarke offers comfort to anyone disturbed by the reflection that he is guilty of the unpardonable sin. While there is no specific evidence that Johnson was disturbed by this particular scruple, it is at least possible that in periods of strong self-abnegation it may have occurred to him that he was guilty of this worst of all offenses. If so, he could have received assurance from Clarke's interpretation that this sin pertained only to the Pharisees who had accused Christ of casting out devils by the power of Beelzebub, and that it is impossible for Christians to commit any sin that is unpardonable.

There was one sermon from which Johnson apparently derived particular solace. On December 5, 1784, just eight days before his death, he retired after dinner and asked John Hoole to read to him "a sermon of Dr. Clarke's 'On the Shortness of Life.' "[29] The full title of this work is "The Shortness and Vanity of Human Life." Because Johnson had probably consulted it on many previous occasions, it is interesting to examine what Clarke says in it. The sermon is prefaced by a text from Job (5:6–7): "Although affliction cometh not forth of the dust, neither doth trouble spring out of the ground; Yet man is born unto trouble, as the sparks fly upward." Clarke begins by explaining that the particular purpose of the Book of Job is to provide an example of "a man perfect in his generation and of unspotted integrity . . . whose strength God was pleased to try with one of the greatest ca lamities." Under this trial Job "sinned not nor charged God foolishly, nor suffered his integrity to depart from him." Instead, throughout his affliction he maintained that it "was by no means an evidence of his being wicked and forsaken of God, but an effect of the divine power and providence which governs the world, and brings about his own designs by wise, though ofttimes (for the present) secret and inscrutable methods."

Clarke then quotes several passages of Scripture to show that misery and afflication are the lot of human kind, whether they be wicked or virtuous. These sufferings come not by chance, but by the wise dispensation of God. "And this indeed," he adds, "is the only true and solid comfort that can possibly be afforded to a rational and considerate mind, in order to support him both under the troubles of life, and against the fears of death." Although Clarke is seldom impassioned in his style, there is a little more fervor than usual in this sermon when he concludes: "I say, the thought of God's governing the world is such a consideration as is sufficient to cause to vanish all the tragical complaints of the miseries and vanities of human life. For, though we could not conjecture at any reason why he has made us thus, though we were not able to discern any kind and gracious designs in the afflictions that he lays upon us, though the ways of Providence had been still more inextricable than they are, and his judgments far more unsearchable than we now apprehend them to be, yet certainly infinite wisdom and infinite goodness might well be trusted and relied upon by any reasonable and considerate mind."

Anyone acquainted with the works of Johnson need not be reminded how frequently he echoes this message. It appears in his essays, notably *Adventurer* 126, in *The Vanity of Human Wishes,* and in other works. The importance of resignation is particularly set before readers in two of his sermons, XV and XVI. Like Clarke's sermon, both are prefaced by quotations from the Book of Job. Although Johnson is not plagiarizing Clarke, there is a similarity in emphasis. For instance, Clarke writes: "That Power which in the frame and construction of the natural world has adjusted all things by weight and measure; that Power which with exquisite artifice has made every thing in the exactest harmony and proportion, to conspire regularly and uniformly towards accomplishing the best and wisest end, in completing the beautiful order and fabrick of the material universe; that Power might surely in his government of the moral world likewise, in his disposing of intelligent and rational creatures, even though we could give no account at all of his ways, yet with the justest reason be believed to direct all things for the best, and in order to bring about the noblest and most excellent ends." Johnson's reasoning on this subject is much the same: Every man who murmurs under afflictions "knows when he reflects calmly, that the world is neither eternal, nor independent; that we neither were produced, nor are preserved by chance. But that heaven and earth, and the whole system of things, were created by an infinite and perfect Being, who still continues to superintend and govern them. He knows that this great Being is infinitely wise, and infinitely good; so that the end which he proposes must necessarily be the final happiness of those beings that depend upon him, and the means, by which he promotes that end, must undoubtedly be the wisest and the best" (Sermon XVI).

Although Johnson already knew all that Clarke had to say in his sermon on "The Shortness and Vanity of Human Life," he was apparently comforted by Clarke's presentation of the message that although every man endures afflictions, there is a meaning to suffering. He must also have found a measure of consolation in Clarke's frequent assertions that salvation is not so difficult of attainment and that one can err in being overscrupulous. Nevertheless, there was something more important that he got from reading Clarke. That was an interpretation of the significance of the Atonement, a subject treated in the following chapter.

III · THE ATONEMENT

Whoever reviews the state of his own mind from the dawn of manhood to its decline, and considers what he pursued or dreaded, slighted or esteemed, at different periods of his age, will have no reason to imagine such changes of sentiment peculiar to any station or character.

Johnson, Rambler *196*

The doctrine of the Atonement, when viewed in the light of a long history of theological discussion, is an exceedingly complex subject. There is no need here to review the various interpretations of why Christ's sacrifice was necessary or on what grounds God was pleased to accept it. We shall be concerned chiefly with two interpretations of what the Atonement meant to humanity. The Church of England teaches that by his death on the Cross, Christ redeemed man from past sin and so reconciled him with God that salvation is made possible on the condition of obedience to the commandments and, when that fails, on true repentance for sin. In this doctrine is embedded the traditional Christian idea that Christ performed a vicarious sacrifice in that he took upon himself the burden of sin and suffered in the place of man. A secondary and related concept is that Christ's sacrifice set before mankind an ideal example of goodness and godliness for all to follow.

The significance of the Atonement, both as a vicarious sacrifice and as a supreme example, is emphasized throughout the Book of Common Prayer. For instance, the Collect for the Second Sunday after Easter reads: "Almighty God, who hast given thine only Son to be unto us both a sacrifice for sin, and also an ensample of godly life; Give us grace that we may always most thankfully receive that his inestimable benefit, and also daily endeavour ourselves to follow the blessed steps of his most holy life, through the same Jesus Christ our Lord."

Both doctrines, that of the vicarious sacrifice and that of the example set by Christ, are fundamental to Christianity. But of the two, the doctrine of the vicarious sacrifice, containing within it the very essence of the Atonement, has seemed more important to most Christians, for, it is reasoned, if Christ had not first removed the burden of sin, frail humanity could not by its own efforts have qualified for salvation. On this subject, however, there has not always been agreement. Some, while recognizing the great personal sacrifice of Christ, have held that he did not suffer in man's *stead* and therefore did not take upon himself the sins of mankind. They reason that Christ set a great and noble example and by following his light man is enabled, through his own efforts, to attain salvation. There are various modifications of this belief, but, stated here in its simplest terms, it may be called the doctrine of the exemplary sacrifice, as opposed to the more generally stressed doctrine of the vicarious Atonement.

Among those who have attached primary importance to the exemplary nature of the sacrifice was William Law. As we have seen, this eighteenth-century clergyman was a devout High Churchman, but he did not subscribe fully to the doctrine that Christ suffered primarily in the *stead* of mankind. He did believe, and very firmly, that Christ died on *behalf* of mankind, that he is the Saviour and Redeemer, and that through him and by him alone man can attain salvation. But this was to be accomplished by following Christ's example. To Law, the death on the Cross was a wondrous mystical act, unique and unparalleled, that made possible the redemption of man through its inspiring exemplary force. Several times in his writings he uses the image that Christ is "the Captain of our salvation." He is the One who leads the way on the steep road to salvation, who inspires faltering and sinful humanity, and who, by investing them with something of his own spiritual nature, makes possible their ultimate victory.

Since any paraphrase of Law is likely to do him less than justice, it will be well to quote one of his many comments on the Atonement. The following passage, taken from *A Serious Call,* shows the kind of emphasis he accords the exemplary nature of the sacrifice.

> The Christian's great conquest over the world is all contained in the mystery of Christ upon the cross. It was there and from thence that He taught all Christians how they were to come out of and conquer the world, and what they were to do in order to be His disciples. And all the doctrines, sacraments, and institutions of the Gospel are only so many explications of the meaning, and applications of the benefit of this great mystery.
>
> And the state of Christianity implieth nothing else but an entire, absolute conformity to that spirit which Christ showed in the mysterious sacrifice of Himself upon the cross.
>
> Every man, therefore, is only so far a Christian as he partakes of this spirit of Christ. It was this that made St. Paul so passionately express himself. "God forbid that I should glory, save in the cross of our Lord Jesus Christ." But why does he glory? Is it because Christ had suffered in his stead, and had excused him from suffering? No, by no means. But it was because his Christian profession had called him to that honour of suffering with Christ, and of dying to the world under reproach and contempt as He had done upon the cross.[1]

Law's belief was not the superficial notion of an unthinking or unspiritual man. Nor was it promulgated with the intent of diminishing the significance of Christ's dying on the Cross. Furthermore, although he usually rules out the idea of a propitiatory sacrifice, sometimes he merely subordinates it. As Stephen Hobhouse observes, in Law's writings "the substitutionary idea ('Christ died in our stead') is not rejected entirely; it is in effect swallowed up in the new birth of Christ in us." This new birth proceeds, moreover, not merely from the example of Christ but also from "his inspiration, and ultimately through man's response and identification with Himself."[2]

Law's emphasis on the exemplary character of the sacrifice was closely related to his teachings on Christian perfection. According to this doctrine, man's purpose in life is to work towards his salvation by imitating Christ. This is to be accomplished by renouncing the world and by an ascetic dedication of self to a life of sanctity. Implicit in Law's view of the Atonement is the notion that a strong emphasis on the vicarious sacrifice, by which Christ takes on the sins of mankind, diminishes the importance of what man must do for himself. On the other hand, by stressing the importance of the exemplary sacrifice, Law is better able to support the doctrine of perfection, by which man through his own strenuous efforts to imitate Christ attains salvation. Seen in this light, Law's belief in the primary importance of Christ's example can be better understood. Nevertheless, as another sturdy Christian pointed out, this view of the Atonement departed from the orthodox interpretation.

Although John Wesley's Evangelical conversion appears to have been influenced by his reading of William Law, and although he continued to admire much of Law's writing, he expressed strong disapproval of his reasoning on the Atonement. In his published "Extract of a Letter to the Reverend Mr. Law," Wesley insisted that Christ's death was first and foremost a vicarious sacrifice. It had to be, he explained, in order to remove the guilt of past sins and to reconcile man to God; moreover, if Christ had not assumed the burden of future sin, man could not by repentance and amendment alone attain salvation. Although Wesley conceded that the example set by Christ is a secondary benefit accruing from his sacrifice, he maintained that the chief benefit resides in the propitiatory nature of the act.[3]

What were Johnson's views of the Atonement? This question yields to no simple explanation, for nowhere does he write at length on it. Furthermore it was a topic on which he would hesitate to be dogmatic. Presumably he had read widely on the Atonement, as he had on other religious questions. Inasmuch as he owned the works of St. Anselm, he was undoubtedly acquainted with such a fundamental treatise on the Atonement as Anselm's *Cur Deus Homo*. He was familiar, too, with the writings of Grotius on this subject. As a boy he had tried to read the *De Veritate Religionis Christi*, and he returned to it later in life. Although he admitted in 1773 that he had never yet read Grotius' *De Satisfactione Christi*, he recommended it to Boswell and at the same time expressed the intention of reading it himself.[4] Johnson would also have encountered discussions of the Atonement in William Law and in numerous other religious writers. From his reading he would perceive that it is an exceedingly complex theological question that has been variously interpreted since the early centuries of Christianity. Knowing this, he would be reluctant to dogmatize in a narrow way on such an important Christian belief.

Although Johnson never wrote at length on the Atonement, there are various allusions to it in his works, and on two different occasions he discussed his interpretation with Boswell. His comments, when carefully studied, indicate that during the course of his life his views changed. This change, though highly significant, did not result in a complete reversal of his position. It represented, rather, a shift in emphasis and a development in his thinking. As we shall see, it appears at one stage to have reached a climactic point, but it was not the kind of experience the Evangelicals called the new birth. Although Johnson's altered view of the Atonement may have affected other aspects of his religion, and although it may ultimately have helped to mitigate his fear of death, he remained the person he had always been, a man of genuine piety, inclined to be overscrupulous, never yielding to despair, but never for any length of time completely at peace.

For many years, probably during most of his adult life, Johnson favored the interpretation that the Atonement was in the nature of a penal and an exemplary sacrifice. The clearest evidence in support of this statement appears in Boswell's *Tour to the Hebrides*. On August 22, 1773, while they were visiting at Aberdeen, Boswell engaged Johnson in a discussion of religion. "I spoke of the satisfaction of Christ," Boswell reports. "He said his notion was that it did not atone for the sins of the world. But by satisfying divine justice, by showing that no less than the Son of God suffered for sin, it showed men and innumerable created beings the heinousness of sin, and therefore rendered it unnecessary for divine vengeance to be exercised against sinners, as it otherwise must have been. In this way it might operate even in favour of those who had never heard of it. As to those who did hear of it, the effect it should produce would be repentance and piety, by impressing upon the mind a just notion of sin. That original sin was the propensity to evil, which no doubt was occasioned by the Fall."[5] Boswell adds: "He presented this great subject in a new light to me and rendered much more rational and clear the ideas of what our Saviour has done for us, as it removed the notion of imputed righteousness in the usual sense, and the difficulty of our righteousness co-operating; whereas by his view Christ has done all already that he had to do, or is ever to do, for mankind, by making his great satisfaction, the consequences of which will affect each individual according to the particular conduct of each. I would illustrate this by saying that Christ's satisfaction is like there being a sun placed to show light to men, so that it depends upon themselves whether they will walk the right way or not, which they could not have done without that sun, 'the sun of righteousness.' "[6]

The view expressed here, as one may see, rejects the idea of a vicarious sacrifice. Boswell's elaboration on Johnson's words suggests the notion of the exemplary sacrifice. In this respect the interpretation resembles William Law's. It differs, however, in that it fails to incorporate Law's mystical belief that man receives a new birth through Christ's death on the Cross. Furthermore, Johnson's own explanation, by stressing such terms as "justice" and "vengeance," suggests that Christ paid a kind of legal penalty for mankind. There is none of this legalistic emphasis in the author of *A Serious Call*. It does appear, in different forms, in various writers of the Reformation period. Even Grotius, though seeing the Atonement as motivated by divine love, favored the idea that God is a "supreme governor, who must preserve law and order. Christ, as head of the Body of which we are members, is punished for the maintenance of authority."[7] Very likely the view that Johnson expressed in 1773 represented a blending of ideas he had read in other writers, in addition to Law. In any event, it seems clear that at this period, at least, he did not fully subscribe to a belief in the vicarious or propitiatory nature of the sacrifice.

Where does one find support for this statement in his works? Until late in life he says relatively little of a positive nature on the Atonement, but certain inferences may be drawn from the treatment of related topics in his earlier writings. Of particular significance are his remarks in *Rambler* 110. The theme of this essay is the importance of repentance. God is merciful and will forgive the sins of a truly repentant person, he affirms, but curiously there is no mention of Christ and his mercy. Several times in the course of the essay the word "propitiation" is employed, but, significantly, always in the sense that it is man who must atone for his offenses. In the past, he observes, people have used various forms of propitiation and atonement that fear has dictated. Nevertheless, these practices show that in all ages man has believed in the principle of "the placability of the divine nature." If man must rely on self-atonement, however, his propitiatory acts must presumably be in proportion to his sins. But how may one be certain when the proper balance has been achieved? The attempt to solve this difficulty produces a conflict, as Johnson indicates when he remarks that man must always fear the possibility of deciding in his own favor and of failing thereby to atone sufficiently for his offenses. In this discussion one seems to be near the very heart of Johnson's conflicts.

Certain religious terms in Johnson's *Dictionary* also reflect his emphasis on man's rather than on Christ's expiation. For instance, he defines "Atonement," in the religious sense, as "expiation; expiatory equivalent; with *for*." What seems chiefly significant is the passage selected to illustrate how the word is employed. The quotation is from the Bible, but from the Old rather than the New Testament. Furthermore it refers to the atonement of men, not to the Atonement of Christ: "And the Levites were purified, and they washed their cloaths, and Aaron offered them as an offering before the Lord; and Aaron made an *Atonement* for them to cleanse them" (Num. 8:21). Similarly, when he defines the term "expiation" there is no reference to Christ's sacrifice. It is only in connection with the adjective "expiatory" that the specific Christian allusion appears. Even here the reference is made, not in the definition, but in the illustrative passage that accompanies it. After defining "expiatory" as "having the power of expiation or atonement," he quotes Hooker, one of his favorite writers, to the effect that, "His voluntary death for others prevailed with God, and had the force of an *expiatory* sacrifice."

It is interesting to see how Johnson deals in his *Dictionary* with the words "redemption" and "redeem." He defines "redemption" first as "ransome, release;" and secondly as "purchase of God's favour by the death of Christ." The emphasis here seems to be on the penal nature of the sacrifice. In the 1755 edition of the *Dictionary* he supported the second definition by quotations from Shakespeare and Dryden. In the revised 1773 edition he added a third illustrative quotation. This was taken from Robert Nelson, a devout layman and Nonjuror of the early eighteenth century. The sentence is: "The salvation of our souls may be advanced by firmly believing the mysteries of our redemption; and by imitating the example of those primitive patterns of piety." Why did Johnson add this quotation? We must keep in mind that in compiling the *Dictionary* he selected passages not only to illustrate the meanings of words but also to provide readers with strikingly beautiful or strongly didactic gems of thought. Although the excerpt from Nelson adds nothing that further clarifies the meaning of "redemption," it does stress both the mystical nature and the exemplary character of Christ's sacrifice. The fact that he provided this additional quotation may be an indication that Johnson was at this period giving particular thought to the Atonement.

There is further evidence pointing in this direction in his treatment of "redeem." In the first printings of the *Dictionary* five definitions are given for this verb. Only the last of these, "To save the world from the curse of sin," makes an allusion to Christ's sacrifice. In the revised edition of 1773, however, he added a sixth definition: "To perform the work of universal redemption; to confer the inestimable benefit of reconciliation to God." The terms employed here are taken from the Book of Common Prayer. The phrase "inestimable benefit," for instance, appears in the Collect, quoted above, for the Second Sunday after Easter. The added definition, with its allusions to the broader implications of the sacrifice, shows that Johnson was not entirely satisfied with his first explanations. It may be taken as a further indication that by 1773 he had started to restudy Christian doctrine and to reassess his own beliefs, particularly his idea of the Atonement.

The most positive evidence that Johnson changed his notion of the Atonement is supplied by Boswell. We have already quoted from his conversation of 1773, in which Johnson expressed the opinion that Christ did not expiate the sins of mankind. Eight years later, on June 3, 1781, the two friends again entered into a discussion of this subject. At this time Johnson, having altered his views, stressed the expiatory character of the sacrifice. Furthermore, he seemed eager to go on record as believing that Christ had atoned for the sins of mankind, for he asked Boswell to remember his words, and when the latter suggested that he dictate his thoughts, he readily complied. Since the whole passage appears in Boswell's *Life,* only the most significant parts will be reproduced here:

> The great sacrifice for the sins of mankind was offered at the death of the MESSIAH, who is called in scripture, "The Lamb of God, that taketh away the sins of the world." To judge the reasonableness of the scheme of redemption, it must be considered as necessary to the government of the universe, that God should make known his perpetual and irreconcilable detestation of moral evil. He might indeed punish, and punish only the offenders; but as the end of punishment is not revenge of crimes, but propagation of virtue, it was more becoming the Divine clemency to find another manner of proceeding, less destructive to man, and at least equally powerful to promote goodness. The end of punishment is to reclaim and warn. *That* punishment will both reclaim and warn, which shews evidently such abhorrence of sin in God, as may deter us from it, or strike us with dread of vengeance when we have committed it. This is effected by vicarious punishment. Nothing could more testify the opposition between the nature of God and moral evil, or more amply display his justice, to men and angels, to all orders and successions of beings, than that it was necessary for the highest and purest nature, even for DIVINITY itself, to pacify the demands for vengeance, by a painful death; of which the natural effect will be, that when justice is appeased, there is a proper place for the exercise of mercy; and that such propitiation shall supply, in some degree, the imperfections of our obedience, and the inefficacy of our repentance: for, obedience and repentance, such as we can perform, are still necessary. . . . The peculiar doctrine of Christianity is, that of an universal sacrifice, and perpetual propitiation. Other prophets only proclaimed the will and the threatenings of God. Christ satisfied his justice.[8]

This statement reveals an important change. Johnson no longer believes that it is man alone who must make propitiation for his sins. Christ by his universal sacrifice has made a perpetual propitiation. And this propitiation supplies the imperfections of man's obedience and repentance. True, Johnson qualifies the statement by saying that Christ makes up for man's inadequacy "in some degree," a qualification that implies, as we have indicated, a shift in emphasis rather than a complete reversal of opinion. Nevertheless, by 1781 his idea of the Atonement had clearly altered and the former view that it served chiefly as an exemplary act is no longer predominant. Instead, he has now arrived at the more generally held Christian belief that the death on the Cross was truly an expiatory sacrifice.

What other evidence is there that Johnson changed his view of the Atonement? There is some, but none so specific as that which Boswell supplies. Johnson's prayers are notable, as we have observed, for the frequent supplications that the Holy Spirit may fortify him with grace. On the other hand, until the last few years of his life, there are relatively few allusions to Christ, except in the formal liturgical ending of the prayers. Despite Law's urging that one address his prayers directly to Christ, Johnson never does. There are also fewer references to Christ in the main context of his prayers than to the Holy Spirit. This seems strange in a pious person who firmly believed in the Trinity. When he wrote, on April 21, 1764, "I will pray to God for resolution, and will endeavour to strengthen my faith in Christ by commemorating his death," certainly it was not because his faith in the divinity of Christ was weak. More likely it was because he could not at this time fully subscribe, as did most devout churchmen, to a strong belief in the propitiatory nature of the sacrifice. This possibility is strengthened by the consideration that later, on April 19, 1778, he petitioned in a prayer before taking the Sacrament, "Almighty and most merciful Father, suffer me once more to commemorate the death of thy Son Jesus Christ, my Saviour and Redeemer, and make the memorial of his death profitable to my salvation, by strengthening my Faith in his merits, and quickening my obedience to his laws."

This prayer, coming as late as 1778, was composed, I believe, sometime after he had developed a belief in the doctrine of the propitiatory nature of the sacrifice, but even at this stage he appears not completely convinced of all its implications. In the earlier prayers there are only a few references that can be construed as allusions to the merits of Christ. On Easter Eve, 1757, he asks, "Grant me resolution for the sake of Jesus Christ, to whose covenant I now implore admission, of the benefits of whose death I implore participation." And on March 28, 1762, he petitions that he may "be received into thine everlasting kingdom through the merits and mediation of Jesus Christ thine only son our Lord and Saviour." After 1770, Christ's merits are mentioned more frequently in his prayers, but positive and specific allusions to the propitiatory nature of the sacrifice are not evident until the last few years of his life. Most of these, as we shall see, appear in the Latin prayers he composed as he prepared for death, though specific references to Christ's disburdening mankind from sin also appear in a few of his later English prayers of this period. One of these he composed at Ashbourne on August 1, 1784. He writes: "O, God, most merciful Father who by many diseases hast admonished me of my approach to the end of life, and by this gracious addition to my days hast given me an opportunity of appearing once more in thy presence to commemorate the sacrifice by which thy son Jesus Christ has taken away the sins of the world, assist me in this commemoration by thy Holy Spirit that I may look back upon the sinfulness of my life past with pious sorrow, and efficacious Repentance."

Although his belief in the propitiatory nature of the sacrifice developed gradually over a period of years, one date seems to mark a climax in his thinking on the subject. It was Easter Sunday, 1776. On this day he received the Sacrament, as he had each year since his wife's death. His customary Holy Week preparations included fasting, the forming of good resolutions, and attendance at church on Good Friday. He also followed his usual practice of composing a penitential prayer. This is remarkable chiefly for the opening supplication: "Almighty and most merciful Father, who hast preserved me by thy tender forbearance, once more to commemorate thy Love in the Redemption of the world, grant that I may so live the residue of my days, as to obtain thy mercy when thou shalt call me from the present State." Unfortunately the next two lines in the manuscript are deleted, for they might have indicated something unusual. In its mutilated form the prayer differs from earlier ones chiefly in the allusion to God's expression of love for mankind in accepting Christ's sacrifice. Even this reference might not be significant, were it not for Johnson's experience in church on this particular Easter Sunday.

He reports that he read the prayer in his pew, commended his friends and departed relatives, and, at the altar, renewed his resolutions. He continues: "When I received, some tender images struck me. I was so mollified by the concluding address to our Saviour that I could not utter it." He adds, "Since my return [home], I have said it." Johnson here records an intense kind of religious experience such as appears nowhere else in his writings. The words that he could not utter, because they so profoundly moved him, form a regular part of the Communion service. They are: "O Lord, the only-begotten Son, Jesus Christ; O Lord God, Lamb of God, Son of the Father, that takest away the sins of the world, have mercy upon us. Thou that takest away the sins of the world, have mercy upon us, Thou that takest away the sins of the world, receive our prayer. Thou that sittest at the right hand of God the Father, have mercy upon us."[9] This was a familiar supplication. From childhood Johnson must have known this part of the Book of Common Prayer, and most certainly must have recited it whenever he received the Sacrament. Yet never before had this address, containing in essence the doctrine of the propitiatory sacrifice, come home to him in its full significance. Never before, probably, had he experienced so deeply the "mollifying" realization that Christ had died for his sins, and that the burden of expiation did not rest on himself alone.

This emotional experience, as we have observed, appears to mark a climax in the development of Johnson's belief in the propitiatory nature of the sacrifice. But even after this date he seems to have had some doubts on the subject, some reluctance to believe wholeheartedly in the doctrine. It was not, apparently, until the closing year or two of his life that he arrived at a full and unwavering assurance of the vicarious nature of the sacrifice.

That such a change in Johnson's religious thinking did occur has been noted by several writers, although no one has properly emphasized its significance. Boswell, for one, referred to it in his *Tour to the Hebrides*. After quoting what Johnson had said in 1773 in support of the exemplary view of the sacrifice, Boswell remarked, with an allusion to the conversation that was to take place in 1781: "What Dr. Johnson now delivered, was but a temporary opinion; for he afterwards was fully convinced of the *propitiatory sacrifice*, as I shall shew in my future work, *The Life of Samuel Johnson, LL.D.*"[10]

In the third decade of the nineteenth century, several contributors to a religious periodical called *The Christian Observer* also commented on Johnson's altered view of the Atonement. Although they erroneously interpreted the change as evidence that Johnson had experienced an Evangelical type of conversion, they were convinced that he did not accept the idea of the propitiatory sacrifice until late in life. The discussion was initiated by Christian Ignatius Latrobe, son of Benjamin Latrobe, a Moravian clergyman with whom Johnson was on friendly terms in his last years. The younger Latrobe wrote: "Indeed for several years my father had observed in him, not only an increasing knowledge of the way of salvation, freely through the merits and atonement of the Redeemer . . . but also a growing humility and piety." This comment stimulated an anonymous writer to add further remarks on the subject.

He observed that an old clergyman of his acquaintance who had known the elder Latrobe had "described the revolution which took place in the mind of the moralist as 'extraordinary and truly Christian.' Far from trusting, either wholly or in part to his own merits, he became distinctly and, it is trusted, experimentally, acquainted with Him who is 'the end of the law for righteousness to everyone that believeth.' "[11]

A third contributor to *The Christian Observer*, the Reverend S. C. Wilks, asserted that Johnson did not read the most enlightening religious writers, that even William Law is defective in providing a proper idea of the all-sufficient sacrifice of Christ. Wilks writes that Johnson "seems in point of fact, for many years, to have viewed the Atonement rather as a medium through which God is pleased to accept our imperfect services, and to make them adequate by the conditions of a remedial law, to the purchase of heaven, than as a sacrifice by which *alone* heaven is fully secured and freely given to the believing penitent." Wilks adds, however, that before his death Johnson did come to accept the orthodox belief in "the sacrifice and mediation of Jesus Christ."[12]

What brought about the change in Johnson's interpretation of the Atonement? The Evangelical writers implied that it was the result of his association in the last year or two of his life with clergymen like Latrobe, but Boswell indicates that the positive shift in opinion had occurred by June, 1781. Ironically it was probably Samuel Clarke, the rationalist, who did most to convert him to the more orthodox understanding of the Atonement.

We have remarked earlier that Clarke gave Johnson a measure of comfort by his reassurance that only a moderate degree of piety is required of the Christian and that salvation is not so difficult to attain. But this message, however consoling to one of Johnson's disposition, would hardly have appealed to his critical intellect unless it was supported by a pattern of thought that seemed reasonable and convincing. "If Christ has taken away the sting of death," Clarke writes, "and gives us the victory over it; then good Christians ought not to be afraid and terrified at death." But how did Christ remove the sting of death? Clarke answers, "Our Saviour by his death and sufferings has purchased this grace for us, that real repentance and sincere renewed obedience shall be accepted instead of innocence."[13] In short, Clarke's most comforting message is that salvation is made relatively easy because Christ performed a propitiatory sacrifice that lifted the burden of guilt from mankind.

More than anything else, apparently, it was Clarke's explanation of the Atonement that created Johnson's esteem for this sometimes unorthodox clergyman. To be sure, Johnson had encountered in other writers a similar explanation of the expiatory nature of the sacrifice. Yet, for some reason, he appears never to have favored this interpretation until he began to read the sermons of Clarke. But, one may ask, how can we be sure Johnson read the clergyman on this particular subject? Fortunately, there is definite evidence that he did.

In the last fifteen years of his life Johnson studied Clarke with care. Hawkins reports that on the near approach of death he devoted himself to reading "Erasmus on the New Testament, Dr. Clarke's Sermons, and such other books as had a tendency to calm and comfort him."[14] Still stronger evidence appears in his private manual of religious devotions, where Johnson records several occasions on which he turned to Clarke. In some instances, moreover, he indicates the specific sermons. He first mentions having read one of these on March 28, 1766. He examined another on May 7, 1769. On neither of these dates does he supply the title, but on April 14, 1770, he notes he has read Clarke "on the Death of Christ"; on April 15, Easter Sunday, 1770, "Clarke's Sermon of the Humiliation of our Saviour"; and on Good Friday, 1773, his sermon "on Faith."[15] These are not exact designations. Clarke's work on faith is entitled "Of Faith in God"; the two sermons consulted at Easter time, 1770, were doubtless two paired sermons (Nos. 16 and 17, Vol. VIII of the 1732 edition), entitled "Of the Nature of the Sufferings of Christ" and "Of the Humiliation and Sufferings of Christ." The first of these is particularly significant because it deals chiefly with the Atonement. Although Clarke discusses this topic elsewhere, in no other place does he treat it so fully as in this particular work.

In this sermon Clarke observes that Christ's death "was truly and properly in the strictest meaning of the word, an expiatory sacrifice. . . . God was graciously pleased to accept this vicarious suffering of his Son, in the *stead* of the punishment that was due to the sinner in his own person; which is the express and most proper notion of an Expiatory Sacrifice." Because Christ's satisfaction was perfect and sufficient, Clarke reasons, it was in the truest sense an Atonement that God freely appointed and accepted. Furthermore, it resulted in a new covenant, based on the merits of Christ's suffering, that enables "all true penitents to continue in the favour of God, by obeying the conditions of that covenant." The conditions, of course, are obedience and, when that fails, true repentance.

Clarke not only emphasizes that the propitiatory interpretation of the sacrifice is primary; he specifically asserts that to attribute chief importance to the exemplary implications of the act is a dangerous error. Although he concedes that the sacrifice serves secondarily as an example to men, he insists that "to say that Christ died for our advantage, but not in our stead; that his death was not properly a Sacrifice for sin, but merely a testimony to his doctrine and an example to encourage us to suffer persecution cheerfully for the will of God, is really to diminish from the grace and mercy of God, and from the exceeding love of our Saviour to mankind." Here, of course, Clarke is refuting the kind of interpretation which William Law favored.

Ironically, although Clarke was unorthodox on some matters of faith, on the Atonement his views were those of the

Church; Law's were those of an individual. This thought may have occurred to Johnson, especially if his own earlier notion of the exemplary nature of the sacrifice had been influenced by what Law had said on the subject. Perhaps that is why, after coming under the influence of Clarke, Johnson remarked late in life, "William Law, Sir, wrote the best piece of Parenetick Divinity; but William Law was no reasoner."[16]

Because Johnson obviously admired Clarke's method of reasoning, it is interesting to observe how closely the remarks that he dictated to Boswell in 1781 (*supra,* p. 55) correspond with a summary statement of Clarke on the Atonement. Johnson discusses the following points in this order: (1) Why mankind's offenses to God had to be punished. (2) Why God elected not to punish man directly. (3) Why Christ was chosen to pay the penalty. (4) How humanity benefits from Christ's sacrifice. Johnson is not quoting Clarke directly, but his reasoning, both in the order and substance of his remarks, is strikingly similar to a summary passage in Clarke's sermon "Of the Nature of the Sufferings of Christ." Clarke writes:

> 1st, that it was from the beginning infinitely reasonable that all possible honour and obedience should at all times be paid by all creatures to all the laws and commands of God. 2ndly, that this honour due to the laws of God is diminished, as much as in us lies, by the sins and impieties of men. 3dly, that it is highly reasonable and necessary, after such presumptuous transgression, that God should make some proper vindication of his divine authority. 4thly, that the first and most obvious method of doing this is by the punishment or destruction of the offenders. 5thly, but because God hates not the persons of sinners, and hath no pleasure in their destruction, but only a just zeal for the honour of his divine and righteous laws, therefore when that is by any means vindicated, his wrath is appeased. Lastly, that our Saviour by his obedience and humiliation even unto death, *has* in the most glorious manner vindicated the honour and authority of God; and, by establishing a covenant of grace upon the merits of his sufferings and obedience, has secured to all that truly repent, pardon and remission of sin consistent with the honour of divine laws.

In addition to this marked similarity in their reasoning on the Atonement, there is further evidence that it was Clarke's exposition of this doctrine that chiefly attracted Johnson to him. We return to the earlier quoted statement of R. G. Robinson, who wrote that a few months before his death Johnson observed that "if he was saved, he should be 'indebted for his salvation to the sermons of Dr. Clarke.' " Normally, as Mrs. Thrale tells us, Johnson did not believe in extravagant or hyperbolic expressions of sentiment.[17] He must therefore have felt that he had discovered a pearl of great price in Clarke's writings when he expressed himself so unequivocally. What could he have meant except that, having misinterpreted the significance of the Atonement during much of his life, he had been saved from dangerous error by reading Clarke?

Johnson's belief in the propitiatory nature of the sacrifice seemed to develop, with increasing conviction, until the very end of his life. During the last months before his death he made various comments showing that he now felt the vicarious sacrifice to form the central core of Christianity, but we shall confine ourselves here to what he said to his friend and attending physician, Dr. Brocklesby. According to Hannah More, who received her report from Mr. Pepys, Johnson offered up an urgent prayer for the conversion of his somewhat sceptical friend and said, "My dear doctor, believe a dying man, there is no salvation but in the Sacrifice of the Lamb of God."[18] Because of her Evangelical enthusiasm, Hannah More might be given to exaggeration, but when Boswell interviewed Brocklesby, he also received the report that at the end Johnson particularly urged upon his doctor the importance of understanding that Christ's sacrifice was of a vicarious nature. Boswell writes:

Dr. Brocklesby, who will not be suspected of fanaticism, obliged me with the following accounts:

"For some time before his death, all his fears were calmed and absorbed by the prevalence of his faith, and his trust in the merits and *propitiation* of JESUS CHRIST.

"He talked often to me about the necessity of faith in the *sacrifice* of Jesus, as necessary beyond all good works whatever, for the salvation of mankind.

"He pressed me to study Dr. Clarke and to read his Sermons. I asked him why he pressed Dr. Clarke, an Arian. 'Because, (said he,) he is fullest on the *propitiatory sacrifice*.'·"[19]

In view of what has already been said about Johnson's interest in Clarke, this dying statement—so simple, so direct, so final—seems to confirm the evidence that Johnson's admiration for the clergyman was based chiefly on his interpretation of the Atonement. This made such a deep impression that it led him in later years to exaggerate the importance of Clarke as a religious thinker and to magnify the influence that the clergyman had on his own faith, although in reality he probably owed more to William Law.

IV · REPENTANCE

A man may be safe as to his condition, but, in the mean time, dark and doubtful, as to his apprehensions; secure in his pardon, but miserable in the ignorance of it; and so passing all his days in the disconsolate, uneasy vicissitudes of hope and fears, at length go out of the world, not knowing whither he goes.

South's Sermons, *quoted in Johnson's* Dictionary

An important key to Johnson's religious position is an understanding of what repentance meant to him. The exploration of this subject requires a brief consideration of various interpretations of this doctrine, for in the Church of England there existed different opinions, ranging from the Roman Catholic position to that of the Protestant Reformers. Furthermore, Johnson's own beliefs represent a peculiar and distinctive combination of various teachings on this subject.

After the Reformation the Church of England modified the Roman Catholic doctrine of penance in various ways. Penance ceased to be a sacrament; the regulated and formal procedure associated with auricular confession largely disappeared; and "repentance" rather than "penance" became the common term. To confess one's sins to a clergyman was not forbidden, but the obligation to do so was abrogated, and provision for private confession remained, chiefly in connection with visits to sick persons. The duty existed, however, for the penitent to examine his conscience, to feel true sorrow for sin, and to express his contrition in private prayers, as well as at public worship.[1]

The relative significance of contrition and amendment was

also altered by the Reformation. In the Roman Catholic Church, forgiveness of sin follows upon an act of the will that results in a thorough detestation of past sins. When contrition, or sorrow for sin, is genuine, it is considered that the penitent must necessarily will and resolve to refrain from offending God in the future. Thus the desire to amend one's life is implicit in the act of detestation of sin. Luther and the other Continental reformers introduced an important change. They taught that the sinner is forgiven, not because of contrition, but because of faith in God's promise of pardon. Although sorrow for sin was assumed, what was chiefly important was a turning away from sin, for repentance was now interpreted in the Greek sense of *metanoia,* or a change of mind. Consequently, the emphasis shifted from contrition to amendment, and the test of a penitent's sincerity became, not his genuine detestation of sin, accompanied by a resolve to avoid it in the future, but rather a personal reformation, evidenced by his turning from sin and leading a new life.[2]

The position of the Church of England on such questions is not easy to state, chiefly because there was and is no strictly dogmatic interpretation of doctrine in the Establishment. A commission of Anglican clergymen, appointed in 1922 to review and, so far as possible, to reconcile differences in interpretation, observe in their *Report:* "There are systems of Catholic Theology and of Protestant Theology. To them we have, of course, owed much. But there is not, and the majority of us do not desire that there should be, a system of distinctively Anglican Theology."[3]

As upon other matters, the attitude in the Establishment towards contrition and amendment incorporated both Catholic and Protestant views. For instance, in the Book of Common Prayer the petition for forgiveness recited by the congregation during the Communion service places strong emphasis on sorrow for sin. It reads, in part: "We do earnestly repent, And are heartily sorry for these our misdoings; The remembrance of them is grievous unto us; The burden of them is intolerable. Have mercy upon us, most merciful Father, For thy Son our Lord Jesus Christ's sake. Forgive us all that is past; And grant that we may ever hereafter Serve and please thee In newness of life, To the honour and glory of thy Name."

The importance of contrition has also been stressed in expositions of the catechism of the Church of England and in similar instructional works. But frequently, if not commonly, still greater emphasis has been accorded the view that to be valid repentance requires, not merely a resolve to amend, but an actual reformation. Because this interpretation was one that Johnson favored, it will be well to glance at the views expressed in several instructional books, some of which presumably helped to shape his thinking.

The first is the Reverend John Goodman's *The Penitent Pardoned.* Originally published in 1679, it was reprinted in several editions. One copy is listed in the *Sale Catalogue* of Johnson's library. Regarding the importance of true sorrow for sin, Goodman writes that a state of contrition calls for "the sinner bewailing his sin, taking shame to himself, under agonies of mind, pricked to the heart, humbly imploring the divine favour, and crying earnestly for mercy." On the other hand, he adds, "But this is not all that repentance means,—the principal part of it is yet behind (*viz.*) actual Reformation. This is that which every awakened Conscience in its agonies promises and resolves upon; this God expects, and every sincere Convert really performs: for without this all the rest is empty pomp and pageantry, and mere hypocrisy."[4] Thus it is not sufficient merely to resolve to amend; the test of one's sincerity is an effected amendment.

A second writer whom Johnson admired and frequently quoted was the Reverend Henry Hammond. His *Practical Catechism,* which first appeared in 1644, also became a popular instructional work. Like Goodman, Hammond emphasizes the importance of feeling sorrow for sin. Nevertheless, he defines repentance in much the same manner as the Protestant Reformers when he writes that it is "A change of mind, or a conversion from sin to God. Not some *one* bare *act of change,* but a *lasting,* durable state of *new life,* which I told you was called also *regeneration.*"[5] This definition, significantly, Johnson quotes in his *Dictionary,* under "repentance."

A third book of this nature, and one that was also widely read, is Bishop William Nicholson's *An Exposition of the Catechism of the Church of England.* In this treatise, first published in 1655, the author leans more towards the Roman Catholic position in stressing that what is chiefly important for the penitent is to feel sorrow and to have a firm intention of amending his ways. Although he asserts that "it is not enough to resolve to be good, but we must be good," he does not, like Goodman, make the sincerity of one's repentance rest solely on reformation, for he adds that if "through ignorance, infirmity, sudden surreption, or violent temptation, the same sins steal upon us, yet we must humble ourselves, confess them, be contrite and beg pardon for them, resist and fight against them."[6]

On the other hand, Bishop Gilbert Burnet, who was more the Broad Churchman than either Hammond or Nicholson, favored the interpretation of the Protestant Reformers. "*Penitence,*" he writes, "is formed from the Latin translation of a Greek word that signifies a change or renovation of mind, which Christ made a necessary condition of the New Covenant." Forgiveness of sin, he observes, depends not just on acts of sorrow, but upon the efficacy of contrition to reform the sinner.[7]

When we examine Johnson's beliefs on repentance, we find that on a few aspects of the subject he favors Catholic views; on others, distinctly Protestant notions. As we have indicated in Chapter I, contrition to Johnson was extremely important. In his prayers we see him strictly examining his conscience, calling his sins to mind, and reflecting with sorrow upon the offense given to God. Each of his penitential prayers implies, if it does not explicitly state, sorrow for transgressions. Similarly, in his sermons he alludes to the necessity of feeling deep compunction for past sins. Johnson went beyond the Church of England teachings on contrition, however, in recognizing the Roman Catholic belief in the efficacy of both attrition and contrition. The distinction made by Roman Catholicism is that "perfect contrition" is sorrow for sin based on a love of God; "attrition" is sorrow for sin motivated by some other reason, such as fear of damnation or the loss of heaven. Although attrition is termed "imperfect contrition," it is regarded as valid in obtaining remission of sin through priestly absolution, and, since it allows the penitent to receive Communion, it opens for him an important means of grace through which he may ultimately arrive at a state of perfect contrition.

Writers like Samuel Clarke, Goodman, Hammond, and Gilbert Burnet were strongly opposed to the Catholic doctrine of attrition. They denounced it either as a distinctly Papist notion, or because they believed mere sorrow for sin cannot effect a true reformation. Burnet says it is positively harmful, because attrition encourages men to return with calmness to evil ways.[8] Jeremy Taylor, another writer whom Johnson admired, deals at length with this subject. He recognizes that attrition or sorrow for sin can be a logical first step towards contrition, but, because he rejects the Roman Catholic belief in the validity of priestly absolution, he asserts that attrition cannot itself be effective for salvation. On the other hand, Taylor shows a degree of psychological insight in being aware that a scrupulous person may question whether his repentance is based on a true love of God or merely on fear or attrition. Such a person, he writes, need not be unduly concerned. If one has a heartfelt and constant desire to please God by obedience, the sincere wish to keep his commandments is itself evidence that one is motivated by love.[9]

Johnson may have had Taylor's remarks in mind when he composed Sermon II. Here he observes that a truly repentant person "needs not recollect whether he was awakened from the lethargy of sin by the love of God, or the fear of punishment." But Johnson seems somewhat more sympathetic to attrition than Taylor. "The Scripture applies to all our passions," he adds, "and eternal punishments had been threatened to no purpose, if these menaces were not intended to promote virtue." He also defines "attrition" and "contrition" in the *Dictionary,* without designating the first as a peculiarly Catholic doctrine. To be sure, he calls "attrition" "the lowest degree of repentance." Though not an inaccurate definition, it sounds characteristic of one who had never forgotten the high ideals taught by William Law in connection with Christian perfection.

While believing in both attrition and contrition, Johnson also accepted the doctrine of the Protestant Reformers that the test of repentance is regeneration. This idea is frequently reiterated in his writings. The discussion in *Rambler* 110 is particularly interesting, for here he shows a realization that, strictly interpreted, forgiveness of sin based on contrition conflicts with the idea of forgiveness resulting solely from the sinner's reformation. Temporarily he resolves the difficulty by saying that sorrow for sin is efficacious in obtaining pardon only when it produces a change. He writes: "*Repentance is the relinquishment of any practice from the conviction that it has offended God.* Sorrow, and fear, and anxiety, are properly not parts, but adjuncts of repentance; yet they are too closely connected with it to be easily separated; for they not only mark its sincerity, but promote its efficacy." Here we seem to have a basically Protestant view tempered and qualified by Roman Catholic doctrine. Nevertheless, this is not the statement of a man merely trying to straddle an issue. It represents, rather, the position of one who throughout his mature life thought deeply about the subject of repentance, who consistently expressed deep contrition for his offenses, and who valiantly tried to amend even slight faults.

In the *Dictionary* Johnson calls "amendment" (1) "a change from bad for the better" and (2) "reformation of life." "Repentance" he defines first in the more general sense as "sorrow for any thing past," secondly, more in accord with Protestant theology, as "sorrow for sin, such as produces newness of life." Even more significant, perhaps, are the passages selected to illustrate the correct use of these terms. The most pertinent are the following. In support of his definition of "repentance," he quotes Dr. South: "This is a confidence, of all the most irrational, for upon what ground can a man promise himself future *repentance,* who cannot promise himself futurity." He also quotes, with negligible variation, Hammond's explanation, to which we have already referred: "*Repentance* is a change of mind, or a conversion from sin to God; not some one bare act of change, but a lasting, durable state of new life, which is called regeneration." In connection with "amendment," he provides the following statement from Hammond's *Practical Catechism:* "Though a serious purpose of *amendment,* and true acts of contrition before the habit, may be accepted by God; yet there is no sure judgment whether this purpose be serious or these acts true acts of contrition." These three passages, it will be observed, point to the idea that forgiveness depends, not on sorrow for sin, or upon the resolve to amend, but upon the successful accomplishment of a reformation.

In view of these quotations it might be argued that Johnson derived his beliefs on repentance from respected Church of England writers like Hammond. No doubt this was true, but it also appears that he went to pains to select passages that accorded with his own conviction that man alone must atone for his sins. Significantly, Johnson's belief that repentance entails a complete and thorough reformation is stated without the qualifications that Hammond supplies in his *Catechism.*

Like Nicholson and other clergymen, Hammond realized that, for most men, complete, unsinning obedience to the laws of God is impossible. Indeed, most of the Protestant Reformers who insisted that repentance was to be judged by real amendment expected, not that the penitent would live without any blemish of sin, but that he would avoid a regular or habitual state of sinfulness and live in the main uprightly. For instance, in Hammond's *Catechism* the question is asked if any sins are compatible with a regenerate state. The answer is "yes." Understandably one may be guilty of "sins of infirmity," "sins of ignorance," those of "sudden surreption," or those committed by "daily incursions of temptation." Hammond adds that even if we are in a regenerate state, we may commit "some one wilful act of deliberate sin which we might have resisted, if it be presently retracted with contrition and confession, and reinforcing of our resolution and vigilance against it."[10]

Johnson's failure to append such important qualifying statements to his definitions of "amendment" and "repentance" in the *Dictionary* was not merely a matter of limitations of space. His own interpretation of these terms appears to have been more literal and more rigid than that of the divines who produced expositions of the Church catechism. To be sure, his knowledge of human frailty and his sense of charity could allow him to temper the conditions of salvation for others. "To imagine that everyone who is not completely good is irrecoverably abandoned," he observes, "is to suppose that all are capable of the same degrees of excellence; it is, indeed, to exact from all that perfection which none ever can attain" (*Rambler* 70). Nevertheless, the ideal of Christian perfection as described by William Law was never far removed from his thoughts. And so long as he believed that man alone must atone for his sins, he was inclined to think that repentance must include not only true sorrow and a firm resolve to amend one's ways but also the fulfillment of a reformation so thorough as to counterbalance past iniquities.

As we have indicated earlier, his conviction that man alone must expiate his sins grew logically out of his earlier belief that Christ's sacrifice, being chiefly of an exemplary nature, did not remove the burden of sin from mankind. It should be emphasized, however, that the whole question of personal expiation seems to have been a confused as well as a troubling question to Johnson. His uncertainty is particularly apparent in *Rambler* 110, where he appears to be arguing the issue with himself. He writes: "The expiation of crimes, and renovation of the forfeited hopes of divine favour . . . constitute a large part of every religion." But the problem of how to practice expiation and how to know when one has sufficiently atoned for sin perplexed him. He says: "He that reviews his life in order to determine the probability of his acceptance with God, if he could once establish the necessary proportion between crimes and sufferings, might securely rest on his performance of the expiation; but while safety remains the reward only of mental purity, he is always afraid lest he should decide too soon in his own favour; lest he should not have felt the pangs of true contrition; lest he should mistake satiety for detestation, or imagine that his passions are subdued when they are only sleeping."

Throughout the essay he appears to be weighing the arguments for and against the validity of expiatory acts of satisfaction. He remarks that history reveals, among various nations at widely separated periods of time, "a general and uniform expectation of propitiating God by corporeal austerities, of anticipating his vengeance by voluntary inflictions, and appeasing his justice by a speedy and cheerful submission to a less penalty, when a greater is incurred." Such an attitude is understandable, he observes, although he expresses neither agreement nor disagreement with it. Later in the essay he recommends the value of self-imposed austerities, mortifications, and abstinence. On the other hand, although he does not specifically mention the Catholic practice of allotting a specific penance or satisfaction for sin, he alludes to it when he speaks of a deplorable "disposition to confound penance with repentance, to repose on human determinations, and to receive from some judicial sentence the stated and regular assignment of reconciliatory pain." His objection to such practices rests chiefly on the assertion that repentance consists in reformation, not on satisfaction performed for past sins.

At this stage Johnson's position on repentance is a curious one, neither strictly Catholic nor Protestant. Both communions believe as a central part of Christian faith that Christ performed a propitiatory sacrifice that removed the burden of sin from men. To the typical Protestant, the assignment and performance of penance are not necessary, because one is saved by faith in God's pardon, by obedience, and when that fails, by amendment. To the Catholic, Christ's propitiatory act is equally important, but doing penance (in later periods usually the recital of assigned prayers) serves as an expression of contrition and as an act of satisfaction which may be joined to the great expiatory satisfaction of Christ. Because Johnson did not, apparently, believe in the propitiatory nature of Christ's sacrifice until late in life, he was inclined to the view that man must alone atone for his sins. So long as he held this opinion, the self-imposition of a much more rigorous and austere form of penance than Catholics usually perform would appear to be the logical course for him to have followed.

There is evidence that he did at times engage in severe acts of self-atonement. During a discussion with Henry White, a young clergyman of Lichfield, Johnson remarked that he had not generally been an undutiful son, but he added, "Once, indeed, I was disobedient; I refused to attend my father to Uttoxeter-market. Pride was the source of that refusal, and the remembrance of it was painful. A few years ago, I desired to atone for this fault; I went to Uttoxeter in very bad weather, and stood for a considerable time bareheaded in the rain, on the spot where my father's stall used to stand. In contrition I stood, and I hope the penance was expiatory."[11] The act of disobedience had been a boyish misdemeanor, which had occurred, presumably, some sixty years earlier in his life. Only a person of tender conscience would have remembered it that long, and only one with an almost *quid pro quo* sense of the importance of compensating for offenses would have performed this particular act of expiation.

If Johnson admittedly felt so scrupulous about an early act of disobedience, it would seem likely that he frequently engaged in mortification to atone for offenses and to assuage a troubled conscience. "No disease of the imagination," remarks Imlac in *Rasselas* (Ch. XLVI), "is so difficult of cure as that which is complicated with the dread of guilt." Is it possible that the man who wrote that statement may have been driven at times to adopt desperate remedies in an attempt to palliate his sense of sin? In an essay entitled "Johnson's Vile Melancholy," Katharine C. Balderston produces evidence that a curious relationship was established between Johnson and Mrs. Thrale during one period when he was particularly disturbed. According to Miss Balderston's interpretation, he sometimes insisted upon being padlocked by his reluctant hostess and may even have persuaded her to inflict physical punishment on him in the form of flagellation. The whole subject is clouded with uncertainty, but it is possible that further light may eventually be shed upon it. If Johnson, at near approaches to insanity, was driven to extremities, at the root of his trouble lay a profound feeling of guilt, coupled with a compulsion to expiate his misdeeds. Miss Balderston suggests that it was a masochistic kind of performance, with erotic implications. Strong sexual proclivities undoubtedly contributed to Johnson's state of abjection, but other offenses, often of a trivial nature, could, as we have seen, prove equally harassing to one of his great scrupulosity. One suspects that if he had lived in the Middle Ages he would have welcomed the opportunity to wear a hair shirt.[12]

One might expect that, when Johnson became convinced of the vicarious nature of Christ's sacrifice, there would appear some modification of his rigid beliefs on the necessity for self-atonement. For imbedded in the doctrine of the propitiatory sacrifice is the idea that man is a weak creature who cannot by his own efforts sufficiently atone for his iniquities, as well as the belief that it is not necessary for him completely to atone, inasmuch as Christ has made up for his deficiencies. In the last year or two of his life, as we shall see, Johnson did at times interpret the meaning of repentance in terms more in accord with the doctrine of the vicarious sacrifice, but apparently he did not alter his views on these two subjects simultaneously. For one thing, the high ideal of Christian perfection stressed by William Law always remained in his mind, and at the core of Law's teaching is the belief that contrition and amendment should be so complete that virtual saintliness will result.

Law's admonitions on the attitude of the penitent seemed to be clearly in Johnson's mind during a discussion that took place on April 15, 1778, when he and other guests were present at the Dillys'. Boswell, as he so frequently did, "expressed a horrour at the thought of death." In reply Mrs. Knowles, the Quaker lady, quoted from Scripture: "The righteous shall have *hope* in his death." Johnson then commented: "Yes, Madam; that is, he shall not have despair. But, consider, his hope of salvation must be founded on the terms on which it is promised that the mediation of our SAVIOUR shall be applied to us,—namely, obedience; and where obedience has failed, then, as suppletory to it, repentance. But what man can say his obedience has been such, as he would approve of in another, or even in himself upon close examination, or that his repentance has not been such as to require being repented of? No man can be sure that his obedience and repentance will obtain salvation."[13] Here, although Johnson now subscribes to the vicarious nature of the sacrifice, his reasoning, even his choice of words, parallels Law's discussion of perfection.

Samuel Clarke also expressed the belief that true repentance requires a complete reformation. In his sermon entitled "Of Forgiveness of Injuries," he remarks, "by true repentance is always meant an actual forsaking and amending of the fault repented of." But elsewhere Clarke qualifies this view, as did most English Churchmen. He writes: "The condition of the Gospel-Covenant is not perfect unsinning obedience, but a sincere endeavour to obey all the commands of God to the utmost of our power. . . . If through the frailty and infirmity of our nature, we be at any time, notwithstanding our sincere endeavours to the contrary, surprized into the commission of sin; God accepts real repentance and a renewed obedience, instead of an uninterrupted course of holiness."[14] This explanation resembles the one quoted from Hammond. Characteristically, however, Johnson tended to read religious writers eclectically, to remember and to try to live by the most rigid rules, and to forget or to disregard, so far as his own religious life was concerned, those conditions tempered by an understanding of human frailty and by the concept of a God of mercy.

The intensity of his religious convictions is revealed not only by his rigid interpretations but also, at times, by his terminology. Sometimes, as in *Rambler* 110 and in his prayers, he refers to moral offenses as "*crimes.*" Similarly, in his Latin prayers he may use "*crimina*" instead of "*peccata.*" His language is also distinctively his own in a discussion of reparation; that is, the idea that the truly repentant person must compensate, so far as possible, for any harm done to others. Although Johnson's views accord with traditional Christian precepts, the urgency of his diction in arguing the importance of reparation is remarkable. In *Rambler* 54, he observes that restitution should be made as promptly as possible, lest death intervene and frustrate the accomplishment of one's good intentions. He adds (italics mine): "There is not, perhaps, to a mind well instructed, a more painful occurrence than the death of one whom we have injured without reparation. Our *crime* seems now *irretrievable;* it is *indelibly recorded,* and the *stamp of fate* is fixed upon it."

In Sermon II he deals with specific acts of reparation that should be performed. "If we have been guilty of the open propagation of errour, or the promulgation of falsehood, we must make our recantation no less openly; we must endeavour, without regard to the shame and reproach to which we may be exposed, to undeceive those whom we have formerly misled. If we have deprived any man of his right, we must restore it to him; if we have aspersed his reputation, we must retract our calumny."

Another way to atone for faults is by exercising charity towards those whom one has not injured. In Sermon IV Johnson writes, "If thou wilt hear the voice of God calling thee to repentance, and by repentance to charity, harden not thy heart." Although he does not develop this point, it may, in view of his emphasis on self-atonement, have motivated in part his notable acts of charity. At least one of his contemporaries thought that his purpose in performing them was to compensate for his faults. Laetitia Hawkins, who knew Johnson well, comments interestingly and perhaps shrewdly: "He certainly considered the unbounded exercise of charity as atonement; and his almost indiscriminate application of it, proved that he added by every opportunity to his store. He always seemed to me in the situation of a man who, meaning well, but having never kept any accounts, gives up all that he has to spare, and adds his superfluities whenever they occur, to discharge debts the amount of which he has never calculated."[15]

Although the sermons generally accord with the religious principles observable in his private prayers and diaries, when addressing others, he tempers somewhat the strictness of his views. In *Perilous Balance,* which provides one of the most penetrating appraisals of Johnson's religion, W. B. C. Watkins remarks that Johnson could always be easier on his fellow men than on himself.[16] For instance, in his meditations he frequently alludes to his lack of tranquillity when receiving the Eucharist, but in Sermon IX he cautions others against being unnecessarily fearful about partaking of the Sacrament unworthily. He reminds them that "God will accept unfeigned repentance, sincere intentions, and earnest endeavours, though entangled with many frailties." He adds, "Heaven itself will be accessible to many who died in their struggles with sin; in their endeavours after virtue, and the beginning of a new life."

Sometimes the encouragement he gives to others may seem almost inconsistent with the strictures he applied to himself, but it was perfectly consistent with his strong sense of charity. He also had another motive. Although unable to overcome his own scruples, he was aware of how much they contributed to his melancholy. The man who told Mrs. Thrale that scruples "seldom make a Man good, but they certainly make him miserable,"[17] knew that scruples might drive one to despair, and that to close the door to hope was to erect the final barrier against salvation. Consequently, despite his troubled uncertainty of his personal salvation, in the sermons he could cheer others by reminding them that "He who falleth seven times a day may yet, by the mercy of God, be numbered among the just."[18]

Johnson's comments on whether or not a deathbed repentance is efficacious are particularly interesting when compared with the prevailing opinion in the Establishment. As we have seen, the English clergy favored the idea that the test of a sincere repentance was a genuine reformation. The question then arose as to the status of a repentant sinner who had no time to amend his life. Most of the writers, while not ruling out the possibility of salvation, express grave doubts on the subject. John Goodman, for instance, observes that a man who feels remorse only at the end of his existence "can give no proof to himself of his own sincerity, because he cannot repair God's honour, he can make no conquest over Satan, he can leave no example to the world . . . he cannot be said to have lived the life of the righteous, and therefore cannot comfortably conclude that he shall die the death of such." Similar reservations appear in the works of Hammond, Gilbert Burnet, and in Johnson's contemporary, Daniel Waterland.[19]

Samuel Clarke was not only sceptical of the value of a deathbed repentance; he may have also acted on the principle that it had no validity. Several years after his death there appeared in the *Gentleman's Magazine* an account that reflected his views on this subject. According to the story, Sir John Germain, who was thought to be the illegitimate son of William II, the Prince of Orange, suffered great mental distress when he knew he was dying. Besides having been publicly charged with adultery with Lady Mary Mordaunt, Sir John had been involved in various other scandals, and his transgressions had become notorious. Disturbed on his deathbed by thoughts of his past, he sent for Samuel Clarke, and when the clergyman arrived, he described his anxiety. "Shall I receive the Sacrament," he inquired, "and do you think it will do me any good to receive it?" Clarke, knowing that Sir John's sins had been scarlet, did not bother to ask if he was now truly repentant. Instead he told him "he could not advise him to take the Sacrament, as likely to be of any avail to him with respect to his final welfare; and so, commending him to the mercy of God, did not administer it."[20]

With this attitude Johnson would not have agreed. He himself deals with the business of a deathbed repentance in two places. In Sermon II, although he repeats the customary assertion that reform is necessary for true repentance, he qualifies this view when he arrives at a discussion of the possibility of salvation for a dying sinner. It is dangerous, he observes, to wait so long to repent, and no one who feels remorse only at the end of life can be certain of his acceptance; at the same time, he eagerly grasps at an explanation that allows him to reconcile the efficacy of a deathbed repentance with the idea that repentance requires an effected amendment. "All reformation," he writes, "is begun by a change of the temper and inclinations, which, when altered to a certain degree, necessarily produces an alteration in the life and manners; if God, who sees the heart, sees it rectified in such a manner as would consequently produce a good life, he will accept that repentance." In other words, a dying sinner who feels truly contrite may be saved without amendment, provided that through foreknowledge God is assured that he would have reformed had he lived.

This explanation may sound too metaphysical to be Johnson's own. Furthermore, although his view of Christianity was somewhat distinctive in its totality, he had too much respect for tradition and authority to venture upon individual interpretations of doctrine. Various theologians may have offered the explanation he provides, but his specific source was probably Hammond's *Practical Catechism,* where a similar provision, based on God's foreknowledge, allows some hope for the efficacy of a deathbed repentance.[21]

A practical test of Johnson's attitude on a late repentance presented itself when he wrote *The Convict's Address* for William Dodd. This sermon was intended for prisoners, many of whom were condemned to die within a few days or weeks. No matter how sincere their remorse, the time left to them was insufficient to prove they had reformed their lives. In this message, written relatively late in life, Johnson again alludes to Hammond's argument. He writes: "Of the efficacy of a deathbed repentance many have disputed, but we have no leisure for controversy. Fix in your minds this decision, 'Repentance is a change of the heart of an evil to a good disposition.' When that change is made, repentance is complete. God will consider that life as amended, which would have been amended if he had spared it. Repentance in the sight of man, even of the penitent, is not known but by its fruits; but our Creator sees the fruit, in the blossom, or in the seed."[22]

Although Johnson repeats the argument based on God's foreknowledge, the sermon written for Dodd emphasizes more than Sermon II the importance of a "good disposition," based on contrition. Correspondingly, there is less emphasis on reformation as a test of repentance. Was Johnson tempering his views in order to hold out hope to the condemned prisoners, or had his own ideas changed by 1777, when he wrote *The Convict's Address?*[23] Certainly, as the whole tone of the sermon shows, he was concerned to keep the prisoners from despair, but, in my opinion, his own beliefs, especially about the necessity of self-atonement, had been modified by a deeper realization of the significance of Christ's vicarious sacrifice. Thus the duty of making reparations for injuries, a point he had urgently stressed in *Rambler* 54, is treated quite differently in *The Convict's Address.* He writes: "If we are tempted to think that the injuries we have done are unrepaired, and therefore repentance is vain; let us remember that the reparation which is impossible is not required; that sincerely to will, is to do, in the sight of Him to whom all hearts are open; and that what is deficient in our endeavours is supplied by the merits of Him who died to redeem us."[24]

Here Johnson seems more trustful of Christ's mercy than he had been in the *Rambler* period. Some years later he quoted a passage that held out even stronger hope for the possible validity of a very late repentance. On April 28, 1783, Boswell raised the question of what chance of salvation could exist for a man who, after being the aggressor in a duel, was killed by his opponent. Johnson replied, "Sir, we are not to judge determinately of the state in which a man leaves this life. He may in a moment have repented effectually, and it is possible may have been accepted by God. There is in 'Camden's Remains,' an epitaph upon a very wicked man, who was killed by a fall from his horse, in which he is supposed to say,

> Between the stirrup and the ground,
> I mercy ask'd, I mercy found."[25]

This allusion to the possibility of a valid last-minute or last-second repentance may seem surprising in view of what Johnson had said earlier on the importance of amendment. But it should be observed that he was merely speculating on the subject. His only positive affirmation, characteristically, is that no one can judge another's spiritual state. Meanwhile, whatever changes may have occurred in his opinions, he continued to judge himself by the strictest standards and to act on the principle that one's whole life, as William Law had asserted, should be devoted to repentance. A year after repeating the epitaph from *Camden's Remains,* he prayed in his customary vein, "Give me such sorrow as may purify my heart, such indignation as may quench all confidence in my self, and such repentance as may by the intercession of my Redeemer obtain pardon."[26]

V · JOHNSON'S SERMONS

We have no sermons addressed to the passions that are good for any thing.

Johnson, *quoted in* Boswell's Life of Johnson, *III, 248*

J ohnson's sermons, from which we have already quoted, are fundamental to an understanding of his religion. In this chapter, therefore, we shall examine them more closely, considering particularly the circumstances of their composition, their distinctive tone, and the extent to which, in two areas, they reveal changes in Johnson's views.

Most of the sermons attributed to Johnson were published a few years after his death. They appeared in two volumes in 1788 and 1789 with the ambiguous title, *Sermons On Different Subjects, Left For Publication by John Taylor, LL.D., Late Prebendary of Westminster.* Taylor and Johnson had known each other since their boyhood days in Lichfield. They had remained friends, and Johnson frequently visited his old companion at his country estate in Ashbourne. Although possessed of a personal fortune, Taylor used his position as a clergyman and whatever other influence he could command to add to his income. His biographer observes, "His desire for preferments was insatiable."[1] When he died in 1788, besides being Prebend of Westminster, he had accumulated several other church livings. Taylor is mentioned as a vigorous preacher; nevertheless, when the sermons appeared shortly after his death, many believed that most of them, if not all, had been written by Johnson.[2] During his lifetime he admitted to intimates that he had composed sermons for various clergymen. In his *Meditations,* under the date, September 21, 1777, he had specifically alluded to writing one for Taylor. Both John Hawkins and his daugh-

ter Laetitia, whose parish church was St. Margaret's, Westminster, report having heard Taylor preach sermons they knew
to have been written by Johnson.[3] Finally, with certain excep-
tions,[4] both the style and the treatment of the subject matter
seem to bear Johnson's characteristic stamp.

Johnson, with his copious fund of religious knowledge, probably found sermon-writing a congenial occupation. Because of
his genuine zeal, he could also feel he was accomplishing some
good by his exhortations. Thus he would be inclined to re-
spond favorably to a clerical friend who called upon him to
compose a sermon. But Johnson also wrote homilies as a
means of adding to his precarious income as a man of letters.
This practice was not uncommon at a time when there appears to have been a considerable demand for such services.
In addition to borrowing from the large stock of printed sermons, Anglican clergymen frequently commissioned writers
more expert than themselves to compose an address. Johnson
alludes to this custom in a letter to a young clergyman, where
he observes, "Few frequent preachers can be supposed to have
sermons more their own than yours will be."[5]

Johnson wrote many more sermons than those that have
been identified as his. Some were probably printed under the
names of the persons who delivered them. Apparently this ar-
rangement was satisfactory to Johnson, for after being paid
for a sermon, generally at the rate of two guineas, he surren-
dered the copy and all rights in it to the clergyman who had
enlisted his services. Boswell reports that in 1773 Johnson told
him he had written "about forty sermons."[6] Later, on April
20, 1778, Johnson recorded in his private diary, "I have made
sermons perhaps as readily as formerly." Presumably this practice continued until the last few years of his life, but because
of his better financial circumstances, his later sermons were
likely to have been composed for friends, like Taylor, and
written, not for a fee, but as a favor.

Altogether twenty-five sermons are included in the two volumes left for publication by Taylor. Only one of these was specifically attributed to Johnson, a composition he wrote on the death of his wife, with the intention of having Taylor preach it at her funeral.

In addition to those left by Taylor, two other printed sermons have been definitely identified as Johnson's. The first is entitled *The Convict's Address to His Unhappy Brethren.* The circumstances of its composition are well known. It was written for the unfortunate clergyman, Dr. William Dodd, who stirred Johnson's compassion when he was imprisoned and later condemned for forgery. This work was first printed in 1777. According to Boswell, Dodd wrote only the introduction and the concluding prayer.[7] A second composition, identified as Johnson's in more recent years, is entitled *A Sermon Preached at the Cathedral Church of Saint Paul, Before the Sons of the Clergy.* Dealing with charity, it was written for his Lichfield friend, Henry Hervey Aston. Originally printed in 1745 under Aston's name, it is now available in the Augustan Reprint Series (No. 50, 1955), with an introduction by James L. Clifford.[8]

Some of the sermons were, quite clearly, composed for particular occasions. The one for Dodd expresses the point of view of a prisoner addressing his fellow convicts. The Aston sermon was delivered before members of an organization concerned with supporting the sons of deceased clergymen, as evidenced by allusions in the text to the plight of the children. Similarly, Sermon IV in the *Works* of Johnson seems from the context to have been an appeal to visitors at Bath to support a charity school in that city. A school of this kind had been in existence there since 1711, and two sermons were customarily delivered each year on its behalf.[9] Sermon XVIII, which bears the notation that it was preached at Ashbourne, must have been written for John Taylor. Towards the end of the discourse there are allusions to the local scene. As Jean Hagstrum observes, this material was probably added by Taylor himself.[10] Presumably, then, several of the sermons were intended for different kinds of congregations. Nevertheless, most of the sermons are addressed to an audience of about the same sort intellectually as that Johnson had in mind when writing his *Idler* essays.

Johnson shared the prevalent assumption of his age that sermons should be directed, not to the emotions, but to the reason. Like his essays, his sermons are intellectual in tone, and, in fact, contain opinions he had expressed elsewhere. Apart from the one composed on the death of his wife, however, the sermons lack the personal allusions found in his religious diaries. Most of the sermons do not even attempt to establish a close rapport with readers or listeners, though in this respect *The Convict's Address* is an exception. When it was published, the *Gentleman's Magazine* commended it in terms that must have caused Johnson to smile. The reviewer wrote: "As none but a convict could have written this, all convicts ought to read it; and we therefore recommend its being framed, and hung up in all prisons."[11]

It is interesting to note that in three instances Johnson and Swift have sermons on the same topics—on brotherly love, on bearing false witness, and on the anniversary of the death of Charles I. But the tone is markedly different. Swift's sermons give the impression of being addressed to a particular group. Although his comments sometimes appear condescending, presumably he had before him a particular congregation of whose intellectual abilities he had formed a distinct judgment. Johnson, on the other hand, seems to be addressing, not a special congregation, but mankind as a whole. To illustrate, we may compare the sermons each wrote on the text, "Thou shalt not bear false witness against thy neighbour." Swift's address has strong political overtones. What he discusses chiefly is the evil of informing on others. This topic takes on special meaning when it is recalled that he was living in a country conducting a form of guerrilla warfare with England, a war in which he himself had participated by writing the pseudonymous *Drapier's Letters*. In this kind of struggle secrecy is paramount, and the chief danger is exposure. Consequently Swift's sermon warns not only against bearing false witness but against any looseness of tongue that might endanger one's neighbor. Johnson's interests are quite different. After dealing briefly with perjury, he concentrates on what he terms the more common sense in which men bear false witness, namely by calumny. Even to listen in silent assent while another's reputation is under attack, he urges, makes one guilty of conniving at evil. The best way to avoid engaging in calumny, he admonishes, is to examine with greater care one's own faults and to remember "that charity is the height of religious excellence; and that it is one of the characteristicks of this virtue, that it thinketh no evil of others."

Johnson's sermons are distinguished from the typical sermons of his time, and from most at any time, by the terse and memorable comments woven into the fabric of his discourse. As in his essays, these are usually naked precepts, unembellished by illustration. For instance: "All violence, beyond the necessity of self-defence, is incited by the desire of humbling the opponent, and, whenever it is applied to the decision of religious questions, aims at conquest, rather than conversion" (XXIII). Or again: "In all matters of emulation and contest, the success of one implies the defeat of another, and, at least half the transaction terminates in misery" (XII). Sometimes the effect is heightened by a rhetorical device, such as parallelism: "As cruelty looks upon misery without partaking pain, so envy beholds increase of happiness without partaking joy" (XI). Occasionally he employs analogy, as in, "He that blows a fire for the destruction of a city, is no less an incendiary than he that kindled it" (XVII).

Particularly arresting are some of the psychological observations on the human condition. In Sermon VI he writes: "Pride is a corruption that seems almost originally ingrafted in our nature. . . . It mingles with all our other vices, and without the most constant and anxious care, will mingle also with our virtues." He observes that humanity often follows a pattern of behavior that no logic can explain. For instance: "Nothing is more common than for men to make partial and absurd distinctions between vices of equal enormity, and to observe some of the Divine commands with great scrupulousness; while they violate others equally important, without any concern, or the least apparent consciousness of guilt" (XVII).

Johnson is especially concerned with what may be termed psychological irony. In *The Vanity of Human Wishes* the whole structure of the poem is built on the disastrous outcome of having one's wishes fulfilled. Here the irony results from the failure, through pride or lack of foresight, to know what is best for oneself. In the sermons he is more often inclined to emphasize the way men delude themselves through wishful thinking or by a process of rationalization. "So tenaciously does our credulity lay hold of life," he remarks, "that it is rare to find any man so old as not to expect an addition to his years, or so far wasted and enfeebled with disease, as not to flatter himself with hopes of recovery" (X).

The perception deepens in Sermon XX, where he comments on the reciprocal nature of thought and action. "Not only our speculations influence our practice, but our practice reciprocally influences our speculations. We not only do what we approve, but there is danger lest in time we come to approve what we do, though for no other reason but that we do it." One should not get the impression, however, that such observations, quoted here out of context, are mere asides; they are closely integrated with the main topics of his sermons. The remark just quoted, for instance, leads up to his explanation of why mankind so often fails to heed religious precepts: "A man is always desirous of being at peace with himself; and when he cannot reconcile his passions to his conscience, he will attempt to reconcile his conscience to his passions; he will find reason for doing what he resolved to do, and rather than not 'walk after his own lusts,' will scoff at religion."

Johnson's concern with self-delusion has been attributed to William Law's influence.[12] Because Law frequently warns against this and other forms of sophistry, he may very well have shared in directing Johnson's attention to it. But the dangers inherent in self-deception have been a common topic of various religious writers. Two other authors in whose works Johnson would have encountered similar admonitions are Sir Thomas Browne and Thomas à Kempis. When Johnson edited Browne's *Christian Morals,* he particularly commented on the following passage: "To magnify our minor things, or hug ourselves in our apparitions; to afford a credulous ear unto the clawing suggestions of fancy; to pass our days in painted mistakes of ourselves; and tho' we behold our own blood, to think ourselves the sons of Jupiter; are blandishments of self-love, worse than outward delusion."[13] A similar thought appears in *The Imitation of Christ* by à Kempis, a work Johnson read at least twice: "We judge oft times after our heart and our affections and not after truth, for we lose the true judgment through our private love . . . commonly there is in us some inward inclination or some outward affection that draweth our heart with them from the true judgment."[14]

It is not always easy to trace Johnson's thoughts to a specific source, but one thing appears certain. As Miss Balderston has remarked, even when his reflections are derivative, he manages to give them a distinctive vitality.[15] Whatever its origin, his awareness of the tendency to engage in rationalization left its impact on his sermons and, in my opinion, upon his conduct as well. He himself remarked that a favorite notion often "takes such an entire possession of a man's mind, and so engrosses his faculties, as to mingle thoughts perhaps he is not himself conscious of with almost all his conceptions, and influence his whole behaviour" (Sermon XVI).

Inasmuch as the sermons were written over a period of several decades, they might be expected to reveal some differences, however slight, in Johnson's point of view. But to detect such changes it is necessary to know at what stage in his career the particular sermons were composed. With the exception of the one written on his wife's death, none of those left by Taylor can be ascribed, on the basis of external evidence, to a definite year. There is, however, a test that may indicate the general period in which a sermon was composed. This test depends on an aspect of style. Various studies made in the past have shown that as Johnson advanced in years his prose grew simpler. In particular, his sentences became shorter, diminishing from an average of 43 words in the *Rambler* period (1750–52) to an average of about 30 words in his *Lives of the Poets* (1779–81). The same kind of evidence emerges from a study of the three sermons that can be specifically dated—the Aston sermon (1745), the one on the death of his wife (1752), and *The Convict's Address* (1777). In these, the average sentence length diminishes significantly, according to the order of time in which the sermons were composed.

This same test can, I believe, give an indication of the general period in Johnson's career when he composed the undated sermons. In the Appendix, pages 209–12, I have discussed at greater length, the dating of the sermons.

The chief reason for emphasizing the chronology of the sermons is its importance to testing whether or not Johnson's religious views changed over the several decades in which the sermons were produced. On this point there is some new evidence, in addition to what may be inferred from a study of sentence length. This new evidence is related to Johnson's two sermons on Communion, numbered IX and XXII in the *Works*. Both deal with the sin of partaking of the Eucharist in an unworthy frame of mind. Each stresses the seriousness of this offense, though each also warns against being overscrupulous on this score. Similarly, both emphasize the necessity of self-examination before receiving the Sacrament. They are alike also in affirming that Communion is an important means of grace, though Sermon XXII deals at greater length with this point. Because both sermons treat the same subject in much the same manner, the indication is that Johnson's views on Communion changed little, if at all, in the time between writing the two sermons. This deduction would be of little significance if the two works were written within a few weeks or months of each other, but it can be shown that Sermon IX was probably composed several years after Sermon XXII. In the first place, by the test of sentence length, Sermon XXII is earlier, averaging 56.5 words to a sentence as compared with an average of 43.1 in Sermon IX. Secondly, and of more interest, is new evidence which indicates that Sermon IX borrows certain materials from Samuel Clarke, whose writings Johnson came to admire relatively late in life.

To prove this point we shall have to examine certain heretofore unpublished notes which are inscribed in a copy of the first edition of Johnson's *Prayers and Meditations*. This volume was once owned by Edmond Malone, and the notations are his.[16] In the end leaves of the book Malone wrote:

Among Dr. Johnson's papers together with several prayers composed at Ashbourne in the Sepr before his death was one on the Eucharist, which I have here copied from the original:

> First end of the Sacrament
> Remembrance of the death of Christ

Remember {
The love of God, the father
The love of God, the son
The heinousness of sin
}

Christ's death is remembered or commemorated,
   As a motive to obedience
   As an acknowledgment that the death of Christ is the only
      ground of assurance of pardon
   As a publick declaration of our faith in Christ
   As an act of thanksgiving for the death of Christ
   An Obligation to universal charity and benevolence

Obligation—Christ's command
Benefits—God's assistance
Preparation—to examine himself

The Eucharist is not a constant Sacrifice; a grant of remission, like baptism, not an expiation of sins, even to those that repent; certainly not of unrepented sins. No grace is annexed to the more material action.[17]

Malone's reference to several prayers composed at Ashbourne may indicate that there were prayers of which we have no knowledge. But more to our immediate purpose is the transcript of Johnson's notations. Because the material was unlabeled, Malone assumed it to be an original composition by Johnson himself. This assumption was erroneous. The material consists of jottings or notes, partly in outline form. Furthermore, they are notes on four closely related sermons of Samuel Clarke. Each of these is entitled "The Nature, End, and Design of Holy Communion."[18] The evidence that Johnson was annotating these sermons becomes clear when we see how closely he used Clarke's wording and how specifically he outlined the clergyman's topics. For instance, Johnson lists five reasons under the caption, "Christ's death is remembered and commemorated." These correspond to the reasons outlined and discussed in Sermons IX and X, except that Clarke supplies six reasons, *viz.* (1) "as a Motive to Obedience," (2) "the only Ground of our Hope of Pardon," (3) "a declaring publickly to the World, our Faith in him," (4) "a returning Thanks to God . . . in sending his Son into the World for the redemption of Mankind," (5) "a confirming on our part, our Covenant with God," (6) "a Profession of our Communion one with another, and a strong Obligation to mutual Love, Charity and Good-will."[19]

The remaining notes Malone copied are also based on a close study of Clarke's discussion of Communion. The captions, "Obligation," "Benefits," and "Preparation," as well as the subtopics under these headings, correspond to topics

Clarke discusses in Sermon XI. Again, the three points listed under "Remembrance of the death of Christ" follow, and in the same order, points that Clarke introduces in Sermon VIII. Finally, Johnson's statement on the Eucharist paraphrases remarks that appear in various places in the four sermons.

In view of this parallelism, I believe it must be granted that Johnson had studied Clarke's ideas on the Sacrament. According to Malone, the notations were found with various manuscript materials that Johnson had presumably penned while at Ashbourne during the last few months of his life. But the outline of Clarke's sermons on Communion was probably made earlier. The reasons for so thinking are: the indication that Johnson used these notes in preparing his discussion of Communion in his own ninth sermon; and the inference, based on the test of sentence length, that this sermon belongs to the middle period of his writing career. Furthermore, it docs not sccm likcly that, ill as hc was in the last year of his life, Johnson would have been occupied at this late date with composing sermons.

The indication that Johnson used his notes on Clarke in preparing Sermon IX is seen first in the fact that his three main divisions in the sermon are (1) "the nature and end of this institution," (2) "the obligations," and (3) "What things are required of them that come to the Lord's supper." These are paralleled in his notes by the reasons: "Christ's death is remembered or commemorated," "Obligation," and "Preparation." Furthermore, in discussing the nature and end of Communion, Johnson deals with the first four points listed as subtopics in his notes, under reasons for commemorating the death of Christ. But even if it is granted that Johnson had the outline of Clarke's sermons before him when composing his sermon, it must not be presumed that he leaned very heavily on Clarke. His notes served chiefly to provide topics for discussion. To the extent that there is a duplication of subject matter, most of it can be explained by the circumstance that both are expressing commonly held views on the sacrament of Communion.

More striking is the fact that Johnson excluded from his discussion various controversial points that Clarke treats, such as his denunciation of the belief in transubstantiation and his objections to the Roman Catholic practice of taking the Eucharist in one form only. Furthermore, on some issues Johnson definitely disagrees with the clergyman. Although in his notes he copied Clarke's assertion that Communion is not, like Baptism, a means of remitting sin, he does not repeat this view in his own sermon. On the contrary, he emphasizes the similarity between the two sacraments, saying that both serve to admit one into the fellowship of Christ and to remove sin. Again, while Johnson's manuscript notes contain the statement that "no grace is annexed to the mere material action," this paraphrase of Clarke's view is in complete contradiction to what Johnson says in Sermon IX. Unlike Clarke, he considers the Sacrament not merely as a commemorative rite but as an important means of obtaining "the supernatural and extraordinary influences of grace."

As we have indicated above, the substance of Johnson's two sermons on Communion is much the same, even though Sermon XXII may have been written as much as twenty years earlier. This similarity would indicate that Johnson's views on the Sacrament did not change perceptibly. Although he read with interest Clarke's four sermons on Communion, it does not appear that the Low Church position of this clergyman materially altered his own beliefs on this subject. Despite the admiration he developed for Clarke, he continued to examine with critical eyes every interpretation of Christian doctrine that he encountered. The chief, perhaps the only real, influence of Clarke on Johnson was the change brought about in his interpretation of the Atonement. We shall now examine Johnson's treatment of this subject in his sermons.

As we have shown, in middle life Johnson apparently felt

that the burden of expiation for sin rests on man. In his view, Christ's death opened the door to salvation, but to be assured of attaining it, man must obey his commandments, or if he fails to do so, he must practice self-atonement, to compensate for his sins. This emphasis upon self-atonement, it would appear, was closely associated with a belief that Christ's sacrifice was not of a propitiatory nature. What evidence exists in the sermons that Johnson did not develop a deep conviction about the vicarious nature of the sacrifice until relatively late in life? One should not expect to find a clear instance of his reversing his views, for in none of his works does he specifically deny the propitiatory character of the sacrifice. It seems significant, however, that in what appear by the test of sentence length to be earlier sermons, there are virtually no clear references to the Atonement as an expiatory act. There are, to be sure, various references to Christ's "merits," but these may be taken as allusions to the redemption of man from the Fall or to his merits in setting an example for men to follow by his life and death. On the other hand, in what may be deemed late sermons, those probably composed in the last ten years of his life, Johnson makes several specific allusions to the sacrifice as a vicarious act.

In Sermon VI, averaging 29 words to the sentence (see Appendix), Johnson concludes his discussion of spiritual pride with the comment: "But it may be hoped that a sufficient remedy against this sin may be easily found, by reminding those who are infected with it, that the blood of Christ was poured out upon the cross to make their best endeavours acceptable to God; and that they, whose sins require such an expiation, have little reason to boast of their virtue." This is one of his strongest affirmations on the vicarious nature of the sacrifice, and I believe it could have been made only in the last ten years of his life. He concludes the sermon with a paragraph in which he describes the humiliation Christ suffered. "At length," he writes, "having borne all the cruel treatment that malice could suggest, or power inflict, he suffered the most lingering and ignominious death.—God of his infinite mercy grant, that by imitating his humility, we may be made partakers of his merits!" This, of course, is a reference to the exemplary character of the sacrifice, but this belief, which had been so strongly emphasized by William Law, now accompanies a conviction that the death on the Cross was truly propitiatory.

A reference to the Atonement in Sermon XXI (averaging 35.3 words to a sentence) is particularly interesting because of the peculiar character of this sermon. It is distinguished from all the other sermons by its tone. The text, "The Lord is good to all, and his tender mercies are over all his works," is developed by allusions to man and nature in terms popular with the Deistical writers of the age. God is called "the eternal Parent"; and creation, "this regular and grand machine, this finished and stupendous fabrick." There are even approving allusions to the Chain of Being, a theory with which Johnson expressed strong disagreement elsewhere. Furthermore, there are many more quotations from Scripture than is customary in his sermons. Because of these circumstances, Jean Hagstrum doubts that Johnson wrote it and believes it may be one of Taylor's compositions.[20] I, too, find it difficult to ascribe any considerable portion of this sermon to Johnson. Whoever the author, he combined, just as Clarke did, a belief in the perfection of the universe with a strong belief in the vicarious nature of Christ's sacrifice. The author writes: "Were the mercies of the Lord limited to the tenure of our present existence, great and glorious as they are, the human mind would be clouded by the consciousness that a very few years must exclude us forever from the participation of them. But since the gracious rays of life and immortality have dissipated the gloom that hung upon futurity, since, by the propitiatory sacrifice of the Son of God, death is disarmed of his sting, and the grave deprived of its victory, Divine goodness hath received its perfect consummation."

We are on more certain ground when we come to *The Convict's Address,* for we know it was composed in 1777, after Johnson's view of the Atonement had apparently changed. Furthermore, this sermon may be considered as one of the important sources of information on Johnson's religious beliefs late in life. Sometime after writing it, probably not long before his death, he is said to have inscribed the following postscript on a copy of that work: "Ambition and Vanity are, I hope, now at an End. I desire no praise as the Authour of the foregoing Discourse, but I desire to leave behind me these Thoughts, by whomever collected and expressed, as the genuine Opinion of my last Hour."[21]

The sermon is addressed to convicted criminals, and since Dodd was one of them, the first person is used throughout. The theme is: we are assured of salvation on the basis of faith, obedience, and repentance. In order to avoid despair, we must have particular recourse to faith. In the short time left, we can show our obedience only in a limited way, but we may still benefit the public by setting an example of patience and true contrition. In this sermon, more than in any other work published in his lifetime, Johnson stresses the propitiatory nature of the sacrifice. Towards the conclusion of his exhortation he writes: ". . . we must commend and entrust our souls to Him, who died for the sins of men; with earnest wishes and humble hopes that he will admit us with the labourers who entered the vineyard at the *last hour,* and associate us with the thief whom he pardoned on the cross!"

Particularly significant is the emphasis placed in this sermon on the Atonement in a definition of "faith." When Johnson dealt with this term in the *Dictionary,* he provided three brief definitions: (1) "Belief of the revealed truths of religion"; (2) "The system of revealed truths held by the Christian church"; (3) "Trust in God." In *The Convict's Address* he writes, with a note of strong affirmation: "Faith is a full and undoubting confidence in the declarations made by God in the holy Scriptures; a sincere reception of the doctrines taught by our blessed Saviour, with a firm assurance that he died to take away the sins of the world, and that we have, each of us, a part in the boundless benefits of the universal Sacrifice." This expanded definition, with its notable emphasis on the propitiatory sacrifice, seems, in view of what has been said heretofore, excellent evidence that Johnson's interpretation of this doctrine had changed by 1777.

At this point we shall terminate a particular consideration of the sermons, though we shall continue to quote from these works which constantly serve to ratify Johnson's religious position. It seems possible that someday various other sermons, hitherto unidentified as his, may be definitely ascribed to Johnson. Such a discovery would be most welcome. Doubtless they would supply certain further insights into his beliefs. Yet I venture to predict that any such additions to the canon would supplement rather than materially change our impressions of the man. No matter for whom his sermons were written, their tone and substance seem to be a true index of his own solemn meditations.

VI · JOHNSON'S
SENSE OF CHARITY

It was not only in his book, but in his mind, that orthodoxy was united with charity.

Johnson, Life of Isaac Watts

S amuel Johnson had a special liking for the history of manners.[1] His own observations on the passing scene suggest that he might have written an excellent social history of his times. Keenly aware that a transformation was taking place, he frequently commented on various novel developments of the age, such as the changes occurring in the education of women, the treatment of crime, and new attempts to deal with the problem of poverty. Particularly arresting, because it sets the subject in an historical context, is one of his remarks on charity. "The present age," he writes (*Idler* 4), "though not likely to shine hereafter among the most splendid periods of history, has yet given examples of charity, which may be very properly recommended to imitation. . . . no sooner is a new species of misery brought to view, and a design of relieving it professed, than every hand is open to contribute something, every tongue is busied in solicitation, and every art of pleasure is employed for a time in the interest of virtue."

Johnson is here alluding to the philanthropic impulse that led to the establishment of special schools for the poor, asylums for the aged and indigent, hospitals, orphanages, and other charitable institutions. In the same essay he remarks that previous times had been notable for great single benefactions, made by wealthy individuals. In his own era philanthropy was more often the product of collective efforts of charitably disposed persons. This was a proper distinction, for the eighteenth century seems to have been the first period in which various influences led to the development of co-operative public charities.[2]

The philanthropic impulse was not limited to establishing institutions to harbor the needy. It found expression in many individual acts of generosity,[3] it formed an important motif in plays and novels, and became both in literature and in life a yardstick for measuring the worth of a man. This virtue was generally given a special name. "Benevolence" and, to a lesser extent, "beneficence" were the terms commonly used to describe an active interest in the welfare of others. Frequently, "benevolence" was substituted for the word "charity," as, for instance, in Edward Harwood's *Liberal Translation of the New Testament*. In this curious work, published in 1768, Harwood attempted to improve on the language of the King James version by translating it into contemporary terminology. Although his efforts were to result in a ridiculous jargon, it is revealing to see how Harwood renders some of the notable scriptural passages on charity. "And above all these things put on charity, which is the bond of perfectness" (Col. 3:14) becomes: "And besides all these virtues above mentioned, do you adorn yourselves with benevolence, which is the great bond and cement of perfection." For the familiar "Charity shall cover the multitude of sins" (I Pet. 4:8) he substitutes: "Benevolence throws a vail over a multitude of faults and follies." The famous precept of St. Paul, "Charity suffereth long, and is kind; charity envieth not; charity vaunteth not itself, it is not puffed up" (I Cor. 13:4), reads in Harwood's version: "Benevolence is unruffled, is benign; Benevolence cherishes no ambitious desires; Benevolence is not ostentatious, is not inflated with insolence." Occasionally the word "charity" is allowed to remain in context, but, like so many others of his time, Harwood clearly prefers the term "benevolence."

As we shall see, "benevolence" did not always connote the same thing as Christian charity. Nevertheless, it was the favored word for a form of humanitarianism that the eighteenth century considered its chief and sometimes its only notable virtue.

The development of a special interest in benevolence may be attributed to various causes. The economic historian might indicate that the growth of capitalism, resulting in greater national wealth and a wider dispersal of riches among the upper classes, made it possible for more people to give to the poor than formerly. He might emphasize still more that greater demands were being placed on private charities. Although poverty was nothing new, certain situations had increased the difficulties of relieving the poor by the traditional method of local taxation; that is, by providing for them out of the parish rates. In the first place, the population was increasing more rapidly than ever before, chiefly because there were no longer devastating plagues and because advances in the knowledge of obstetrics meant fewer deaths at birth.

Also in process was an agricultural revolution that led large numbers of village workers to drift to the towns and cities, where low wages and unemployment made it impossible for many to support their families. Because of the Settlement Act these displaced persons were ineligible for assistance from the public rates, except in the communities of their origin. This complex of factors meant that without private donations many could not even sustain life. In 1779 Johnson remarked about the situation in London: "Saunders Welch, the Justice, who was once High-Constable of Holborn, and had the best opportunities of knowing the state of the poor, told me, that I under-rated the number, when I computed that twenty a week, that is, above a thousand a year, died of hunger; not absolutely of immediate hunger; but of the wasting and other diseases which are the consequences of hunger."[4]

Economic changes were important, but the historian of ideas provides another explanation for the special interest in benevolence, namely, the background of philosophical optimism.

Basic to this school of thought was the belief that man is naturally good. The development of this idea has been attributed to the third Earl of Shaftesbury, more than to any other single man. Believing that morality may operate independently of religion, he had argued that man has a native disposition to good. This natural affection, especially when fortified by reason, issues in benevolence towards one's fellow man.[5] Although Shaftesbury's writings undoubtedly had much to do with promoting this belief, the rise of the benevolent movement was clearly more complex, more broadly based, and of earlier origin.

In an important article on the subject, R. S. Crane has convincingly shown that the vogue of benevolence may be traced initially to the influence of various Latitudinarian divines of the late seventeenth century. While the Christian ideal that man should strive to imitate God's universal love for mankind underlay their beliefs, the stress they placed on good works was, in part, a reaction against Puritanism, with its emphasis on faith as opposed to works. On the other hand, when the Latitudinarians urged that man has a native inclination to good, they seem to have been particularly concerned to negate Thomas Hobbes's view that man is basically selfish. They were also anti-Stoical to the extent that they wished to invalidate a reliance on reason alone and to combat the notion that the passions are necessarily evil. Consequently, they preached the idea that pity and compassion are natural to man and that he should find joy in his benevolent disposition.[6]

Quite clearly the growth of a new form of humanitarianism was complex both in its origins and in its effects. Shaftesbury's influence was probably the greater because many of his ideas already existed in the intellectual milieu when his works were published. In any event, numerous advocates of benevolence were to follow him. Praised alike by the Deists and their opponents, this virtue eventually came to be regarded by many as man's noblest characteristic. The impact of benevolence upon the eighteenth century was so varied and of such scope that it has never been properly assessed. Socially it did much good by the impulse it gave to the founding of hospitals and asylums for the ill, the aged, the needy, and the neglected. In the field of politics it played an important role in furthering democratic theories and the establishment of democratic forms of government. In literature its influence was a mixed blessing. On the one hand, the concomitant esteem for the emotions helped to restore a proper regard for the passions. On the other hand, as so many plays, novels, and poems of the mid-eighteenth century attest, benevolence became such a popular theme, so highly extolled, and so frequently sentimentalized that, as Leslie Stephen remarked, it spread like a kind of mildew over the surface of literature.[7]

Although related to Christian concepts of charity, benevolence probably got its sentimental coloring from the non-Christian idea that man is naturally good. Therein lay a main difference between the two. Love of one's fellow man as taught in the New Testament was based on an important religious principle, the love of God. Love of others, conceived of as a native impulse of the heart or glands, was based on a relatively new assumption of the native nobility of mankind. It is interesting to observe how two of Johnson's biographers differ in their views of benevolence. Sir John Hawkins, objecting to the idea that it is an inborn quality, comments that Fielding was the "inventor of a cant phrase, 'goodness of heart,' which means little more than the virtue of a horse or a dog." In his essay on Johnson, Arthur Murphy criticizes Hawkins for this observation. Indicating his own inclination toward the school of sentimental benevolence, he insists that a disposition to kindness is "implanted in our nature."[8]

Johnson would not have agreed with Murphy. Like Hawkins, he felt that men have no more native goodness than animals. When Lady Macleod asked him "if no man was naturally good," he replied, "No, Madam, no more than a wolf." Although he sometimes used the term "benevolence" to indicate an acquired disposition to charity, he was strongly opposed to regarding benevolence as a natural instinct. When Boswell attempted to defend a person whose "principles had been poisoned by a noted infidel writer" by saying he was "nevertheless, a benevolent good man," Johnson objected: "We can have no dependence upon that instinctive, that constitutional goodness which is not founded upon principle." This belief he held to consistently. As early as 1753 Mrs. Chapone wrote: "I had the assurance to dispute with Mr. Johnson on the subject of human malignity, and wondered to hear a man who by his actions shews so much benevolence, maintain that the human heart is naturally malevolent, and that all the benevolence we see in the few who are good, is acquired by reason and religion." Even under these circumstances he doubted that true goodness of heart could exist unadulterated by other motives. When someone remarked that Mrs. Montagu's notable acts of kindness were performed from a sense of vanity, he defended her: "I have seen no beings who do as much good from benevolence, as she does, from whatever motive. . . . No, Sir; to act from pure benevolence is not possible for finite beings. Human benevolence is mingled with vanity, interest, or some other motive."[9]

This attitude has led some to think of Johnson as a pessimist.[10] By contrast to the philosophical optimists who asserted that man was naturally good, his view might be termed pessimistic. He believed man to be a frail creature, morally weak, and intellectually unstable. Consequently, he thought it impossible for man to be altruistically inclined by nature. But there was nothing singular or cynical in this position. He was merely adhering to the traditional Christian belief that whatever goodness man attains is the result of the operation of grace.

Like William Law, and millions of other Christians before him, Johnson regarded charity or *caritas* as a theological virtue, linked with faith and hope. These specifically Christian virtues were to be distinguished from temperance, fortitude, wisdom, and justice, all of which had been known and practised in pre-Christian eras. Similarly, benevolence, when motivated by a prudential sense of doing good to others, might be cherished in a pagan society, or in any community where man has cultivated the power of reason. Charity, on the other hand, was a higher virtue that could exist only among Christians or possibly among those influenced by Christian teaching. The point is emphasized in *Idler* 4. Johnson observes that the bounty bestowed on citizens and soldiers by the Roman emperors was motivated by a desire to win favor, and not by any religious purpose. The Mohammedans, he believes, were encouraged to practice charity, only because Mohammed had learned about this virtue from Christianity. He concludes, therefore, that "Charity, or tenderness for the poor, which is now justly considered, by a great part of mankind, as inseparable from piety and in which all the goodness of the present age consists, is, I think, known only to those who enjoy either immediately or by transmission, the light of revelation."

Johnson's interpretation of charity as a theological virtue is, of course, completely in accord with Christian teaching. That it is a unique Christian virtue is strongly emphasized in his writings. For example, in his edition of Shakespeare he makes an acute observation on the lines in *King Lear* where Edgar says to his dying brother:

> Let's exchange charity,
> I am no less in blood than thou art, Edmund.
> (V, iii, 168)

Believing that the word "charity" is anachronistic in a pagan society, Johnson remarks, "Our authour by negligence gives his heathens the sentiments and practices of Christianity. In *Hamlet* there is the same solemn act of final reconciliation but with exact propriety, for the personages are Christians."

The fundamental difference between Christian charity and benevolence in a secular sense is seen in Johnson's treatment of the two words in his *Dictionary*. "Benevolence" is defined first as "disposition to do good; kindness; charity; good will;" and secondly as "the good done; the charity given." For the word "charity" he provides several definitions: "1. tenderness, kindness, love; 2. goodwill, benevolence, disposition to think well of others; 3. the theological virtue of universal love; 4. liberality to the poor; 5. alms; relief given to the poor." Obviously there is an overlapping of meaning. Both benevolence and charity can be a disposition to do good, kindness, or the performance of specific acts. But charity means much more than benevolence. In the first place it is love. In the second place it is a theological virtue, by which he means the love of God and, subsumed under that, the love of one's fellow man. Under his definition of charity as "the theological virtue of universal love" Johnson appends quotations from Hooker, Jeremy Taylor, and Milton. The quotation from *Paradise Lost* is especially significant, for here again is the allusion to charity as a distinctly Christian virtue. In his admonitions to Adam, the Archangel Michael says:

> Only add
> Deeds to thy knowledge answerable; add faith,
> And virtue, patience, temperance; add love,
> By name to come called charity, the soul
> Of all the rest.
>   (XII, 581–85)

As Johnson indicates, the ultimate source of his knowledge about charity is the Bible. Nevertheless, his views may have been reinforced by his familiarity with *A Serious Call*. Both William Law and Johnson, it will be noted, commonly use the term "Universal love" as an equivalent for Christian charity. Both writers insist that charity in its true meaning is a distinctly Christian virtue. Both believe it to be the highest Christian virtue, though Law is more specific in asserting, as St.

Thomas Aquinas had done centuries earlier, that charity is the chief element in Christian perfection. Because of his concern with perfection, Law constantly emphasizes the doctrine of Christian love. His most detailed discussion, however, appears in Chapter XX of *A Serious Call,* where he writes: "There is no principle of the heart that is more acceptable to God than a universal fervent love to all mankind, wishing and praying for their happiness, because there is no principle of the heart that makes us more like God, Who is love and goodness itself, and created all beings for their enjoyment of happiness."[11]

Johnson similarly believed charity to be the cornerstone of Christianity. In connection with his definition of charity as a theological virtue he quotes Bishop Atterbury's statement: "Charity or love of God, which works by a love of our neighbour, is greater than faith or hope." Again, in Sermon XI Johnson writes: "Charity, or universal love, is named by St. Paul, as the greatest and most illustrious of Christian virtues; and our Saviour himself has told us, that by this it shall be known that we are his disciples, if we love one another."

Johnson is especially clear in his sermons on the motives for practising this virtue. Even without the advantage of religion, he writes, prudence should teach us to relieve the distress of others, for no one knows when he himself may need assistance. Charity is also a duty we are exhorted to perform in numerous passages of Scripture. But the most important reason of all, Johnson points out, is given by Christ, who has informed us "that those who have shown mercy shall find mercy from him, that the practice of charity will be the great test by which we shall be judged, and that those, and those only, who have given food to the hungry, and raiment to the naked shall, at the final doom, be numbered by the Son of God amongst the blessed of his Father" (Sermon XIX). Thus the most specific and the most urgent motive for being charitable is to attain salvation.

It may seem strange that Johnson nowhere in his sermons

quotes the statement, "Charity shall cover the multitude of sins." His failure to do so may have been owing to a realization that this was the favorite text of the benevolists, though, as we have seen, among his contemporaries, Laetitia Hawkins, at least, believed his own acts of charity were partly motivated by a desire to atone for his offenses. He does stress the point that charitable acts may be used as a means of offsetting temptations to sin. For this reason, he comments, "we should consider every opportunity of performing a good action as the gift of God, one of the chief gifts which God bestows upon man, in his present state" (Sermon XIX).

In addition to the all-important motive of personal salvation, Johnson observes, there is also a great social incentive to prompt one to charity. That is to preserve others from falling into sin. "The chief advantage which is received by mankind from the practice of charity," he urges, "is the promotion of virtue amongst those who are most exposed to such temptations as it is not easy to surmount, temptations of which no man can say that he should be able to resist them, and of which it is not easy for any one that has not known them to estimate the force, and represent the danger" (Sermon IV). He is here making a point the advocates of secular benevolence would be inclined to neglect. What he is saying is: If we pity our neighbor, we provide him with food and clothing because we are moved by his temporal sufferings; but if we have Christian love for our neighbor, we feed and clothe him still more because we wish to keep him from falling into sin and thereby risking his salvation. "Let any man reflect," he says, "upon the snares to which poverty exposes virtue, and remember how certainly one crime makes way for another, till at last all distinction of good and evil is obliterated; and he will easily discover the necessity of charity to preserve a great part of mankind from the most atrocious wickedness" (Sermon IV).

Despite the great importance he attached to charity, Johnson never lost sight of the fact that it is only one of several virtues. There is, for instance, an interesting discussion and comparison of justice and charity in *Rambler* 81. Justice, Johnson says, is that which is "indispensably and universally necessary, and what is necessary must always be limited, uniform and distinct." Charity, "though equally enjoined by our religion," is "for the most part, with regard to its single acts, elective and voluntary." Consequently there are rules to maintain justice. It is something that can be measured, whereas charity is not definable by limits. The best guide to justice, he remarks, is found in the precept, "Whatsoever ye would that men should do unto you, even so do unto them." In the light of these distinctions he shows that justice should sometimes take precedence over charity. For instance, a judge who answers a plea for mercy and grants a pardon to a confirmed criminal betrays the community he represents and commits an act of injustice to society. Similarly, if a conflict exists as to which should be discharged first, debts of justice or debts of charity, the former have prior claims by the rule of doing right to others.

In contrasting Johnson's views with those of the secular benevolists we do not intend to imply that his position was singular in his own time. Others, especially High Churchmen, were aware of what charity in the biblical sense means. They could also recognize that it is but one of several Christian virtues. Even the advocates of benevolence would doubtless have agreed in theory, yet they were inclined, especially in the plays and novels of the time, to extol goodness of heart to the exclusion of other virtues. In doing so, they were going to one extreme, just as the Calvinistic Puritans had gone to another. Ronald Knox in his book *Enthusiasm* comments that "traditional Christianity is a balance of doctrines, and not merely of doctrines, but of emphases." He adds, ". . . in itself enthusiasm is not a wrong tendency but a false emphasis."[12] If the Puritans, by asserting the importance of internal monitions, became enthusiasts of one kind; then the sentimental benevolists, by stressing that goodness of heart is native to man, tended towards enthusiasm of another form. Johnson, who was alsways on guard against irrational extremes, could subscribe to neither position.

So far in this chapter we have attempted to show the common meaning of "benevolence" in the eighteenth century and to indicate that Johnson, though sometimes employing this word as an equivalent for "charity," never uses "charity" in the sense of a virtue native to man. True charity, he believed, develops from Christian teaching, and its basis is the love of God and of one's neighbor. Having seen what his theory was, we shall in a later chapter discuss the extent to which the love of God influenced his religion. More immediately, we shall be concerned with his conduct in relation to his neighbor. For convenience this subject may be divided into three subtopics: (1) almsgiving, (2) the performance of other acts of kindness, and (3) forbearance.

As we have indicated above, in the eighteenth century many people had to depend on alms if they were to sustain life. "The Poor," a common designation for the lower economic segment of society, included not only paupers and itinerant workers but all those in the humble walks of life. The number of such persons was extremely large. In 1696 Gregory King had classified the population into two groups. He estimated that there were 2,675,500 members of families helping to increase the wealth of the nation, and 2,825,000 persons decreasing the wealth of the nation. During the latter half of the eighteenth century, because of a substantial increase in population, the total number of indigent persons became still larger. Furthermore the cost of living was rising. Because of these conditions, the parish rates levied to support the needy increased from about £700,000 at the end of the seventeenth century to £4,267,000 in the first decade of the nineteenth century. By this time, moreover, no fewer than 1,040,716 per-

sons were being supported from the parish rates, to say nothing of those dependent on charity.[13]

In having a system of local taxation for the relief of the indigent, England undoubtedly made better provision for them
than most countries. Johnson observed that "The French have
no laws for the maintenance of the poor." Believing that "a
decent provision for the poor is the true test of civilisation,"
he proudly asserted that "the poor in England were better provided for, than in any other country of the same extent."[14]
Nevertheless, he knew that, despite substantial increases in
the parish rates, misery and want were widespread. Although
important developments were occurring in science and industry, there seemed to be little real advancement in the conquest
of poverty. To most Englishmen, including Johnson, it appeared inevitable that a large section of the population would
either be unemployed or able to earn so little that they must
be supported by the parish rates or by private charity.

The frustrating problem was that not enough jobs existed.
Some writers, like Defoe, believed that the able-bodied poor
who expected public support should be assigned to labor in
the workhouses. With this idea Johnson could not agree. He
considered the demand for manufactured goods to be relatively stable. Consequently, to allot the task of producing materials to the indigent in workhouses could only result in de-
priving others of their customary labor. Under these circumstances the only means of keeping a large number from starva-
tion was to support them by public rates or by private charity.
These methods did not solve the problem; at best they could
but mitigate the misery of the poor. Keenly aware of this,
Johnson observed almost despairingly, "It is an unhappy circumstance that one might give away five hundred pounds in
a year to those that importune in the streets, and not do any
good."[15]

By not doing any good, Johnson meant, of course, that small
donations contributed but little to the relief of the total mis-

ery. This did not keep him from doling out money to the
needy. According to his friend Dr. Maxwell, "He frequently
gave all the silver in his pocket to the poor, who watched him,
between his house and the tavern where he dined."[16] His compassion for the poor has been so strongly emphasized by his
biographers that it seems superfluous to repeat more than a
few examples. Mrs. Thrale calculated that he never spent
more than seventy or eighty pounds a year on himself. The
rest of his pension of three hundred pounds and presumably
some of the earnings from publications were devoted to the
support of various dependents and to the bestowal of alms on
the needy. Miss Reynolds reported that, when returning home
at night, "he often saw poor children asleep on thresholds and
stalls, and that he used to put pennies into their hands to buy
them a breakfast." There is also the well-known story of the
prostitute he discovered early one morning. Ill and nearly
naked, she had just been turned out by her landlord. Johnson
wrapped her in his greatcoat and carried her to his house. The
next day, when it became evident that she was suffering from
a venereal disease, he summoned a doctor. During the next
thirteen weeks he provided her with shelter and care. When
she recovered, he raised money from friends and established
her in the millinery business.[17]

"He loved the poor as I never yet saw anyone else do, with
an earnest desire to make them happy," Mrs. Thrale commented. Nevertheless, though strongly moved by compassion
for them, Johnson seldom spoke in sentimental terms about
their plight. To him poverty was a great evil. To treat it as
an occasion for pious platitudes would have seemed almost as
culpable as to neglect the poor altogether. When a lady asked
why he gave money to beggars, he avoided the opening to
preach a sermon and answered curtly, "Madam, to enable
them to beg on."[18]

In conversation he sometimes showed a concern for the
practical aspects of charity. "It is a duty to give to the poor,"

he said; "but no man can say how much another should give to the poor, or when a man has given too little to save his soul. . . . no man is obliged to strip himself to the shirt in order to give to charity. Because he realized that poverty was so extensive that no amount of charity could relieve all the needy, he urged that one should be judicious about distributing alms. "A man should first relieve those who are nearly connected with him, by whatever tie," he affirmed, "and then, if he has any thing to spare, may extend his bounty to a wider circle."[19] In practice he also included among the recipients of his own charity those likely to be neglected by others. When asked how he could bear to be surrounded by such indigent and quarrelsome people as he sheltered in his home, he answered, "If I did not assist them no one else would, and they must be lost for want."[20]

His compassion often led him to be indulgent, but his sense of charity was never befuddled by the kind of sentimentalism we see in Goldsmith's Man in Black or in Smollett's Matthew Bramble. These fictional characters, as if ashamed of their good deeds, engage in hypocritical evasions in order to conceal their acts of charity. Johnson deals with this subject in a common-sense way. Giving in order to win esteem, he writes, or because one expects gratitude or favors is to act on false motives of charity. "True charity arises from faith in the promises of God, and expects rewards only in a future state. To hope for our recompense in this life, is not beneficence, but usury" (Sermon IV). On the other hand, he sees the folly of going to ridiculous extremes to conceal one's charitable acts. The biblical precept on this point, he observes, is to be interpreted as a warning against giving *in order that* we may be seen by others. It is not to be understood as a mandate to conceal true acts of charity (Sermon XIX).

Johnson believed it the duty of the Christian not only to give alms but to seize upon every opportunity to perform other acts of kindness. "Every degree of assistance given to another, upon proper motives, is an act of charity," he writes, "and there is scarcely any man, in such a state of imbecility, as that he may not, on some occasions, benefit his neighbour." Those who cannot give alms to the poor may instruct them. Those unable to tend the sick may assist in reforming the vicious. Those without funds may solicit money for good causes from others. "The widow that shall give her mite to the treasury, the poor man who shall bring to the thirsty a cup of cold water, shall not lose their reward" (Sermon IV).

Because his income was limited, Johnson frequently called upon friends to assist the needy. His appeals to wealthier associates, like the Thrales, Reynolds, Langton, and Garrick, were usually answered. In fact, it was largely through these requests that his intimates came to understand his own deep sense of charity. Besides seeking donations, he also asked friends to perform various other favors for those in want. Boswell, for instance, notes that he requested Bennet Langton and the Reverend Dr. Vyse to use their influence in having an old acquaintance, the eighty-three-year-old De Groot, admitted to the Charter-House Hospital.[21]

Frequently his pen was employed in a more public manner, as in the petitions he wrote for the forger, Dr. Dodd. Here, as in other instances, his rule was to be guided, not by the merits of a situation or by personal esteem for the individual, but by his commiseration for anyone in distress. For instance, he had little respect for the talents of the dramatist Hugh Kelly, but when Kelly died, Johnson cheerfully contributed a prologue for a benefit performance to aid his wife and children.

Johnson also wrote innumerable prefaces and dedications for friends, but these literary performances were acts of friendship rather than of charity, and he distinguished between the two. In friendship, he observes, both affection and duty naturally lead to reciprocated acts of kindness. But friendship was known even to the Ancients who lived before Christ introduced the idea of charity. Christianity did not abolish friend-ship; rather it broadened the private obligations to include the general duty to promote the happiness of all mankind.[22] The real test of charity was not to love one's friends but to fol-low the exhortations of the Sermon on the Mount—to love one's enemies.

Johnson had at least one opportunity to become the spe-cific advocate of this more difficult form of charity. In 1759 a group of about eleven hundred French prisoners of war were incarcerated near Bristol. Poorly clothed and half starved, they were in a desperate situation until their suffering was publicized. A committee was designated to receive donations and, much to the credit of the times, there was a widespread response to the appeal for funds. Nevertheless, in some quar-ters objections had been raised to giving aid and comfort to the enemy. Johnson, who was commissioned to write an intro-duction to a report on the contributions, replied to these ob-jections. What particularly distinguishes his comments is his ability, so often revealed in other works, to see in a particular situation the broader, more universal implications. He pleads the cause not only of the French prisoners but of all victims of war. Reminding his readers of the Christian obligation to do good even "to them that hate us," he suggests that the best hope for the termination of wars lies in the achievement of a universal sense of brotherhood. "That charity is best," he says, "of which the consequences are most extensive: the relief of enemies has a tendency to unit mankind in fraternal affection; to soften the acrimony of adverse nations, and dispose them to peace and amity; in the mean time, it alleviates captivity, and takes away something from the miseries of war."[23]

When Thomas Tyers wrote that Johnson "was at the head of subscription in cases of distress,"[24] he was referring specifi-cally to the support Johnson gave to various philanthropic un-dertakings. Though his interest in them has never been fully explored, his subsidy of the Associates of Dr. Bray supplies an example of the financial aid he gave to such organizations. This small society, formed to provide books for poorer members of the clergy and to establish schools for free Negroes in the American Colonies, had enrolled Johnson as a member in 1760. In addition to paying annual dues of a guinea, he made a special contribution of ten guineas to the society in 1784, and when he died he left to it the proceeds of the first edition of his posthumously published prayers and meditations.[25]

Besides giving financial assistance to the philanthropies of his time, he frequently encouraged the growth of public charities. In the *Idler* (May 6, 1758) he commends his age for the support given to the relief of so many species of misery. Although he does not mention any specific institution, he probably had in mind places like the Foundling Hospital for orphans; the British Lying-In Hospital, instituted in 1749; St. Luke's Hospital for Lunatics, established in 1751; and the Magdalen House, which opened its doors a few months before the *Idler* paper appeared. While he praised the philanthropic impulse that had led to the building of so many asylums for the needy, he was nevertheless disturbed by the thought of what might happen to such institutions if "the blaize of charity, which now burns with so much heat and splendour, should die away for want of lasting fuel." Perhaps he was alluding favorably to the grants that Parliament had started making in 1756 for the support of the Foundling Hospital when he added, "Whatever is left in the hands of chance must be subject to vicissitude; and when any establishment is found to be useful, it ought to be the next care to make it permanent."

Johnson may have helped to initiate certain charitable foundations by early calling attention to specific forms of misery. A letter in *Rambler* 107, for instance, points out that, in the absence of a refuge to which prostitutes could turn for assistance, those who wished to renounce their course of life had no means of abandoning it. Six years later, Jonas Hanway and

Robert Dingley, in an attempt to solve this problem, established the Magdalen House for reclaiming prostitutes. Johnson also appealed to the public conscience when he described
the plight of persons imprisoned for debt. Two of his *Idler* essays (22 and 38) are devoted to this topic. In these he vigor-
ously attacks the barbarity of the law which allowed creditors
to send to prison those who owed even small sums. He comments: "A debtor is dragged to prison, pitied for a moment,
and then forgotten; another follows him, and is lost alike in
the caverns of oblivion; but when the whole mass of calamity
rises up at once, when twenty thousand reasonable beings are
heard all groaning in unnecessary misery, not by the infirmity
of nature, but the mistake or negligence of policy, who can
forbear to pity and lament, to wonder and abhor?" (*Idler* 38).
England did not repeal the laws providing for the imprison-
ment of debtors until the nineteenth century, but in 1773
James Neild and others instituted a Society for the Relief and
Discharge of Persons Imprisoned for Small Debts. Because
public opinion had been aroused to the injustice of this practice by works such as Johnson's, the society was so well supported that in the first fifteen months of its existence it was
able to secure the release of 986 victims.[26]

Many readers of Boswell find in the accounts of the household Johnson maintained the most striking evidence of his
charity. The chief dependents who lived with him were Anna
Williams, the blind poetess; Dr. Levet, the slum physician;
Mrs. Desmoulins, daughter of Dr. Swinfen of Lichfield; a Miss
Carmichael, of whom little is known; and Francis Barber, the
Negro servant. Some of these, like Mrs. Williams and Dr. Levet, Johnson harbored for thirty years or more. They were
frequently a quarrelsome set. Mrs. Thrale reports that, "he
really was oftentimes afraid of going home, because he was so
sure to be met at the door with numberless complaints; and he
used to lament pathetically to me . . . that they made his life
miserable from the impossibility he found of making theirs

happy, when every favour he bestowed on one was wormwood to the rest. If however I ventured to blame their ingratitude, and condemn their conduct, he would instantly set about softening the one and justifying the other; and finished commonly by telling me, that I knew not how to make allowances for situations I never experienced."[27]

Obviously the poverty of his dependents and the likelihood that they would otherwise be homeless made an appeal to his deep sense of charity, but in this instance he probably had an additional reason for his generosity and tolerance. He himself had remarked that "benevolence is mingled with vanity, interest, or some other motive." One consideration that counted with him was his fear of solitude. There were times when he could not bear to be alone. Under these circumstances he probably preferred returning to a noisy, quarrelsome group of companions to entering a dark and silent home.

The real proof of his charity lay not in that fact that he supported several dependents, but rather in the way that he treated them. In the first place, he never demanded gratitude. According to Hawkins, ". . . he neither sought nor expected praise for those acts of beneficence which he was daily performing, nor looked for any retribution from those who were nourished by his bounty."[28] His conduct in this respect was no doubt partly a matter of tact on the part of one who could be notably untactful in other situations, but it was even more a matter of principle. When we have relieved the needy, he writes in Sermon XIX, "we should never upbraid them with our kindness, nor recall their afflictions to their minds by cruel and unseasonable admonitions to gratitude or industry. He only confers favours generously, who appears, when they are once conferred, to remember them no more."

Furthermore, although Johnson complained of the quarrelsome habits of his dependents, he gave them both respect and love. As Boswell attests, he treated Mrs. Williams with almost courtly courtesy. He took pains to instruct Francis Barber in religion, and left him most of his small fortune. Dr. Levet, as he indicates in the elegy on his death, he regarded not as a dependent but as a friend. This, in spite of the evidence that Levet had little to recommend him to others. In Hawkins' *Life* he is described as "middle-sized and thin, his visage swarthy, adust, and corrugated. His conversation, except on professional subjects, barren. When in deshabille, he might have been mistaken for an alchemist, whose complexion had been hurt by the fumes and crucible, and whose clothes had suffered from the sparks of the furnace." Hawkins adds: "The consideration of all which particulars almost impels me to say, that Levett admired Johnson because others admired him, and that Johnson in pity loved Levett, because few others could find anything in him to love."[29] Here Hawkins puts his finger on an essential trait of Johnson's character. He could not only sympathize with the unfortunate; he had, it would appear, a special ability to love the unlovable.

The forbearance Johnson accorded his dependents was not always exercised towards others. Because of his contentiousness in society, he gained the reputation in some quarters of being a bear or a bully. Despite Boswell's balanced picture of the man, readers sometimes come away from a first perusal of the *Life* with the impression that Johnson was an overbearing and highly egotistical person. There is no doubt that he was quick to anger, and in argument a strong competitive sense impelled him to overcome his opponents, even if he had to shout them down.

His rudeness may be partly explained as a rare kind of compulsive honesty that led him spontaneously to attack a shamming pose or an erroneous opinion, but there was more to it than that. Even his kindest critics felt he too often disagreed for the sake of disagreement. After meeting him, Richard Farmer, author of the essay on Shakespeare, wrote: "I can excuse his *Dogmatisms* and *Prejudices;* but he throws about rather too much of what some *Frenchman* calls the *Essence* of But; in plain *English,* he seems to have something to *except* in every man's character."[30] Sir Joshua Reynolds, though an intimate of Johnson for thirty years, also commented on this unpleasant side of his character. In a mixed group, Reynolds wrote, he fought with all his weapons, and "the most light and airy dispute was with him a dispute on the Arena. . . . If he was foiled in argument, he had recourse to abuse and rudeness." Reynolds adds that his conduct among small groups of friends was quite different; otherwise they could never have held him in such deep affection.[31]

Johnson's contentiousness, when contrasted with his many acts of kindness, reveals a marked ambiguity in his disposition. An excellent insight into the nature of this duality is provided by Herman W. Liebert. Johnson's childhood, he reminds us, was beset by illness. This, combined with his physical handicaps, his unprepossessing appearance, and his years of poverty, made him aware that if he was to excel, it must be by his superior intellect. As a result, he was led to be aggressively competitive when among his intellectual peers. With them he felt a compulsion to demonstrate and to prove his mental prowess. With the poor and unfortunate there was no such need. Liebert even suggests that perhaps he was never completely at home, except among those who, like himself, had experienced the miseries of sickness and suffering.[32]

Johnson himself attributed discourtesy and lack of forbearance chiefly to pride. In Sermon XI he writes: "For courteous some substitute the word humble; the difference may not be considered as great, for pride is a quality that obstructs courtesy." A further and more analytical discussion of bad manners appears in *Rambler* 56. Some men alienate themselves from others, he remarks, because selfish interests cause them to be heedless of the opinions and feelings of their associates. A still larger number give offense, not because they have some personal objective, but merely because of an unpleasant, imperious disposition. Such people, though sometimes merely negligent or stupid, are often the victims of pride, men who have "spent their lives amidst the obsequiousness of dependants, and the flattery of parasites." Johnson interrupts this discussion, however, in order to observe that one may be too humble. "It is common," he writes, "for soft and fearful tempers to give themselves up implicitly to the direction of the bold, the turbulent, and the overbearing; of those whom they do not believe wiser or better than themselves; to recede from the best designs where opposition must be encounterd, and to fall off from virtue for fear of censure." If his own lapses from forbearance were owing to pride, it was not because he was accustomed to the flattery of parasites. He knew his intellectual ability was the surest means of proving his superiority, and, preferring honesty to tact, he was determined not to be classed with the timid who too easily submit to "those whom they do not believe wiser or better than themselves."

To what extent was he aware that he lacked forbearance? One anecdote might indicate that he was unconscious of this failing. During an illness he asked his friend Bennet Langton to tell him sincerely what his faults were. Langton, attempting to be kind, brought him a list of several scriptural texts that recommend the exercise of charity. Johnson later described his reaction to Boswell, who reports the following conversation. Johnson: "When I questioned him what occasion I had given for such animadversions, all he could say amounted to this,—that I sometimes contradicted people in conversation. Now what harm does it do any man to be contradicted?" Boswell: "I suppose he meant the *manner* of doing it; roughly,—and harshly." Johnson: "And who is the worse for that?" Boswell: "It hurts people of weak nerves." Johnson: "I know no such weak-nerved people." When Joshua Reynolds heard this story, he commented that "it was a scene for a comedy, to see a penitent get into a violent passion and belabour his confessor."[33]

Boswell's anecdote and Reynolds' comment would both indicate that Johnson himself was unaware of how offensive his conduct sometimes was. Yet this seems unlikely. His momentary anger at Langton's inferences was perhaps genuine, but as he reflected on the incident, he no doubt saw the irony of his own position, and when he reported the episode he appears to have been engaging in a sly bit of humor at his own expense— a kind of humor that Boswell frequently failed to detect. That Johnson was acutely conscious of his rudeness is borne out by Boswell's own observations elsewhere that, after offending someone by his harshness, he "was not only prompt and desirous to be reconciled, but exerted himself to make ample reparation."[34]

Johnson was not only aware of his failing; he was deeply disturbed by it. Hawkins reports that after his death an anonymous letter was found among his papers. In it the writer had reminded him of "his propensity to contradiction, his want of deference to the opinions of others, his contention for victory over those with whom he disputed . . ." Although written in a spirit of charity, Hawkins observes, it was the kind of letter most recipients would have destroyed. But "Johnson preserved it, and placed it in his bureau, in a situation so obvious, that whenever he opened that repository of his papers, it might look him in the face." Hawkins adds: "I have not the least doubt that he frequently perused and reflected on its contents, and endeavoured to correct his behaviour by an address which he could not but consider as a friendly admonition."[35] Whether or not this was the letter Langton had written to Johnson, its import was similar.

In *Rambler* 56 a discussion of bad manners concludes with the comment: "Even though no regard be had to the external consequences of contrariety and dispute, it must be painful to a worthy mind to put others in pain, and there will be danger lest the kindest nature may be vitiated by too long a custom of debate and contest." When Johnson wrote that sentence, his eyes must have been turned inward, for it is a clear echo of what he said in a more personal context. One of his most revealing remarks appears in a letter of November 18, 1756, where he expresses with deep anxiety a guilty awareness that his sharp tongue often betrayed his tender heart. "When I am musing alone," he wrote John Taylor, "I feel a pang for every moment that any human being has by my peevishness or obstinacy spent in uneasiness."

VII · THE FEAR OF GOD AND
THE LOVE OF GOD

Now there is another part of charity, which is the basis and
pillar of this, and that is the love of God, for whom we love
our neighbour; for this I think charity, to love God for him-
self, and our neighbour for God.

Sir Thomas Browne, Religio Medici

In a work dealing with Johnson's religion, his serious and
somber side much appear so often that one may be in danger of forgetting that solemnity and melancholy did not always prevail. As Fanny Burney and Mrs. Thrale attested,
Johnson had a remarkably playful sense of humor. He could
be a cheerful companion, and he possessed an enormous gusto
for life. Despite his many allusions to the human condition as
a "state in which much is to be endured and little to be enjoyed," he treasured existence. Books, friends, conversation
were a constant source of pleasure. Although his reflections
were often painful, he delighted in the play of the intellect: in
the power of his first-rate mind to absorb, to compare, to ana-
lyze ideas—and to shape them into an aphorism, an essay, or a
poem.

Everyone remembers his remark, "When a man is tired of
London, he is tired of life."[1] Johnson never tired of either. In
his last year, when his strength and health were failing, he
passed the summer at Ashbourne and the early fall at Lichfield. By late October he was eager to leave for home. His
friends, fearing the journey might prove too arduous, tried to
dissuade him from making it, but neither disease nor debility
could diminish his gusto at the prospect of returning to the
delights of the city. "I am not afraid either of a journey to
London or a residence in it," he wrote Dr. Brocklesby. "The

town is my element, there are my friends, there are my books
to which I have not yet bidden farewell, and there are my
amusements."[2]

This love of life cannot be neglected in any explanation of
his fear of death. As we shall see, his fear was closely related to
his religious beliefs, but the idea that he had an obsession
about death has been overstressed. Like most people, when
Johnson thought about dying, he preferred to cling to familiar
surroundings and to ontological certainties. In this respect, he
conformed more nearly to the typical human pattern than did
Percy Bysshe Shelley, who, half in love with death, courted it
with neurotic impatience.

There is no denying that during most of his life Johnson
feared the prospect of death. His letters often allude to his apprehensions, and Boswell, Mrs. Thrale, and others have shown
how a discussion of the subject could profoundly disturb him.
But, one point cannot be too strongly emphasized. Except on
a few occasions when Boswell pressed the topic too hard, Johnson never avoided mentioning death. Quite to the contrary,
man's mortality was one of his most frequent themes. There
was a special reason for this interest that had nothing to do
with an obsession. To Johnson, habitual reflection on death
was both salutary and necessary to leading a good Christian
life. He writes: "A frequent and attentive prospect of that
moment, which must put a period to all our schemes, and de-
prive us of all our acquisitions, is indeed of the utmost efficacy to the just and rational regulation of our lives; nor
would any thing wicked, or often any thing absurd, be under-
taken or prosecuted by him who should begin every day with
a serious reflection that he is born to die" (*Rambler* 17).

The view that Johnson had an obsession about dying was
created largely by James Boswell. Although he knew the topic
could disturb his friend deeply, he reverted to it with impor-
tunate insistence. Sometimes a question, especially when reiterated, may be more revealing than the reaction to it. His own

preoccupation with the subject indicates that Boswell was as much disturbed by the thought of death as his learned friend.

When he heard that David Hume was dying, Boswell hastened to his side, because, as he says, "I had a strong curiosity to be satisfied if he persisted in disbeleiving [*sic*] a future state, even when he had death before his eyes." When he learned that his fellow Scot remained sceptical of an afterlife, he was extremely agitated, as his language indicates: "I was like a man in sudden danger eagerly seeking his defensive arms; and I could not but be assailed by momentary doubts while I had actually before me a man of such strong abilities and intensive enquiry dying in the persuasion of being annihilated. But I maintained my Faith."[3]

Curious to learn Johnson's reaction, Boswell introduced the subject by saying "that David Hume's persisting in his infidelity, when he was dying, shocked me much." Johnson, more annoyed than surprised, replied, "Why should it shock you, Sir? Hume owned he had never read the New Testament with attention. Here then was a man, who had been at no pains to inquire into the truth of religion, and had continually turned his mind the other way." The conversation continued, and Boswell reports, "The horrour of death which I had always observed in Dr. Johnson appeared strong to-night." Yet he adds the confession, "I ventured to tell him, that I had been, for moments in my life, not afraid of death."[4]

Boswell's life, it will be remembered, spanned the period of the development of the Evangelical revival. Because of the particular stress they placed upon a personal assurance of salvation, the Evangelicals attached great significance to the manner in which a person expired. Sometimes it almost appeared that one's deportment on the deathbed counted for more than one's conduct in life. A tranquil death, especially if accompanied by pious ejaculations on the part of the moribund person, was taken as a sign that he was saved. On the other hand, if one died in anguish and fear, that was likely to be interpreted as evidence that he was lost. This idea was reiterated so often in Evangelical sermons, periodicals, and tracts during the last decades of the eighteenth century that great attention came to be focused on the deathbed scene.

When the circumstances of Hume's death were publicized, many people were concerned to hear that an infidel, contrary to what they had been taught, had died peacefully. They were equally disturbed after Johnson's demise to learn that this man, celebrated for his piety, had always feared the prospect of death. At least one Anglican clergyman, the Reverend William Agutter, showed an awareness that false inferences were being made. As a corrective he preached a noteworthy sermon at St. Mary's Church, Oxford, on July 23, 1786. In its printed form it is entitled *On the Difference between the Deaths of the Righteous and the Wicked, Illustrated in the Instance of Dr. Samuel Johnson and David Hume.* Although both Johnson and Hume are referred to in footnotes to the printed version, neither is specifically mentioned in the body of the sermon. Apparently those who heard it preached knew to whom the clergyman was alluding when, in denial of current Evangelical beliefs, he observed, "It must be obvious to every reflecting mind that Religion does not always triumph over the fears of death; and, likewise, that the man who is depraved in principle, or profligate in practice, may enjoy an apparent peace, or display a real indifference at the close of life."[5]

Boswell might have profited from this sermon. He was never inclined to Evangelicalism; indeed, like most people of fashion, he expressed distaste for the conduct and beliefs of its adherents. Nevertheless, he was intensely curious about the revival. He knew Whitefield, and unlike Johnson, professed great admiration for his preaching. He begged Johnson for a letter of introduction to John Wesley, and upon receiving it, employed the opportunity to have a private interview at Edinburgh with the religious leader.[6] (Later in life Boswell had a dream about Wesley in which the latter said he had been re-

ceived into the presence of God.)[7] In London Boswell frequently visited dissenting chapels to hear Evangelicals like the
Moravian Benjamin Latrobe. On one occasion he even ex-
cused himself from the cherished society of Dr. Johnson in order to attend a service at St. Dunstan's conducted by the Reverend William Romaine. Since the sermon of the well-known
Evangelical was on death, Boswell heard it with particular relish. He reports: "There was nothing gloomy in his manner,
though the methodistical system is so, and a robust fellow in a
green coat and black wig groaned and sighed often at the end
of sentences, I suppose from habitual sadness contracted by
hearing other preachers of that class. I could not but feel wonder and some degree of contempt for the man. Romaine
seemed to call his audience to heaven as a Birdcatcher does
with a whistle. His manner was quite cheerful. It was as if he
had been singing, 'Will you go to Flanders, my Molly O? /
Will you go to Heaven, my Hearers, O?' "[8]

As this passage indicates, Boswell's concern with death was
not always morbid, but even in his more volatile moments it
appears somewhat obsessive. Perhaps this was partly owing to
the climate which the Evangelicals had created. In any event,
his unabated eagerness to get the reaction of Johnson and
others to the prospect of death clearly reflects his personal preoccupation with this subject.

Johnson himself made carefully discriminated judgments
about the Evangelicals. He admired John Wesley's sincerity
and praised him for bringing his religious message to thou-
sands who without him and his fellow preachers would have
remained unawakened to the importance of Christianity. He
liked the fervor of the Methodists and once remarked that it
might be better for one of them or for a Popish priest to attend
prisoners, because they might succeed better than an Anglican
clergyman in arousing a hardened criminal to the necessity of
salvation. Nevertheless, he felt that Evangelical zeal was too
often dangerously directed. The Evangelicals, he thought,

followed self-imposed rules instead of the practices of an institution like the Church of England. He was especially unsympathetic to their profession of being spiritually directed by an inward light. "If a man (said he,) pretends to a principle of action of which I can know nothing, nay, not so much as that he has it, but only that he pretends to it; how can I tell what that person may be prompted to do? When a person professes to be governed by a written ascertained law, I can then know where to find him."[9]

Another Evangelical principle that he could neither approve nor understand was the belief that a converted person experienced a strong assurance of his own salvation. Because his fear of death was based on an uncertainty of his own merits, to him it seemed like presumption for anyone, even on his deathbed, to have complete confidence that he was accepted by God. In *Rambler* 54 he describes with admiration the way one of his friends parted from this life. When he knew his end was near, the man had put aside all thoughts of "riches, authority, and praise." Detached from worldly vanities, he was gladdened only by the memory of the virtuous acts he had performed and the opportunity to exercise his religious duties. All his thoughts were fixed on futurity, Johnson remarks approvingly, but he reports no pious ejaculations on the part of his dying friend, and no expressions of assurance in his salvation.

Johnson himself did not wait until the approach of death to fix his mind on futurity. But sometimes, horrible as the thought was, he wondered if there would be an afterlife, if death might not mean simply annihilation. Although such considerations probably played no more than a minor role in his fear of death, this subject must be examined.

The three friends whose records have contributed to the impression that thoughts of annihilation weighed heavily on his mind were Boswell, Arthur Murphy, and the Reverend John Taylor. Of these Taylor was chiefly responsible for the attention given to this topic after Johnson's death. The discussion arose as the result of his publishing in 1787 *A Letter to Samuel Johnson, LL.D. on the Subject of a Future State.* This is a curious document. According to Taylor, it was reported to him that Johnson had observed to Dr. Brocklesby "that he would prefer a state of torment to annihilation." In a subsequent discussion Taylor told Johnson that, coming from a man with his reputation for piety, such a remark might prove dangerous. Presumably Taylor meant that people would be shocked to learn that he had even alluded to the possibility of annihilation.[10]

In his Advertisement to the *Letter* Taylor reports that, as a result of their conversation, Johnson asked him "to arrange his thoughts on the subject." The publication of 1787 represents Taylor's reply, though R. W. Chapman believes, on evidence of style, that before his death Johnson himself may have revised or added to the original letter.[11] In any event, this work, intended to refute the notion of annihilation, is not a very impressive piece of Christian apologetics. Taylor merely repeats without any new approach or emphasis the arguments based on reason and Scripture.

What is most amazing about the performance is to find Taylor, for whom Johnson had written so many sermons, posing after the death of his friend as the one who had set him right on futurity. His motive for assuming this posture would seem to be sheer vanity. For proof we have only to glance at a poetic tribute to himself that he allowed to be inserted before his own text. The author of the verses was Brooke Boothby, Jr., a minor poet, brought up in Taylor's town of Ashbourne and later associated with the Lichfield circle headed by Anna Seward.[12] The poem begins:

> When doubts disturb'd the dying Johnson's breast,
> From thee, his long tried Friend, he sought for rest,
> Thy clearer reason chas'd the clouds away,
> And on the senses pour'd the living ray.

> Hence, taught, the path of faith he firmly trod,
> And died in full reliance on his God.

This testimonial to Taylor's influence appears ridiculous. No evidence exists that he contributed to Johnson's religious views. On the contrary, although Johnson esteemed him as an old friend, he seems to have held his clerical abilities and his lack of dedication in contempt.

The most significant statement in Taylor's *Letter* is the reply Johnson gave when chided for having discussed annihilation with Brocklesby. "You said," Taylor writes, "that nothing could be more weak than any such notion; that life was indeed a great thing; and that you meant nothing more by your preference of a state of torment to a state of annihilation, than to express at what an immense value you rated vital existence." This statement sounds authentic; as we shall see, what Johnson most dreaded was the prospect of abandoning any form of existence.

According to Arthur Murphy, when disinclined to enter into the conversation of a group, Johnson could frequently be heard repeating to himself two famous passages, one from *Measure for Measure* and the other from *Paradise Lost*.[13] Murphy mentions this habit in connection with Johnson's apprehensions about dying, without alluding to annihilation, but later writers have interpreted his remarks as evidence that Johnson was preoccupied with this thought. The quotation from Shakespeare is Claudio's speech, beginning:

> Ay, but to die and go we know not where,
> To lie in cold obstruction and to rot,
> This sensible warm motion to become
> A kneaded clod, and the delighted spirit
> To bathe in fiery floods.
>
> (III, i, 118–22)

The passage, taken in its entirety, bears only slightly on annihilation. It is concerned with hell, though more with Virgil's

pagan vision of it than with the Christian conception. Furthermore, Johnson's annotation in his edition of Shakespeare in-
dictates that he interpreted the speech as a reflection, not on
annihilation, but on an afterlife of pain and retribution.[14]

The quotation from *Paradise Lost,* however, is indisputa-
bly concerned with extinction. In a council in hell Belial, the
fallen angel, comments:

> Who would lose,
> Though full of pain, this intellectual being,
> Those thoughts that wander through eternity,
> To perish rather, swallowed up and lost
> In the wide womb of uncreated Night,
> Devoid of sense and motion?
> (II, 146–51)

Belial is here stating his preference for a continued existence
in hell to losing all mental and physical consciousness. This is
just the point Johnson made when he remarked he would
choose a life of torment to annihilation. Like Belial, what he
feared in this connection was the abandonment of "intellectual
being," the play of the mind, the loss of the reasoning faculties—all that made existence worthwhile to him.

In this attitude he was consistent. "No wise man," he told
Boswell, "will be contented to die if he thinks he is to fall into
annihilation. For however bad any man's existence may be,
every man would rather have it than not exist at all."[15] He
made the same point when Miss Seward commented that no
one need fear annihilation because it is only a pleasant sleep.
"It is neither pleasing, nor sleep," Johnson insisted; "it is nothing. Now mere existence is so much better than nothing, that
one would rather exist even in pain, than not exist."[16]

Because sentience meant so much to him, he could not believe that anyone who had no faith in an afterlife could approach death with tranquility. When Boswell reported that
Hume, though professedly believing in annihilation, had no
fear of dying, Johnson replied: "He had a vanity in being

thought easy. It is more probable that he should assume an appearance of ease, than that so very improbable a thing should be, as a man not afraid of going (as, in spite of his delusive theory, he cannot be sure but he may go,) into an unknown state, and not being uneasy at leaving all he knew. And you are to consider, that upon his own principle of annihilation he had no motive to speak the truth."[17]

This spontaneous reply was much more ingenious than might at first appear. It is, indeed, a good example of the mental agility in which Johnson so much delighted and which caused him to detest any thought of surrendering his "intellectual being." He refutes Hume first on his own grounds. The philosopher had argued that there is a "uniform experience" amounting to proof that militates against the existence of miracles.[18] Johnson implies that it is the uniform experience of mankind to fear death; hence it is very improbable that Hume, being a man, should not be uneasy about his demise. Secondly, Hume had observed that a true sceptic must be as sceptical of his own doubts as he is of the affirmations of others. Johnson echoes this point in the parenthesis, where he observes that despite his theory, Hume could have no certitude about annihilation. Next Johnson shifts to an argument related to his own conviction that there can be no valid system of morality except one based on religion. If Hume, he suggests, was so irreligious as to disbelieve in an afterlife, then he had no motive to be truthful.

Johnson's own fear of death was based primarily on his belief in a God who judges humanity strictly according to their deserts and, secondly, upon strong doubts about his own merits. As we have seen, his earlier interpretation of the nature of Christ's sacrifice differed from that of most Christians. Otherwise there was nothing fundamentally unorthodox about his religion. It was distinctive, however, in two respects. In the first place, he was a more devout and more dedicated Christian than most. G. B. Shaw has remarked that "the passionately re-

ligious are a people apart."[19] To this minority Johnson definitely belonged. In the second place, his Christianity was distinguished to a degree from that of other firm believers by the
emphasis he accorded certain precepts and doctrines. We have
already discussed some of them, such as the idea of Christian
perfection, the importance of self-atonement, and his interpretation of penance. These, as we shall see, were closely related
to his strong fear of God.

Johnson's writings make clear that his fear of death and
damnation were ancillary to his fear of God. Both fears were
regarded as necessary aids to salvation. The fear of God, he
says (Sermon III), is a holy fear, for a constant apprehension
of offending the Deity is the best bulwark against sin and
temptation. But, ensnared by worldly distractions, man is
likely to forget how short a time remains before he must account for his transgressions to his Maker. Therefore he should
constantly remind himself of his mortality and of the brevity
of life by meditating on death. Such reflections will naturally
produce fear, but this is a salutary effect, for the fear of death
keeps alive the fear of God, and both constantly remind man
of the importance of being prepared to meet his judgment.[20]

Because it serves such an urgent purpose, Johnson considered meditating on death a positive duty of the Christian. That
it is not a pleasant duty he ruefully concedes in the wry un-
derstatement: "To consider the shortness, or misery, of life, is
not an employment to which the mind recurs for solace or diversion; or to which it is invited by any hope of immediate delight." Rather it is like a nauseous medicine that the "fastid-
iousness of nature prompts us to refuse." Nevertheless, it is a
medicine that must be taken frequently and in large doses, for
"it is our duty, in the pilgrimage of life, to proceed with our
eyes open, and to see our state; not as hope or fancy may de-
lineate it, but as it has been in reality appointed by Divine
providence" (Sermon XV).

How often he reflected on his own demise may be seen in his prayers. Almost every one of them makes some allusion to death. Although these references become more frequent in later life, even as a relatively young man he usually incorporated a reflection on his mortality. For instance, on New Year's Day, 1745, he wrote: "I return thee thanks that Thou hast given me life, and that thou hast continued it to this time, that thou hast hitherto forborn to snatch me away in the midst of Sin and Folly, and hast permitted me still to enjoy the means of Grace, and vouchsafed to call me yet again to Repentance."

One may recall that in his discussions of perfection William Law had counseled the penitent to engage in daily reflections on death. In an earlier chapter we have already suggested that Johnson's habits of prayer were influenced by Law's counsels. The same source may have helped to form his views on the importance of having constantly in mind the fear of God. Nowhere, certainly, does he write more clearly in the spirit and temper of William Law than in Sermon III, on the text, "Happy is the man that feareth alway; but he that hardeneth his heart shall fall into mischief" (Prov. 28:14). It is interesting to see how Johnson deals with the paradox that fear produces happiness. In a notable passage that echoes much of what Law had said about the importance of pursuing an unworldly type of life, he writes:

He is happy that carries about with him in the world the temper of the cloister; and preserves the fear of doing evil, while he suffers himself to be impelled by the zeal of doing good; who uses the comforts and the conveniences of his condition as though he used them not, with that constant desire of a better state, which sinks the value of earthly things; who can be rich or poor, without pride in riches, or discontent in poverty; who can manage the business of this life with such indifference as may shut out from his heart all incitements to fraud or injustice; who can partake the pleasures of sense with temperance, and enjoy the distinctions of

honour with moderation; who can pass undefiled through a polluted world; and, among all the vicissitudes of good and evil, have
his heart fixed only where true joys are to be found.

Such an existence, he adds, can be achieved only "by fearing always, by preserving in the mind a constant apprehension
of the Divine presence, and a constant dread of the Divine
displeasure." One may ask how he could write in this manner
when, quite clearly, in his own experience the fear of God had
brought neither happiness nor tranquillity, but sometimes a
state of anxiety bordering on madness. In the first place, it
goes without saying that by happiness he did not mean ordinary pleasure or even contentment. In *Rasselas* and elsewhere,
he had reiterated the belief that no choice of life can lead to
anything more than a brief and unsatisfying kind of pleasure.
Our chief gratification, he believed, must come from hope.
Even when that deludes us, we must not abandon it, "for hope
itself is happiness, and its frustrations, however frequent, are
less dreadful than its extinction" (*Idler* 58). He was here
speaking of hope in a secular sense. A still greater key to happiness is hope considered as a theological virtue. "This happiness," he writes, "we may expect with confidence, because it is
out of the power of chance, and may be attained by all who
sincerely desire and earnestly pursue it. On this therefore every
mind ought finally to rest. Hope is the chief blessing of man . . ."
(*Rambler* 203).

Similarly the fear of God does not consist merely of a normal
visceral reaction. Theologically, the fear of God is a divine
gift that warns sinful man against the danger of damnation,
unless he repents; and warns a virtuous man against the danger of losing salvation, should he fall from grace. Thus the
fear of God promotes happiness, because, by helping to safe-
guard man from sin and by inciting him to goodness, it provides a strong basis for hope. Hope and fear are therefore not
antithetical elements; instead they are closely related virtues.

Their parallel nature is emphasized by Johnson in *The Vanity of Human Wishes* when he asks, "Where then shall Hope and Fear their objects find?" The answer, of course, lies in a humble submission to the will of God and in the powers of faith and charity—all to be achieved through prayer:

> Pour forth thy fervours for a healthful mind,
> Obedient passions, and a will resign'd;
> For love, which scarce collective man can fill;
> For patience sov'reign o'er transmuted ill;
> For faith, that panting for a happier seat,
> Counts death kind Nature's signal of retreat.
>
> (ll. 359–64)

Although Johnson's fear of God shows his tendency to asceticism, Johnson lacked something important to the true ascetic. The Christian who renounces this world and fixes his thoughts on the afterlife usually maintains a balance. While he is motivated in part by the fear of damnation, equally if not more important is the prospect of an eternity of happiness and the joyful vision of God. In the last year of his life, as we shall see, Johnson did once allude to the Beatific Vision, but generally when he referred to futurity, he spoke of it merely as an undefined state of happiness. "Reason," he remarks, "deserts us at the brink of the grave, and can give no further intelligence." Revelation tells us there is joy in heaven, and we may hope, since it is not disallowed, that there may be a union of souls there. But, "We know little of the state of departed souls, because such knowledge is not necessary to a good life" (*Idler* 41).

A related characteristic of true ascetics and of many other devout Christians is that the love of God may motivate them at least as much as the fear of God. William Law saw these forces as alternating ones. "Sometimes," he writes, "our hearts are so awakened, have such strong apprehensions of the divine presence, are so full of deep compunction for our sins, that we cannot confess them in any language but that of tears." On the other hand, "Sometimes the light of God's countenance shines so bright upon us, we see so far into the invisible world, we are so affected with the wonders of the love and goodness of God, that our hearts worship and adore in a language higher than words, and we feel transports of devotion which only can be felt."[21]

It has sometimes been observed that with Johnson the fear of God predominated over the love of God—that his religious reflections instilled, not peace, but perturbation, and that he seldom experienced the consolation of those whose hearts are filled with divine love. Although generally true, such a statement tends to oversimplify his complex religious position. I therefore propose to add and to develop three important qualifications. In the first place, Johnson was fully aware of the significance of love to the Christian concept of Deity. Secondly, he realized his own shortcomings in this respect and probably felt disturbed by them. Finally, although he never expressed himself on this subject in such ardent terms as William Law employed, it would be a mistake to believe that the love of God was never a motivating principle with him.

Johnson's *Dictionary*, from which we have already quoted, often sheds considerable light on his disposition and values. Frequently the quotations used to illustrate a meaning are more important than the definitions, and not simply because he consciously chose passages with a didactic purpose in mind. The quotations, culled from his extensive reading, were ones he had retained in memory over a period of years or had especially marked for inclusion in the *Dictionary*.[22] Because one is prone to remember and to select what one most values, it may be inferred that he generally supplied extracts that had struck him as particularly significant. To be sure, psychological inferences may be carried too far. It would be dangerous, for instance, to assume that Johnson had romantic tendencies, simply because his *Dictionary* provides fourteen different definitions of the word "love." Nevertheless, several of the quotations dealing with the love of God show his concern with this important aspect of Christianity.

In connection with his definition of "love" as "due reverence to God," he quotes Hammond: "*Love* is of two sorts, of friendship and of desire; the one betwixt friends, the other betwixt lovers; the one is rational, the other a sensitive *love:* so our *love* of God consists of two parts, as esteeming of God, and desiring of Him." Taylor (probably Jeremy) provides Johnson with a second quotation: "The *love* of God makes a man chaste without the laborious arts of fasting and exterior disciplines; he reaches at glory without any other arms but those of *love.*" The tenth definition of "love" is "principle of union." Under this is included a passage from Dr. South which, as we shall see, describes what Johnson meant by "charity" in the sense of a theological virtue: "*Love* is the great instrument of nature, the bond and cement of society, the spirit and spring of the universe; *love* is such an affection as cannot so properly be said to be in the soul, as the soul to be in that: it is the whole man wrapt up in one desire."

The number of quotations related to the love of God shows how much the lexicographer had pondered this subject. He even introduces a passage on divine love under his definition, "tenderness; parental care." Taken from Tillotson, presumably from a context where distinctive aspects of Christianity are under discussion, it reads: "No religion that ever was, so fully represents the goodness of God, and his tender *love* to mankind, which is the most powerful argument to the love of God." This thought is echoed in Johnson's prayers when he writes (April 16, 1775): "Fill my thoughts with aweful love of thy Goodness." He also alludes to the Atonement as a principal reason for reciprocating divine love. On Easter Sunday, 1776, which we have already mentioned as an occasion of particular piety for him, he prays before receiving the Sacrament: "Almighty and most merciful Father, who hast preserved me by thy tender forbearance, once more to commemorate thy Love in the Redemption of the world, grant that I may so live the residue of my days, as to obtain thy mercy when thou shalt call me from the present State."

Johnson's awareness of the importance of love in Christianity is further revealed in several of his sermons. For instance, he concludes Sermon XVI with the pious exhortation, "Let death . . . find us, whenever it shall come, animated with the love of God." Various other brief allusions of this sort are scattered through the sermons, but his most extended and most informative comment appears in Sermon XIII, where he writes:

The power of godliness is contained in the love of God and of our neighbour; in that sum of religion, in which, as we are told by the Saviour of the world, the law and the prophets are comprised. The love of God will engage us to trust in his protection, to acquiesce in his dispensations, to keep his laws, to meditate on his perfection, and to declare our confidence and submission, by profound and frequent adoration; to impress his glory on our minds by songs of praise, to inflame our gratitude by acts of thanksgiving, to strengthen our faith, and exalt our hope, by pious meditations; and to implore his protection of our imbecility, and his assistance of our frailty, by humble supplication; and when we love God with the whole heart, the power of godliness will be shown by steadiness in temptation, by patience in affliction, by faith in the Divine promises, by perpetual dread of sin, by continual aspirations after higher degrees of holiness, and contempt of the pains and pleasures of the world, when they obstruct the progress of religious excellence.

This notable passage, which so clearly echoes William Law's counsels on perfection, shows that Johnson understood the part that the spirit of love plays in Christianity. But this knowledge perhaps made him conscious that he was somewhat wanting in this respect. Earlier in the same sermon he confesses, "To give the heart to God, and to give the whole heart, is very difficult; the last, the great effort of long labour, fervent prayer, and diligent meditation." One suspects that he also had himself in mind when he told Boswell that he disagreed with Dr. Blair's statement that "he who does not feel joy in religion is far from the kingdom of heaven!" "There are many good men," he dissented, "whose fear of God predominates over their love."[23]

It is noteworthy that in his prayers he constantly asks for the grace to overcome this deficiency. Although he occasionally uses the word "love," he also asks that he may be able to fix his "affections on things eternal," that he may "frequent thy worship with pure affection," and that he may serve God "with pure affection and a cheerful mind."[24] The reiteration of "affection" may suggest an awareness that his regard for the Deity fell short of a deep and abiding love. It may also indicate that for him the word "love," when related to the awful majesty of God, was almost an ineffable word. In this connection his observations on the subject of religious verse seem pertinent. He generally disliked it, and the reason he gave was that it attempts to express something inherently inexpressible. Devotional language must always appear inadequate, he says, for "Whatever is great, desirable, or tremendous is comprised in the name of the supreme being." He adds: "The ideas of Christian theology are too simple for eloquence, too sacred for fiction, and too majestick for ornament. . . . Faith, invariably uniform, cannot be invested by fancy with decorations. Thanksgiving, the most joyful of all effusions, yet addressed to a being without passions, is confined to a few modes, and is to be felt rather than expressed."[25] Enforcing these observations was an attitude of deep reverence which, combined with his scruples, restrained him, even in private prayer, from professing any religious sentiment as much as bordering on insincerity.

Because Johnson was reluctant to use the word "love," one may fail to observe how frequently he petitions, by other means, that he may be inspired by a true love of God. He does this chiefly by employing more muted or more technically theological terms. We have previously mentioned the numerous references to the Holy Spirit in his prayers. Sometimes, as we have pointed out, he is asking for the assistance of the Holy Spirit to give him wisdom or the strength to withstand sin. Sometimes he is asking in this context that he may be inspired with a love of God. According to theological interpretation, a special function of the Holy Ghost is to fill man with a sense of God's love and to awaken in his soul a reciprocation of this love. ("The love of God is shed abroad in our hearts by the Holy Ghost which is given unto us" [Romans 5:5].) Johnson must have known this interpretation either from William Law or from some other source.²⁶ Hence he is indubitably alluding to the love of God in supplications such as, ". . . let my heart be surely fixed by the help of thy Holy Spirit on the everlasting fruition of thy presence, where true joys are to be found . . ." or, "Take not thy holy Spirit from me, but let me so love thy laws as to obey them, that I may finally be received to eternal happiness through Jesus Christ, Our Lord."²⁷

Earlier in this chapter we have seen that Johnson describes the power of "godliness" as consisting of the love of God and the love of neighbor. We can therefore understand the allusion to love when he prays, "Take not, O Lord, thy holy Spirit from me, enable me to avoid or overcome all that may hinder my advancement in Godliness."²⁸ Still another theological term for love is "charity," as he indicates in his *Dictionary* when he defines "charity," as "the theological virtue of universal love." What he meant by this virtue is best explained by William Law, who says that "universal love" is a principle first introduced by Christianity and based on the idea that we are to love one another "as Christ loves us." The noblest motive to this love resides in the doctrine that "God is love, and he that dwelleth in love dwelleth in God." In this sense love is a principle of the soul, "founded on reason and piety, which makes us tender, kind, and benevolent to all our fellow-creatures of God, and for his sake . . . The love, therefore, of our neighbour is only a branch of our love to God."[29] Thus when Johnson prays that he may be more strongly moved by charity, he is not asking simply that he may have a greater regard for his fellow men, for this is but one manifestation of one's love of God. When he petitions, "Let encrease of years bring encrease of Faith, Hope, and Charity," he is thinking of charity in the broader theological signification. The same meaning appears in his final prayer, composed when he knew he was dying. In this last week of life the time for benefactions was well-nigh over. Consequently when he prayed for "the enlargement of my Charity," he could mean only one thing—a greater love of God.[30]

As we have seen, when speaking of charity in the sense of kindness to others, Johnson had stated that the motives to this virtue are seldom pure. He no doubt meant that people were often moved by vanity, but he probably meant something else as well, namely, that good deeds are not sufficiently prompted by a basic love of God. He would have included himself in this condemnation, of course, but in view of his awareness of the theological principle involved and of his remarkable acts of kindness to others, there can be no doubt in my mind that he strove to act in accord with the principle that the love of neighbor is a branch of our love of God.

Closely associated in the minds of many who have an ardent love of God is a sense of his divine presence. This may or may not be in the nature of a mystical experience. The true mystic is a rarity, but devout persons, without being complete mystics, may, it has been observed, have flashes or glimpses of God's presence in the soul, constituting an elementary kind of mystical experience.[31] In his *Life of Herman Boerhaave,* which he wrote when he was only thirty, Johnson deals with a spiritual condition of this kind. Boerhaave, as Johnson describes him, was a man of genius, particularly skilled in science and noted for his piety. During the last weeks of his life he received a visit from a friend, the Reverend Mr. Schultens, to whom he imparted his reflections during his final illness. "He had never doubted of the spiritual and immaterial nature of the soul," Johnson wrote, "but declared that he had lately had a kind of experimental certainty of the distinction between the corporeal and thinking substances, which mere reason and philosophy cannot afford, and opportunities of contemplating the wonderful and inexplicable union of soul and body." Despite his physical infirmities, he said "his soul was always master of itself, and always resigned to the pleasure of its maker."[32]

Although Johnson expresses great admiration for the piety of Boerhaave, he never describes this experience before death as being of a mystical nature. One might even say that the terms "mysticism" and "mystic" did not form a part of his vocabulary, for neither word appears in his *Dictionary*. He does define the adjectives "mystical" and "mystick," grouping them together as meaning "sacredly obscure." To this etymological definition he appends two quotations from Hooker by way of illustration. These and his definition indicate that he associated the adjective "mystical," not with "mysticism," but rather with the theological term "mystery," which he also defines as "something awfully obscure."

At this point it would be easy to say that Johnson's rationalism excluded from his mind an understanding of mysticism. Certainly he was no mystic himself, but anyone who had read William Law so thoroughly as he, must have acquired at least a theoretical acquaintance with mysticism. It would therefore be more accurate to say that it was something probably foreign to his experience rather than foreign to his belief.

There is positive evidence that Johnson did believe in a non-mystical sense of God's presence. Furthermore he refers to it as something he himself had experienced. Probably the most common form of non-mystical awareness is a sense of God's universal pervasiveness. It is interesting that Johnson introduces this meaning in his *Dictionary* through a quotation from

William Law. It is the more striking since it appears under the word "presence," which he defines simply as a "state of being present; contrary to absence." The quotation is: "We have always the same natures, and are everywhere the servants of the same God, as every place is equally full of his presence, and everything is equally his gift." Like Law, Johnson also alludes to the sacred presence in the sense of a union between the soul and God, achieved through prayer (Sermon III). In either sense, the awareness is most often stimulated by religious devotions. In Sermon III, for instance, Johnson observes that those who absent themselves from public worship miss an opportunity of "awakening their attention to the presence of God, by hearing him invoked, and joining their own voices in the common supplication." He further remarks that a virtuous existence may be achieved "by fearing always, by preserving in the mind a constant apprehension of the Divine presence, and a constant dread of the Divine displeasure." He also states (Sermon IX) that partaking of the Sacrament and performing other devotions will aid in giving one "an habitual attention to the laws of God, and a constant sense of his presence."

In view of such references one may better understand the spirit in which he prayed, and in which he admonished others to pray, when he composed the following lines in *The Vanity of Human Wishes:*

> Yet when the sense of sacred presence fires,
> And strong devotion to the skies aspires,
> Pour forth thy fervours for a healthful mind,
> Obedient passions, and a will resign'd.
>
> (ll. 357–60)

By "the sense of sacred presence" he never means anything in the nature of pantheism. In at least one place he clearly indicates that he is referring to the Christian belief that God is infinitely concerned for each human soul, and that a strong individual awareness of this may arouse a sense of his nearness and a special reverence for Goodness. He writes: "The man who has accustomed himself to consider that he is always in the presence of the Supreme Being, that every work of his hands is carried on, and every imagination of his heart formed, under the inspection of his Creator, and his Judge, easily withstands those temptations which find a ready passage into a mind not guarded and secured by this awful sense of the Divine presence" (Sermon XVI).

Here he was speaking of a kind of non-mystical realization developed by Christian teaching, and that is what he undoubtedly meant in most instances by a sense of God's presence. Yet his experience at Easter time, 1776, seems to have been of a different order. This experience, which we have mentioned in an earlier chapter, is pertinent to the present discussion. After attending services on Good Friday, he wrote, "In the morning I had at Church some radiations of comfort." "Radiations" was not a customary term for him, but, as we shall see, he employed it on another occasion, and in both instances he clearly meant something more than intellectual awareness. The most striking notation concerns his experience upon taking the Sacrament on Easter Sunday. "When I received, some tender images struck me," he observed. "I was so mollified by the concluding address to our Saviour that I could not utter it."[33] Here for once he seems to have had an inner consciousness of the supernatural, perhaps even approaching an elementary mystical experience.

This unusual incident may have a bearing on an uncharacteristic remark that appears in a sermon he composed the following year. In his address to Dodd's fellow convicts Johnson writes: "The reception of the *holy sacrament,* to which we shall be called, in the most solemn manner, perhaps a few hours before we die, is the highest act of Christian worship. At that awful moment it will become us to drop for ever all worldly thoughts, to fix our hopes solely on Christ, whose death is represented; and to consider ourselves no longer connected with mortality,—And possibly, it may please God to afford *us* some consolation, some secret intimations of acceptance and forgiveness. But these radiations of favour are not always felt by the sincerest penitents." "Intimations" and "radiations" are uncommon terms in Johnson's vocabulary. He might not even have mentioned the possibility of this kind of inner awareness if it had not been for his own unusual experience upon receiving the Sacrament the previous year. To be sure, he cautions the convicts, in an added note, that one must not rely on having such intimations, since to most "nothing is granted in this world beyond rational *hope*."[34] Nevertheless, in this instance Johnson speaks as a man aware of what is meant by the mystical sense of Transcendental Reality.

VIII · JOHNSON AS A
CHURCH OF ENGLAND MAN

That men of different opinions should live at peace is the true effect of that humility, which makes each esteem others better than himself, and of that moderation, which reason approves, and charity commends.

Johnson, Sermon XI

In this chapter we shall discuss Johnson's attitude as an English Churchman from three points of view. We shall deal first with his personal loyalty to the Establishment, secondly, with his attitude towards the dissenting Protestant groups and the Roman Catholics, and, finally, with his position as a Churchman with respect to certain Christian doctrines.

Johnson was not always consistent in what he said about the doctrinal differences existing among various Christian churches. Sometimes he expressed himself in surprisingly unequivocal terms. Boswell, for instance, reports him as saying, "For my part, Sir, I think all Christians, whether Papists or Protestants, agree in the essential articles, and that their differences are trivial, and rather political than religious."[1] Such comments must be considered in relation to the circumstances under which they were uttered. The above observation was made in June, 1763, about five weeks after Boswell and Johnson had first met. Since the two were alone in each other's company, Boswell had seized the opportunity to talk about himself. "I told him," he writes, "how I was a very strict Christian, and was turned from that to infidelity. But that now I had got back to a very agreeable way of thinking. That I believed the Christian religion; though I might not be clear in many particulars." Johnson, obviously pleased to learn that his young friend had turned away from infidelity, cried, "Give me your hand. I have taken a liking to you." His further remarks, as summarized by Boswell, appear to have been made by way of comment on Boswell's statement about not being very clear on the particulars. Johnson assured him it was difficult to know about final causes and then, in apparent enthusiasm at Boswell's declaration of orthodoxy, added his remark about the differences among Christians being "trivial."[2] In a more sober moment he would probably have qualified this assertion, saying something to the effect that differences in interpretation were trivial by comparison with the importance of attaining a firm religious conviction.

When Johnson alluded, as he frequently did, to all Christians agreeing on the "essentials" of faith, he undoubtedly meant the beliefs necessary for salvation, but he never, it appears, specified what he meant by the "essentials." Perhaps the nearest he came to doing so was in his *Life of Thomas Browne.* Here, in refutation of those who had called Browne a condemner of religion, Johnson defends him as "among the most zealous professors of Christianity" for the following reasons— his belief in Scripture; his faith, which was founded on "the principles of grace, and the law of his own reason"; his submission to the authority of Scripture, and, where that is silent, to the interpretation of the Church; his belief in the death and resurrection of Christ; his belief in an afterlife; his reverence for Church ritual and especially for the sacrament of the Eucharist. This was the description of a zealous Christian who was also a member of the Church of England. Quite clearly, the essentials on which *all* Christians concurred could not include Browne's submission to interpretations of the English Church, or, where Dissenters were concerned, a belief in the sacramental nature of the Eucharist. If pressed, Johnson might have said the essentials on which all Christians agree would include a belief in the Bible, a belief in the Trinity, a belief in Christ as the Redeemer of man from the Fall, a belief in the afterlife, and a disposition to practice Christian charity. These he might have termed the basic principles, in that a commitment to them would be necessary for salvation. But this does not mean he considered the differences existing among Christians on other points trivial.

On March 21, 1772, Boswell reverted to the subject he had discussed with Johnson nine years earlier. "We talked of the Roman Catholick religion," Boswell writes, "and how little difference there was in the essential matters between ours and it." Johnson replied, "True, Sir; all denominations of Christians have really little difference in point of doctrine, though they may differ widely in external forms." A few minutes later Johnson virtually contradicted this statement when another topic was raised. Boswell mentioned a petition which had been introduced in Parliament in favor of removing the required subscription to the Thirty-nine Articles of the Establishment. "It was soon thrown out," Johnson commented with approval and then added, "Sir, they talk of not making the boys at the University subscribe to what they do not understand; but they ought to consider, that our Universities were founded to bring up members for the Church of England, and we must not supply our enemies with arms from our arsenal." Even if the boys did not comprehend what they were subscribing to, he reasoned, the custom should be preserved, inasmuch as the Thirty-nine Articles was a basic document, showing the distinctive beliefs of the Church of England. When Boswell asked, "But, Sir, would it not be sufficient to subscribe to the Bible?" Johnson replied, "Why no, Sir, for all sects will subscribe the Bible; nay, the Mohametans will subscribe the Bible."[3]

Johnson's insistence on the importance of the Thirty-nine Articles shows he did not consider the differences among Christian churches as insignificant. Unlike the Latitudinarians of his century, he believed there were real and perhaps irreconcilable points of disagreement among the various Christian faiths. As an English Churchman, he was unwilling to make doctrinal concessions to other groups. Hence his insistence on maintaining the custom of a formal declaration in support of the Thirty-nine Articles, even though he himself, quite clearly, did not subscribe to every one of the articles. For instance, in view of his private practice of praying for the dead, he obviously had reservations about Article XXII, which rejects the Roman Catholic idea of purgatory. And when Boswell alluded to the statement in Article XVII on predestination, Johnson, somewhat embarrassed, explained, "Why yes, Sir: predestination was a part of the clamour of the times, so it is mentioned in our articles, but with as little positiveness as could be." Boswell then confronted him with an important issue by asking if it was necessary to believe all thirty-nine articles. Avoiding a direct answer, Johnson replied, "Why, Sir, that is a question which has been much agitated. Some have thought it necessary that they should all be believed; others have considered them to be only articles of peace, that is to say, you are not to preach against them."[4]

Johnson's defense of the Thirty-nine Articles, despite his reservations about particular statements, shows his veneration for the Establishment as an institution with a distinct set of beliefs. He respected its organization and its practices, and, unlike many of his time, he treated its clergy with particular deference. Furthermore he was strongly opposed to any attack upon the institution or its doctrines. During his interview with George III, in answer to an inquiry about the *Monthly Review,* Johnson told the king that its authors were "enemies to the Church." Upon another occasion he remarked, "I think that permitting men to preach any opinion contrary to the doctrine of the established church, tends, in a certain degree, to lessen the authority of the church, and, consequently, to lessen the influence of religion."[5]

The Thirty-nine Articles were important as a formal declaration, but Johnson's commitment to the Book of Common

Prayer was deeper and more personal. As we have indicated in the Introduction, he regarded the liturgy of the Establishment "as the genuine offspring of piety and wisdom." In the *Dictionary* he quoted Richard Hooker: "We dare not admit any such form of *liturgy,* as either appointeth no scripture at all, or very little to be read in the Church." Like Hooker, he felt that reading the designated text from the Bible was more important than the sermon, since the word of God as handed down in Revelation counted far more than any mere commentary on it.[6] Johnson also had a deep reverence for the traditional prayers recited at public worship. "I know of no good prayers," he remarked, "but those in the 'Book of Common Prayer.' "[7] In keeping with this view, he frequently used the Sunday collects as models for the prayers he composed.

Because he read and admired so many English theologians, it is generally impossible to state just what he drew from particular writers. None of them held such an authoritative position in the Establishment as St. Thomas Aquinas holds in the Roman Catholic Church. On formal interpretations of doctrine and practice, however, no English theologian was more respected than Richard Hooker (1554?–1600). Coming at a relatively early period in Anglican history, his great opus, *Of the Laws of Ecclesiastical Polity,* was a forceful argument for the necessity of a body of dogma and a learned discussion of the position of the Establishment on a wide spectrum of beliefs and practices. Hooker generally followed a *via media* between Roman Catholicism and Protestantism. Although his thinking sometimes veered in the direction of Puritanism, he was deeply concerned with checking the tendency of his church to move in that direction. Consequently he is a strong advocate of the collective tradition of Christianity and often a sharp critic of the newly arisen emphasis on private interpretation. One writer comments: "He was the greatest of a group of Elizabethan divines who saved the Church of England from a destiny of pure Protestantism by reintroducing into her thought some of the great fundamentals of Catholic tradition."[8]

Although Johnson seldom alluded to Hooker's works in his recorded conversation, his familiarity with them is evidenced by the scores of times he quotes Hooker in the *Dictionary*. These citations, while not proving Hooker as a source for his views, show Johnson's agreement with him on various points. Both men, for instance, believed that the Church in its larger sense was composed of all Christians. "It is," says Hooker, "the Mystical Body of Christ made up of all who believe in him."[9] Johnson defines "Church" as "The collective body of Christians, usually termed the catholick *church*." Under this definition he quotes Hooker: "The *church,* being a supernatural society, doth differ from natural societies in this; that the persons unto whom we associate ourselves in the one, are men, simply considered as men; but they to whom we be joined in the other, are God, angels, and holy men."

In a section in which he draws much upon St. Thomas Aquinas, Hooker is particularly concerned with the nature of laws. All laws, he writes, ultimately derive from the eternal law that exists in the mind of God. Other laws are subsumed under this, according to the different things that are subject to it. There are the laws that govern the operations of nature, those that angels observe, and the law of reason which binds humanity and which, through reason, men may understand. (This latter is written in men's hearts and is similar to what St. Thomas terms the natural law.) Hooker also has a category called divine law; this is based on what man knows only by Revelation. Another division is human law, which concerns what men, judging by both reason and Revelation, deem expedient. With this scheme in mind, Hooker proceeds to discuss what the Church may properly rule on. In opposition to the Puritans who insisted that Revelation was the sole basis for law, he argues that the Church may and must legislate on other matters on which God enlightens men through their reason. On some points, he says, the law of Scripture is so clear that it need only be followed; on others for which Scripture does not specifically provide, the Church must rule, though it should not create any laws contrary to Revelation. Consequently the Church has the right and the duty, not to create new doctrines, but to interpret, enforce, and administer doctrinal matters through the laws of polity.[10]

Various quotations in the *Dictionary* indicate Johnson's general agreement with this interpretation. Under "doctrine" he quotes Hooker's statement: "To make new articles of faith and *doctrine,* no man thinketh it lawful; new laws of government, what church or commonwealth is there which maketh not either at one time or other?" Similarly, Johnson shows his support of Hooker's view that the law of reason or nature must at times interpret and supplement what Scripture states. Under "canon" appears the quotation: "The truth is, they are rules and *canons* of that law, which is written in all men's hearts; the church had for ever, no less than now, stood bound to observe them, whether the apostle had mentioned them or no" (Hooker, Bk. III, Ch. vii, Sec. 2). Sometimes an excerpt from Hooker appears under a word unrelated to ecclesiastical matters. For instance, in connection with "uncertain," Johnson takes the opportunity to quote a sentence consonant with his own respect for liturgy: "As the form of our publick service is not voluntary, so neither are the parts thereof *uncertain;* but they are all set down in such order, and with such choice, as hath, in the wisdom of the church, seemed best."

Johnson's admiration of Hooker is further revealed by borrowings which, though not related to church matters, found an echo in his own heart. Johnson quotes with approval Hooker's statement, "Civil society doth more content the nature of man, than any private kind of solitary living; because, in society, this good of mutual *participation* is so much larger." As the author of the *Rambler,* Johnson himself might have observed, "The soul preferreth rest in ignorance before *weari-*

some labour to know." Sometimes a sentiment in Hooker appealed so strongly to him that he shortened a sentence too long for inclusion. Thus he merely prints part of a subordinate clause from Book V of *Ecclesiastical Polity* (Ch. xlviii, Sec. 13), in order to preserve the precept, "The Apostle St. Paul teacheth, that every one which will live *godly* in Christ Jesus must suffer persecution."

It would appear, then, that Johnson was a staunch Church of England man, who admired the structure of the Establishment, who revered its liturgy, and whose views were generally in accord with such orthodox theologians as Richard Hooker. There is also the testimony of his biographers on his loyalty to the English Church. Although they sometimes disagreed on other aspects of Johnson, on this point Mrs. Thrale, Sir John Hawkins, Thomas Tyers, and Arthur Murphy were in hearty agreement with Boswell, who in his summary describes Johnson as "a sincere and zealous Christian, of high Church-of-England . . . principles."

Notwithstanding the evidence of his strong allegiance to the Establishment, it is a curious fact that during his life and after his death various assertions were made to the effect that Johnson was virtually a Roman Catholic, or that he was strongly inclined to Calvinism, or that he came to favor Evangelical principles. None of these allegations rests on substantial evidence, in my opinion, but, because of their persistence, it is pertinent to consider Johnson's posture towards other Christian faiths.[11] Such an examination will also serve to further clarify his position as a Church of England man.

It should be emphasized first that Johnson's attitude towards individual believers of another faith might be quite different from his attitude towards the tenets they held. He sometimes said, quite frankly, that he did not like a particular sect, such as the Quakers, but at the same time he remarked that he liked many members of that sect.[12] This was not simply a matter of friendship overcoming a prejudice. Johnson possessed a tolerance and sympathy, unusual in his day, for all men of good faith, irrespective of the denomination to which they might belong. This tolerance of individuals was based on a recognition of the fellowship existing among all Christians, as well as on the conviction that one must follow the dictates of one's conscience. Still more important, perhaps, was Johnson's firm belief that tolerance constitutes an important part of Christian charity.

His attitude in this regard parallels that of William Law, except that the latter explicitly associates charity towards all Christians with his doctrine of perfection. Law writes: "We must enter into a Catholic affection for all men, love the spirit of the Gospel wherever we see it, not work ourselves into an abhorrence of George Fox, or an Ignatius Loyola, but be equally glad of the light of the Gospel wherever it shines, or from what quarter it comes; and give the same thanks and praise to God for an eminent example of piety wherever it appears, either in Papist or Protestant."[13] Johnson expresses much the same sentiment in Sermon XI, as one may see from the quotation that heads this chapter. He also emphasizes the importance of charity when he comments on tolerance in his *Life of Thomas Browne*. He says: "Men may differ from each other in many religious opinions, and yet all may retain the essentials of christianity; men may sometimes eagerly dispute, and yet not differ much from one another; the rigorous prosecutors of errour should, therefore, enlighten their zeal with knowledge, and temper their orthodoxy with charity; that charity, without which orthodoxy is vain; charity that 'thinketh no evil,' but 'hopeth all things,' and 'endureth all things.' "

Despite his liking for individual believers, and despite his great admiration for certain Nonconformist writers, like Richard Baxter and Isaac Watts, Johnson had little sympathy for the Protestant dissenting groups. As a student of religion, he doubtless was acquainted with the particular tenets that distinguished the various sects from each other. Nevertheless, he was inclined to disregard their individual differences and to lump them together as a body in disagreement with the Establishment. He defines "dissenter" as "one who, for whatever reasons, refuses the communion of the English church," and it was perhaps characteristic that he fails to list in his *Dictionary* such groups as the Quakers and Anabaptists, though he does include the Independents and Presbyterians. Again, in his *Life of Isaac Watts,* while he refers to Watts as a dissenter, the only allusion to his belonging to a particular sect appears in the statement, "With the congregation of his tutor, Mr. Rowe, who were, I believe, independents, he communicated in his nineteenth year." Similarly, in speaking of the Puritans, Johnson seldom discriminates between those within the Establishment and those belonging to separatist groups, or between the Calvinistic and the much smaller body of Arminian Puritans. Perhaps he thought of all Puritans as Calvinistic. In any event, as a staunch Church of England man, he regarded all who dissented from the Establishment as "schismaticks" or "sectaries."

Johnson's dislike of the dissenting groups occasionally appears in his writing. As we shall see, it is particularly pronounced in his *Life* of the Presbyterian Francis Cheynel. It is also evident in his *Life of Samuel Butler,* where he speaks of "the sullen superstition, the gloomy moroseness, and the stubborn scruples of the ancient puritans." On his visit to Scotland he was particularly annoyed at the followers of John Knox for causing or permitting the ancient Catholic churches to fall into ruins. "The malignant influence of calvinism," he wrote, "has blasted ceremony and decency together; and if the remembrance of papal superstition is obliterated, the monuments of papal piety are likewise effaced."[14]

In conversation, Johnson's sense of charity presumably restrained him from attacking the dissenting sects. At least there are few instances in Boswell and Hawkins of his taking a notably belligerent attitude towards them. It is therefore surprising to find Anna Seward, in a letter written a few years after his death, commenting, "Johnson's uncandid and intolerant bluster against the Dissenters has made every High Churchman his idolater and champion."[15] This remark, I believe, must be almost entirely disregarded, in view of Miss Seward's aggressive and perhaps neurotically inspired attempts to disparage Johnson after his death. Nevertheless, his dislike of the Puritans was very genuine. Again the *Dictionary* proves to be a source of interesting evidence.

The number of caustic comments directed at Puritan beliefs and practices is so considerable that only a sampling will be given here. Several of the quotations in the *Dictionary* allude disparagingly to distinctively Calvinistic beliefs. Under "predetermination," for instance, Johnson quotes Hammond: "The truth of the catholick doctrine of all ages in points of *predetermination* and irresistibility, stands in opposition to the Calvinists." Under "election," Atterbury's remark is cited: "The conceit about absolute *election* to eternal life, some enthusiasts entertaining, have been made remiss in the practice of virtue." Johnson himself defines "enthusiasm" as "A vain belief of private revelation; a vain confidence of divine favour or communication." In connection with both "enthusiasm" and "enthusiast" he includes pejorative statements from Locke: "*Enthusiasm* is founded neither on reason nor divine revelation, but rises from conceits of a warmed or overweening brain," and, "Let an *enthusiast* be principled that he or his teacher is inspired, and acted by an immediate communication of the Divine Spirit, and you in vain bring the evidence of clear reasons against the doctrine."

Occasionally Johnson inserts a quotation so slyly that its full import can be understood only in relation to the context from which it is taken. For instance, under "doctrinal" he quotes Hooker: "What special property or quality is that, which, being no where found but in sermons, maketh them effectual to save souls, and leaveth all other *doctrinal* means besides destitute of vital efficacy." This criticism might appear to be pointed at any clergyman who overemphasized the importance of sermons, but it is taken from a section of *Ecclesiastical Polity* (Bk. V, Ch. xxii, Sec. 10) where Hooker is attacking the Puritans for neglecting other means of promoting salvation. They act, he satirically observes, as if the Bible existed merely to supply a text on which to preach. As a consequence, they grossly neglect the word of God as contained in Scripture and seem to assume that the "Sacraments are not effectual to Salvation, except men be instructed by Preaching before they be made Partakers of them."

Johnson's contempt for Puritan preaching and for Puritanism generally is clearly and amusingly revealed in his *Life of Francis Cheynel*. In writing this biography of a seventeenth-century divine, Johnson apparently tried to be fair, as indicated by his concluding remark about Cheynel's "hospitality and contempt of money." But the work begins with a delightfully scornful observation, and throughout its course satiric thrusts keep breaking in. The comment on Puritan preaching appears in a section in which he describes what happened when the forces of Parliament took Oxford in 1646 and, as he observes, "the reformation of the university was resolved." Cheynel and his associates occupied the pulpits and began preaching to highly unresponsive congregations. "Those who had been accustomed to the preachers of Oxford, and the liturgy of the Church of England," Johnson writes, "were offended at the emptiness of their discourses, which were noisy and unmeaning; at the unusual gestures, the wild distortions, and the uncouth tone with which they were delivered . . . and at, what was surely not to be remarked without indignation, their omission of the Lord's Prayer."[16]

To Johnson such preaching was a clear manifestation of mistaken zeal, another subject he treats in the *Dictionary*. Altogether he supplies twenty-eight different quotations under definitions of "zeal," "zealot," "zealous," and "zealously." Not all these are of a pejorative character, because Johnson firmly believed in the kind of zeal reflected in his diaries and prayers. It may be assumed that he wholeheartedly approved of the statement he quotes from William Law: "There is nothing noble in a clergyman but burning *zeal* for the salvation of souls. . . ." Perhaps the definition that best reflected his own view is one cited from Sprat's sermons:" True *zeal* seems not to be any one single affection of the soul; but rather a strong mixture of many holy affections; rather a gracious constitution of the whole mind, than any one particular grace, swaying a devout heart and filling it with all pious intentions; all not only uncounterfeit, but most fervent." Such zeal was to be distinguished from the fanatical type associated with Puritanism. This sort of zeal is alluded to in a quotation from Hammond: "The bare fervour and *zeal* is taken in commutation for much other piety, by many the most eager contenders." Johnson also quotes Hooker's observation on the Puritanism of his time: "The present age, wherein *zeal* hath drowned charity and skill; meekness will not now suffer any man to marvel, whatsoever he shall hear reproved by whomsoever."

Despite the evidence that Johnson regarded the Calvinistic Puritans as despicable enthusiasts, after his death he himself was accused of having Calvinistic leanings. Where the misconception began, I do not know, but it already exists in Robert Anderson's *Life of Johnson*, which appeared in 1795. According to Anderson: "He saw the Almighty in a different light from what he is represented in the pure page of the gospel; he trembled in the presence of Infinite Goodness. Those tenets of the Church of England, which are most nearly allied with Calvinism, were congenial to his general feelings, and they made an early impression, which habits confirmed, and which reason, if ever exerted, could not efface."[17] One asks, Which tenets? Certainly there appears to be no evidence that Johnson favored any of the distinctive doctrines of Calvinism, such as predestination, the witness of the spirit, or salvation by faith alone.

Anderson later mentions that while in Edinburgh Johnson refused to hear Dr. Robertson preach, "because he should be present at a Presbyterian assembly."[18] This incident is reported as an example of Johnson's bigotry, but his refusal fails to accord with an alleged sympathy with Calvinism. What he really said, according to Boswell, was, "I will hear him . . . if he will get into a tree and preach; but I will not give a sanction, by my presence, to a Presbyterian assembly."[19]

This was clearly the statement of a man with a distinct prejudice against Calvinistic Presbyterianism. Nevertheless, the report that he himself was a Calvinist persisted, and came to include some of his friends. According to an anonymous writer in the *Gentleman's Magazine* for 1798, Hawkins, Ryland, and Johnson "all lived in the profession of what is now called Calvinistic Christianity, and died with the supports of it."[20] In subsequent issues of this periodical various other correspondents denied this story, but even today there are those who believe Johnson was inclined in that direction. The basic reason for this misconception seems to be a notion that any Christian who works out his salvation in fear must be a Calvinist.

Turning now to another religious group, we shall briefly examine Johnson's attitude towards Roman Catholics. In the first place, the assertion that Johnson had leanings towards Roman Catholicism must be considered in terms of what is meant by "leanings." If one means he had a slant in that direction in the sense that High Churchmen are generally more in sympathy with Rome than with continental Protestantism, most readers of Boswell would probably agree. On the other hand, if one means he was seriously disposed to the idea of being converted to Roman Catholicism, the evidence for such a belief is extremely slight. The whole question is of interest, however, because Johnson made various pronouncements on the Catholic faith, and his comments sometimes reveal his own stand on various doctrines. In the following pages we shall discuss, first, the kind of evidence that has led some to think he had a strong personal predilection towards Roman Catholicism, and, secondly, his attitude as a High Churchman towards various dogmas, some of which were Catholic in origin.

Much as he enjoyed the busy life of London and the full tide of existence, Johnson had an ascetic streak. As we have indicated, this tendency may have developed partly from reading William Law. Whatever its source, his asceticism is evident in various comments he made on monasticism. Although he had certain reservations about retreating from the world, what is more remarkable is his genuine admiration for monastic existence. During their tour of Scotland, Johnson observed to Boswell, "I never read of a hermit, but in imagination I kiss his feet; never of a monastery, but I could fall on my knees and kiss the pavement."[21] This unusually extravagant remark was made at a time when, presumably, Johnson had never had a chance to visit a monastery, since there was none in eighteenth-century England. The opportunity presented itself two years later, however, when he accompanied the Thrales to France. There he passed considerable time in the company of monks and examined with great curiosity their mode of life. His brief jottings in a diary of this trip indicate his surprise at learning that not all Benedictines were ordained, that they were permitted to sleep eight hours, and that they customarily performed some physical labor. He may also have been astonished at seeing monks and nuns abroad on the streets of Paris, for, as Mrs. Thrale remarked, the typical Londoner assumed they were always confined to a monastery or convent.[22]

Before his trip to France, Johnson may have thought of all members of Catholic religious orders as cloistered and committed to a completely contemplative life. Such a misconception would explain one of his reservations about monasticism. Because of the importance he attached to helping one's fellow men, he could not entirely approve of an existence devoted solely to prayer, and having little knowledge of the active orders dedicated to works of mercy, he perhaps assumed that monks and nuns made no direct contribution to the welfare of others. He also expressed another reservation. While he praised the desire to retreat from temptation, he considered this an insufficient motive for entering a monastery. Though ascetics show a proper fear of sin, he remarks (Sermon III), "it cannot be allowed that flight is victory." Seemingly, it was not the abstinence or the austerities of monastic life to which he was opposed; he felt rather that those who entered religious retreats had adopted an easier course than living a holy life in the midst of worldly temptations. Perhaps the best key to his sentiments on members of monastic orders is the comment, "surely it cannot be said that they have reached the perfection of a religious life."[23] What he meant by "perfection," of course, was the mode of existence described by William Law—a way of life not passed in a cloister, but nonetheless dedicated to qualifying for salvation.

One statement in *Rasselas* particularly shows the attraction that monasteries had for Johnson. He writes: "Those retreats of prayer and contemplation have something so congenial to the mind of man, that, perhaps, there is scarcely one that does not purpose to close his life in pious abstraction, with a few associates, serious as himself" (Ch. XLVII). Because these are Imlac's words, some may question whether Johnson himself is speaking through this character. Nevertheless, it is interesting to compare the view expressed with new evidence provided in James M. Osborn's article, "Dr. Johnson and the Contrary Converts." During his sojourn in Paris with the Thrales, Johnson had been cordially entertained by a group of English Benedictine monks, resident at St. Edmund's Convent. There he had met a young man named James Compton, who had recently entered the order. Several years later, in 1782, Compton left the Benedictines, renounced Catholicism, and came to England. Finding himself destitute, he appealed to Johnson, who supplied his immediate necessities. Johnson also introduced him to the Bishop of London and thus enabled him eventually to become a clergyman of the Established Church.[24]

Of particular interest is a letter Compton wrote to Boswell after Johnson's death. Compton states that he passed many evenings with his benefactor during the winter of 1784, when Johnson was in his last year of life. At this time, according to Compton, Johnson expressed a strong inclination to return to Paris in order to pass his remaining days at the Benedictine monastery, and was dissuaded from doing so chiefly by Compton.

For some reason Boswell omitted from his *Life* all references to Compton. Perhaps the biographer distrusted his testimony, or perhaps he felt that, if printed, it might lead to misconstructions. There is still a question as to how much weight Compton's assertions should carry. It is quite possible, of course, that Johnson did express at least a passing desire to end his days in a monastery, but, as James Osborn points out, if he entertained this idea, he was perhaps thinking of the Benedictine establishment as a place where he had been warmly welcomed and where, now that he was old and ill, he might receive proper care. The monastery would also appeal to him as a retreat where he could converse with religious-minded men and engage in meditation, but that does not necessarily mean he was contemplating a conversion to Roman Catholicism. Indeed, if he had such thoughts, it seems strange that the only person he discussed them with was a recusant monk.

Although Johnson's interest in monasteries gives an insight into his character, it seems chiefly significant as evidence of his ascetic inclinations. But the ascetic ideal is not confined to Roman Catholics. William Law, for instance, was much more genuinely dedicated to an unworldly contemplative life than Johnson, but Law was an ascetic who apparently never considered being anything but a devout Anglican.

The principal reason for thinking Johnson was inclined towards Roman Catholicism was his habit of defending its teachings in conversation. He understood its tenets better than most Englishmen of his time, and he often expressed strong sympathy for many of its doctrines, though sometimes he defended it, perhaps not entirely from conviction, but in order to oppose the canting comments of those who spoke from a conventionally anti-Papist bias. He seems also to have changed his mind over a period of years about certain Catholic practices. For instance, in 1769 he told Boswell it was "criminal" to administer the Sacrament in only one form, but in 1784 he had altered this opinion and said he thought this mode was warranted.[25] Although he definitely had reservations about some aspects of Roman Catholicism, at least one of these may have been more nationalistic than doctrinal. When he warned a prospective visitor to the Continent not to be influenced by "the ostentatious pomp of church ceremonies,"[26] he was probably speaking as an Englishman with an aversion for processions and the elaborate ceremonies favored in Latin countries, but he seems not to have objected to more strictly liturgical practices.

Because he frequently spoke of Roman Catholicism with approval, at a period when this faith was outlawed in England, a few of his contemporaries falsely suspected that he had a genuine commitment to it. Thomas Cooke, the translator of Hesiod, who had known Johnson during his earlier period in London, is reported to have said he was "three parts a Roman Catholic."[27] But Boswell, Mrs. Thrale, and other close friends never doubted his firm adherence to the Established Church. To them the opinion of Bennet Langton's father that he was secretly a Papist would seem ridiculous. Johnson, himself, in reporting the elder Langton's impression, cited it as an example of a narrow mind which had reached this conclusion simply because he had defended certain Roman Catholic beliefs.[28]

The truth is, Johnson could be extremely ambivalent in

what he said about Roman Catholicism. He sometimes referred to it sympathetically, as in his *Life of Samuel Garth,* where he quoted with seeming approval the statement "that a mind, wearied with perpetual doubt, willingly seeks repose in the bosom of an infallible church."[29] On the other hand, he could denounce the Roman Catholic clergy for having "snatched the bible out of the hands of the people" and having thus "precluded great numbers from the highest spiritual consolation."[30] In conversation he seems to have spoken more often in terms of praise. According to Boswell, he even said on one occasion that he would be a Papist if he could, but that an obstinate rationality prevented him.[31] Nevertheless, even in conversation he could take quite a contrary position on Catholicism, just as he could argue for or against various other views, according to the occasion or his mood. Reporting a conversation that took place on October 10, 1779, Boswell writes, "He this evening expressed himself strongly against the Roman Catholicks; observing, 'in every thing in which they differ from us they are wrong.' "[32] This statement, made, as Boswell observes, when "he was in the humour of opposition," contradicts what Johnson had said on other occasions in defense of the Catholic belief in purgatory, masses for the deceased, and the invocation of saints in prayer.[33] Nevertheless, even when the spirit of opposition is discounted, such an inclusive statement could hardly be made by one strongly inclined to Roman Catholicism. It could be made, as indeed it was, by one with a firm commitment to the Church of England.

Among Johnson's writings, the one that shows him following Roman Catholic practices to some degree is his posthumously published *Prayers and Meditations.* This work, the manuscript of which Johnson entrusted to the Reverend George Strahan shortly before his death, provoked considerable comment of an adverse kind when it appeared. Johnson's record of his broken resolutions led to accusations that he was a weak Christian; his scruples created the impression in some quarters that he was superstitious; his Lenten fasts and his prayers for deceased relatives and friends caused some to believe he was dangerously inclined towards Roman Catholicism.[34] Even his editor, George Strahan, felt uncomfortable about printing the petitions for the dead, as indicated by his apology for this practice in the preface. But no such apology had been needed for the works that Johnson published during his lifetime. In them his position is clearly that of an English Churchman. Indeed, when the whole body of his writings is considered, expressions of sympathy for Roman Catholicism are relatively few—much fewer and less pronounced than in the pages of Boswell.

It is also true that none of Johnson's other biographers particularly stressed his Catholic interests. Consequently, most of what we know on that subject appears in Boswell's *Life*. This is not to imply that Boswell gave false reports or that he purposely distorted Johnson's views. Nevertheless, the emphasis in that work on certain topics, such as sex, religion, and the fear of death, partly reflects the particular interests of the biographer. So far as Roman Catholicism was concerned, Boswell's own early conversion to that faith was probably significant.[35] Although Boswell remained a Catholic for only a brief period, he continued to be keenly interested in the church's practices and beliefs. Thus he would be especially inclined to direct the conversation to that area, and to recall and emphasize whatever Johnson had to say on Roman Catholicism.

We repeat, then, that Johnson showed a better understanding of Roman Catholicism than most Englishmen of his era. He also expressed, at times, an unusual sympathy for various Catholic beliefs. But there is little evidence that he ever seriously considered a conversion to that faith. He knew that one must be directed by one's conscience, and his own conscience told him his best hope for salvation existed in the Church of England. Furthermore, because of the latitude the Establishment permits, he could feel relatively free to follow certain practices and to adopt certain beliefs not in favor with most English Churchmen but, on the other hand, not specifically interdicted. Thus on points where writers on religion disagreed, he could select the particular interpretation that seemed right to him, without thinking of himself as an apostate. The fact that some of these interpretations were basically Roman Catholic is not necessarily evidence of a personal predilection for that faith. Frequently, the favor he accorded Catholic beliefs merely indicates the historical and doctrinal orientation towards Rome which he shared with other High Churchmen. In the following pages, therefore, when we allude to his stand on various Catholic doctrines, our purpose is not to show that Johnson was a Roman Catholic at heart, but rather to help define his position as a Church of England man.

Among his many allusions to Roman Catholicism, three, when juxtaposed, seem particularly significant. On one occasion Johnson observed that a Protestant who becomes a Catholic merely adds to what he believes, but a Catholic who becomes a Protestant "gives up so much of what he has held as sacred as any thing that he retains." This is a reference, of course, to the fact that Catholicism is a much more dogmatic faith, in that its adherents specifically subscribe to more doctrines than other Christians. He also observed that "No reasoning Papist believes every article of their faith." Although this remark may be interpreted in different ways, in context it appears he meant that Catholics are not bound to believe everything on a basis of individual reasoning, but may accept certain teachings as a matter of faith or authority. Johnson himself accepted some doctrines, such as the Trinity, on authority, but certain others he could not subscribe to on this basis. Consequently when he added, "I would be a Papist if I could. I have fear enough; but an obstinate rationality prevents me," he did not mean that his own beliefs rested exclusively on individual reasoning. He meant, rather, there were limitations to what he could hold to on tradition, authority, or faith.[36]

According to Boswell, "Johnson at all times made the just distinction between doctrines *contrary* to reason, and doctrines *above* reason."[37] Despite his "stubborn rationality," he firmly believed in the Trinity as a mystery that could be classed as above reason. This doctrine seemed so fundamental to him that, much as he admired Clarke, he called him a condemned heretic for not supporting it. Interestingly, in dealing with the term "mystery" in his *Dictionary,* he quotes Swift, for whom he sometimes expressed scant respect. The quotation, which is based on traditional Christian teaching, is taken from Swift's sermon on the Trinity and reads: "If God should please to reveal unto us the great *mystery* of the Trinity, or some other *mysteries* in our religion, we should not be able to understand them, unless he would bestow on us some new faculties of the mind." This, of course, is not an explanation of the Trinity; it is merely an explanation of why it is inexplicable. But here Johnson is quite willing to accept a doctrine on faith or authority because in its nature it is above reason.

Another belief which he favored, not because he considered it above reason, but rather in accord with reason, was the existence of a middle state between heaven and hell. When Boswell asked about the Roman Catholic doctrine of purgatory, he replied: "Why, Sir, it is a very harmless doctrine. They are of the opinion that the generality of mankind are neither so obstinately wicked as to deserve everlasting punishment, nor so good as to merit being admitted into the society of the blessed spirits; and therefore that God is graciously pleased to allow of a middle state, where they may be purified by certain degrees of suffering. You see, Sir, there is nothing unreasonable in this."[38] That this was not merely a passing remark is evidenced in his prayers, where he frequently petitions for the welfare of his departed relatives and friends, as if they were in some kind of intermediate state. Generally the prayer is of this sort: "O, Lord, so far as it may be lawful, I commend unto thy fatherly goodness my father, brother, wife, and mother, beseeching thee to make them happy for Jesus Christ's sake." The qualifying phrase, "so far as it may be lawful," indicates his awareness that the Church of England at this time did not favor prayers for the dead. Most members regarded it as a Papist custom, based on a belief in purgatory, to which they did not subscribe. Yet William Law and other Nonjurors did believe in an intermediate state, and one of them, Archibald Campbell, wrote a lengthy treatise entitled *The Doctrine of the Middle State.*

According to Campbell, there is no immediate judgment after death; final judgment will not be rendered until the Resurrection; meanwhile souls remain in a middle state, where praying for them is not only lawful but a duty.[39] This view differs from the Catholic doctrine, according to which there is an immediate and particular judgment, and purgatory is a place where souls requiring purgation temporarily remain preliminary to their admission to heaven. The *Sale Catalogue* of his library indicates that Johnson owned a copy of Campbell's book, but when he was in Scotland, he refused to discuss it. He never explained specifically the nature of his own belief in an intermediate state. Probably his ideas on the subject were not very clearly formulated, but there is at least slight evidence that he favored the Catholic belief in an immediate judgment. Upon a couple of occasions he prayed that God "may have had mercy" on the soul of the deceased. The use of this tense would indicate that he subscribed to the Catholic view rather than to Campbell's interpretation of a delayed judgment.[40]

Johnson's belief in some sort of middle state prevailed during his whole adult life. In this instance he was embracing a doctrine that seemed logical, and the fact that only a small group in his own church adhered to it did not deter him from accepting what appeared reasonable to him. In view of his fear of damnation, a belief in an intermediate state must also have appealed to him as a solid basis of hope for salvation.

The Roman Catholic doctrine to which he was most rigidly opposed was transubstantiation. When he was in France and visiting at Douay, he told Mrs. Thrale he would not kneel, with the rest of the congregation, at the elevation of the Host, for the whole city.[41] In a discussion with Boswell he advanced several reasons for discrediting a belief in transubstantiation. He used first an empirical argument based on sense data when he quoted Tillotson's objection that at the consecration we see only bread and wine. When Boswell asked about the "continued tradition of the church upon this point," Johnson replied that tradition counts for nothing where Scripture is plain, and suggested that Christ was speaking only figuratively when he said, "This is my body." Later, when Boswell inquired if the same objections might not be made against the Trinity as against transubstantiation, he said, yes, "If you take three and one in the same sense. . . . but the three persons in Godhead are Three in one sense, and One in another. We cannot tell how; and that is the mystery!"[42]

Here he seems to be defending one mystery on the grounds of metaphysical reasoning and rejecting another mystery for a mixed set of reasons. Just what Johnson believed to be the nature of the Eucharist he never, so far as I know, explicitly stated. As a devout Anglican, he undoubtedly believed Christ to be present in the Eucharist in some sense, but possibly only in a general spiritual sense. If this was his interpretation, he differed from Caroline divines and from English Churchmen of his own and later times who have held that Christ is present in the Eucharist in a more special way. Few if any of these subscribed to the Roman Catholic doctrine of transubstantiation, which, indeed is specifically denied in the Thirty-nine Articles. Nevertheless, while rejecting the Roman Catholic doctrine that a change is effected through which the bread and wine become in substance the Body and Blood of Christ, Anglicans have traditionally believed in some sort of Real Presence. That is, they have held that Christ is present in a devout communicant upon partaking of the Lord's Supper, or that the elements take on the virtues of Christ's Body and Blood, or that Christ is present in some other special way beyond the figurative one.[43]

Johnson never discusses the Eucharist in these terms. In the *Dictionary* he defines "Eucharist" simply as "the act of giving thanks; the sacramental act in which the death of our Redeemer is commemorated with a thankful remembrance." In his sermons he speaks of Communion as an important means of grace and as something more than a commemorative rite, and when he partook of the Sacrament he did so in a most reverent manner, after careful spiritual preparation. Yet his silence on the nature of the Eucharist suggests that he did not believe Christ to be present except symbolically. If this was his position, then he was rejecting the interpretations of contemporary Churchmen, such as William Law, Daniel Waterland, and Bishop Thomas Wilson, and, in this instance, showing himself more in accord with the Nonconformist view than the Anglican one. But on this subject empirical objections probably counted more strongly with him.

In his discussion with Boswell, the first point Johnson had raised was "that we are as sure we see bread and wine only, as that we read in the Bible the text on which that false doctrine is founded. We have only the evidence of our senses for both." A further indication that the empirical objection was his principal one appears in the *Dictionary*. He defines "transubstantiation" as "a miraculous operation believed in the Romish Church, in which the elements of the eucharist are supposed to be changed into the real body and blood of Christ." To this definition he appends, not several illustrative quotations, as he so often does, but only one, taken from John Locke: "How is the Romanist prepared easily to swallow, not only against all probability, but even the clear evidence of his senses, the doctrine of *transubstantiation?*" In view of his acceptance of other Christian mysteries, it is surprising to find Johnson quoting such a blunt, materialistic remark; nevertheless it seems to represent his own point of view on the Eucharist. Normally he did not, because he could not, subject Christian doctrines like the Trinity to an empirical test, but to subscribe to the doctrine of transubstantiation demands that one believe that a change takes places in the elements. Because this change is not confirmed by perception, Johnson was unable to accept the doctrine of transubstantiation, and it is possible that his empiricism made it equally difficult for him to subscribe to an Anglican belief in the Real Presence.

Johnson's faith was obviously not built on any simple plan. It was a blend of many things. Although based on hope and the promises of Scripture, although supported by traditional interpretations of the pre-Reformation church and the Church of England, it was tempered by what seemed to him reasonable in a logical sense or, in a few instances, credible according to empirical considerations. He probably did not accept any religious belief without grave and prolonged consideration, and thinking sometimes raised difficulties. "Every thing which Hume has advanced against Christianity," he remarked, "had passed through my mind long before he wrote." But he fought religious scepticism with philosophical scepticism, reminding himself and others that the intellect is by nature extremely circumscribed. "The human mind is so limited," he said, "that it cannot take in all the parts of a subject, so that there may be objections raised against any thing."[44]

Johnson took a somewhat similar stand in a discussion with the Quaker Mrs. Knowles. When she told him of a young lady who recently has been converted to Quakerism, he became angry and asserted she could not have made the change as the result of conviction, that she knew no more of the religion she had embraced than she did of the one she had rejected. He added that one is generally wise to remain an adherent of the church in which one is raised, for no one has the time to study and compare the tenets of the multiple religions that exist. When Mrs. Knowles inquired if we must then "go by implicit faith," he answered, "Why, Madam, the greatest part of our knowledge is implicit faith."[45] This remark did not mean he had given up the study of dogma or was placing intuition and inspiration above doctrine, but it did emphasize his distrust of reason as a sole guide to faith, the kind of distrust evident in other intensely religious people, like William Law and Cardinal Newman.

In addition to recognizing the natural limitations of the intellect, Johnson was, as we have seen in his sermons, extremely conscious of man's tendency to rationalize; that is, to be guided, not by logic or evidence, but by the vagaries of one's wishes. In short, he saw man as a creature prone to error, first, because of the finite nature of his mind and secondly, because of his predilection to self-delusion. Both shortcomings are stressed in an extract that appears in his *Dictionary* under a definition of "reason," where he again quotes Swift: "It would be well if people would not lay so much weight on *reason* in matters of religion, as to think every thing impossible and absurd which they cannot conceive: how often do we contradict the right rules of reason in the whole course of our lives! reason itself is true and just but the reason of every particular man is weak and wavering, perpetually swayed and turned by his interests, his passions and his vices." Like Swift, Johnson distrusted individual reasoning about the fundamentals of religion. Although given to speculation, he generally avoided making dogmatic pronouncements which had no basis in Scripture or theology.

One more point is significant. Johnson was never anthropomorphic in his thinking. On the contrary, because he regarded God's infinite nature with awe, he deemed it presumptuous for man with his fallible and finite mind to attempt to determine by analogy to his own thought-processes the motives and purposes of divinity. One of his most bitter attacks on another writer was directed at Soame Jenyns for trying to explain the nature and origin of evil. Johnson comments: "When this author presumes to speak of the universe, I would advise him a little to distrust his own faculties, however large and comprehensive. Many words, easily understood on common occasions, become uncertain and figurative, when applied to the works of omnipotence." Although Johnson is critical of Jenyns' loose reasoning, his sharpest satire is reserved for a section in which the author allowed himself to engage in an anthropomorphic form of speculation. While averring he found it impossible to believe the idea himself, Jenyns had toyed with the analogy that, just as men use certain animals for their diversion, so celestial beings might, for a similar purpose, deceive or torment members of the human race. Johnson ridicules both the suggestion and the author of it, but beneath the banter one detects his feeling that to engage in such theorizing approaches blasphemy.

Johnson himself believed in a God whose purposes man cannot fully fathom but in whose infinite goodness and infinite wisdom he must trust. Because of the imbecility of the human intellect, man ought not to engage in "unseemly inquiries into the reasons for His dispensations." Because the finite cannot comprehend the infinite, man is destined to see through a glass darkly. Yet man may trust in the knowledge "that heaven and earth, and the whole system of things, were created by an infinite and perfect Being, who still continues to superintend and govern them."[46]

If Johnson's religion had been a matter of the intellect alone, it would be easy to say there were inconsistencies in it. But consistency belongs to the realm of logic and reason; it has little, if anything, to do with what is considered as above reason. Some might accuse him of being inconsistent in not reconciling these two spheres, in accepting certain mysteries as above reason and rejecting others on a basis of abstract reason or on empirical evidence. But the degree to which one has convictions that may be classed as above reason seems itself to be determined, not by logic, but rather by the will, the temperament, or some other agency.

Taken as a whole, Johnson's religion impresses one by its integrity. Insofar as consistency is itself a virtue, the truest test would appear to be the degree that one lives by his innermost convictions. Johnson sometimes accused himself of failing to do this, but he strenuously endeavored to, and as compared with most, he succeeded conspicuously in following the dictates of his conscience.

IX · END OF THE JOURNEY

To neglect at any time preparation for death, is to sleep on our post at a siege: but to omit it in old age, is to sleep at an attack.

Johnson, Rambler 78

F ew writers appear to have meditated so much on old age as Samuel Johnson. The prospect was much in his mind during his middle years and probably before that time. In the sermon on the death of his wife he had written: "The young man who rejoiceth in his youth, amidst his musick and his gaiety, has always been disturbed with the thought, that his youth will be quickly at an end." In this instance he seems to have generalized erroneously from his private experience. Youth is seldom preoccupied with thoughts of old age and death, but young Sam Johnson evidently was. The prospect may have loomed more clearly in his mind because his parents were already middle-aged when he was born, and because, when he married at twenty-eight, he chose a wife twenty years his senior. But even more important was the fact that, seeing life with greater clarity than most, he could better anticipate the final phase of mortality.

His best-known description of old age appears in *The Vanity of Human Wishes.* He was drawing on Juvenal, of course, but he added much distinctly his own. In Juvenal, senescence is viewed as repellent, avaricious, prurient, and physically revolting. In Johnson the loneliness and more pitiable aspects are emphasized. The vanity of wishing for length of life is also treated in various other works, such as his little-known allegory entitled "The Fountains."

Johnson regarded old age as a period of enfeebled powers, often of declining health, and one saddened by the loss of relatives and friends. His view was optimistic in only one respect. To him the chief advantage of longevity was the additional opportunity it afforded to perfect his repentance. "Piety," he had observed in *Rambler* 69, "is the only proper and adequate relief of decaying man."

During his last two years of life he knew his end was near. Temptations and indulgences, chiefly sensuality and sloth, that had earlier disturbed his conscience were in old age no longer such important concerns. To a degree, also, he appears to have overcome a lack of forbearance. Perhaps the chief conflict now was caused by the realization that illness, suffering, and long periods of confinement made him impatient with his condition. His concern on this score is reflected in his letters. "The sense of my own diseases, and the sight of the world sinking round me," he told Mrs. Thrale (Aug. 20, 1783), "oppresses me perhaps too much." To Robert Chambers he wrote (April 19, 1783), "I am afraid that I bear the weight of time with unseemly, if not with sinful impatience. I hope that God will enable me to correct this as well as my other faults, before he calls me to appear before him." Writing to Joseph Fowke on the same day, he observed, "I have led an inactive and careless life; it is time at last to be diligent. There is yet provision to be made for eternity."[1]

He had never had much respect for mere stoicism. In *Rasselas* he had satirized this philosophy when the young prince discovered that the sage who had descanted on the virtue of stoical resignation was unable to act by his own principles when ill fortune struck home. In *Rambler* 32 he had expressed doubt that the Stoics had really been able to bear calamity and misery with the fortitude attributed to them. This pagan philosophy was false, he concluded, because it was divorced from human experience. Patience, Christian patience, was another thing. To submit to the will of God is not always easy, he observes, but since it is our duty, we must constantly strive to do so. To fret at the evils allotted by Providence can serve no purpose; on the contrary it deprives us of the consolation offered by others, and "it is yet less to be justified, since, without lessening the pain, it cuts off the hope of that reward which he, by whom it is inflicted, will confer upon them that bear it well." Yet, knowing the limitations of human endurance, he makes one reservation. In times of physical suffering, "the nature of man requires some indulgence," he observes, "and every extravagance but impiety may be easily forgiven him."

This statement, written some thirty years earlier, serves as a fitting representation of his own situation during his last two years. As his autopsy was to show, he suffered from a complication of diseases. His nights now were often sleepless, his body became swollen with the dropsy, and asthma interfered with his breathing. Sometimes his patience became exhausted, but his piety, which had always seemed remarkable to his friends, became even more intense.

Two events particularly served as warnings that he had not long to live. In June, 1783, a paralytic stroke temporarily deprived him of his speech. When the attack occurred, the first thing he did, even before summoning assistance, was to compose a prayer, in which he asked, no matter how his body might be afflicted, that his understanding might be spared. This act was characteristic not only of his piety but also of the objectivity with which he could examine himself. A few days later, having partly recovered, he explained to Mrs. Thrale that he had written the prayer in Latin, as a means of determining whether his mind was affected. "The lines were not very good," he wrote, "but I knew them not to be very good, I made them easily, and concluded myself to be unimpaired in my faculties."[2]

The same sort of objectivity led him to keep a daily record of his symptoms and of the methods used in treating his various ailments. It is a diary of a man interested in medicine, not as a hypochondriac, but as one who never excluded from his broad range of interests anything bearing on the human condition. Perhaps, too, this diagnostic attitude in which he played the dual role of patient and physician was psychologically helpful in assisting him to withstand pain and fear.

A second event that made a deep impression on him was his sudden, though temporary, recovery from the dropsy. This occurred in February, 1784. In the preceding months he had been seriously ill and confined to his home. Feeling that his end was near, he told Hawkins he intended to pass an entire day in fasting, prayer, and other devotional exercises. When Hawkins next visited him, he found the patient much better physically and noticeably serene. Johnson explained that on the day set apart for meditation he had unexpectedly been relieved of his bloated condition by evacuating twenty pints of water. This form of relief, Dr. Brocklesby assured him, was most unusual. He himself clearly regarded it as a divine interposition. He discussed it as such with Hawkins and later with Boswell. In his letters he mentioned it as virtually a miraculous occurrence, and in his Easter prayer he offered special thanks for his "late deliverance from imminent death."[3] Grateful as he was for this respite, he regarded it chiefly as a warning. He later said "that when he recovered the last spring, he had only called it a *reprieve* . . . however, he hoped the time that had been prolonged to him might be the means of bringing forth fruit meet for repentance."[4]

After being confined to his home much of the winter of 1784, with the arrival of spring Johnson felt much better. By July he was strong enough to undertake the long journey to Ashbourne to visit his old friend, John Taylor. He passed the summer with him, visited Lichfield for several weeks in the fall, and returned home by November 16. During his absence, he observed, he had alternately seemed to improve and then to relapse but on the whole had "lost ground very much." This was a correct diagnosis, for when he reached London, only four weeks of life remained.

The report quickly circulated that Johnson was very ill. Having always placed a high value on friendship, he must have been comforted by the attention and affection of the many friends who visited him. Several of these were to describe the manner in which he met death. Boswell, who was in Scotland at the time, later pieced together a coherent account of Johnson's last month, but in writing the conclusion of his long work, the biographer was unable to provide the firsthand reporting that gives such distinction to his earlier pages. Although his description of Johnson dying with dignity and calmness, tinged by a degree of melancholy, seems correct, the specific frame of Johnson's mind during his terminal period has ever since been a subject of discussion from Egypt to Peru. Of late, interest has centered on the interpretation of a prayer Johnson wrote on December 5, 1784, the day he received Communion for the last time. The prayer follows:

Almighty and most merciful Father, I am now, as to human eyes it seems, about to commemorate for the last time, the death of thy son Jesus Christ, our Saviour and Redeemer. Grant, O Lord, that my whole hope and confidence may be in his merits and in thy mercy: forgive and accept my late conversion, enforce and accept my imperfect repentance; make this commemoration of him available to the confirmation of my Faith, the establishment of my hope, and the enlargement of my Charity, and make the Death of thy son Jesus effectual to my redemption. Have mercy upon me and pardon the multitude of my offences. Bless my Friends, have mercy upon all men. Support me by the Grace of thy Holy Spirit in the days of weakness, and at the hour of death, and receive me, at my death, to everlasting happiness, for the Sake of Jesus Christ. Amen.[5]

This prayer suggests that Johnson had at last achieved in large measure the reconciliation with God's will for which he had so ardently striven. The controversial point is concerned with what he meant by "forgive and accept my late conversion." In the *Dictionary* he provides three definitions of "conversion." It is generally agreed that he used the word in his prayer in some sense related to the second definition, "change from reprobation to grace, from a bad to a holy life." But the act of conversion, because it is such a distinctly individual experience, means different things to different people.

Perhaps no two conversions are exactly alike, but, insofar as the event can be classified, certain types may be distinguished. First, there is the kind St. Paul experienced. In a conversation at which Mrs. Knowles was present, Johnson remarked, "I should not think the better of a man who should tell me on his death-bed he was sure of salvation. A man cannot be sure himself that he has divine intimation of acceptance; much less can he make others sure that he has it." Mrs. Knowles then cited the case of St. Paul. Johnson replied, "Yes, Madam; but here was a man inspired, a man who had been converted by supernatural interposition."[6] A related form of conversion is that of the mystics. Evelyn Underhill describes this type as usually occurring to people already notably devout, but the conversion itself is commonly a single and abrupt experience. The change that takes place is described as "a sudden, intense, and joyous perception of God immanent in the universe; of the divine beauty and unutterable power and splendour of that larger life in which the individual is immersed, and of a new life to be lived by the self in correspondence with this now dominant fact of existence."[7] While it is true, as Johnson observed, that the heart cannot be known, no one, I believe, has asserted that he was a mystic.

A second kind of conversion is the revivalistic phenomenon. It came into prominence, partly owing to the influence of the Moravians, among eighteenth-century Evangelicals, and, in more recent times, it is the object and often the product of revival meetings. This form of conversion involves a pattern of behavior that has particularly interested psychologists. William James, for instance, discusses it in *Varieties of Religious*

Experience, where he sees as its distinguishing mark the in-stantaneous nature of the experience. In this connection he quotes John Wesley, who, after consulting six hundred and fifty-two of his followers, found each affirming that his sense of liberation from sin was instantaneous. Wesley, though surprised by the unanimity of opinion, commented, "I cannot but be-lieve but that sanctification is commonly, if not always, an in-stantaneous work."[8]

Both the mystical and the Evangelical types of conversion may lead to ecstasy, but where the mystic rejoices in a sense of God's immanence and a feeling of oneness with him, the Evan-gelical is more likely to rejoice in a conviction of being freed from sin and in a personal assurance of salvation. According to psychologists, hysteria, self-suggestion, and other extra-re-ligious factors may be involved in conversion, but when a gen-uine religious motivation for the change exists, the Evangelical type is usually based on a belief in justifying faith. This doc-trine, so dear to the Puritans, asserts that man is saved by faith and faith alone. Though good works should follow the conver-sion, works in themselves are not a means of salvation. Faith, moreover, does not consist simply of "a belief of the revealed truths of religion" and "trust in God," as Johnson had defined the term in the *Dictionary.* Instead, faith is regarded as the sole avenue to grace and the sole means by which one may be justified or saved.

If the Evangelical type of conversion is often instantaneous, that is chiefly because the convert's belief in his sanctification emanates from within, and the experience is essentially a mat-ter of the heart rather than the head. Nevertheless, William James seems to have overstressed the importance of the spon-taneous nature of the act; other writers have asserted the change may occur as the culmination of an extended period of dissatisfaction and distress. More significant is the emotional basis of the experience, of which the instantaneousness seems to be only one attribute. In his comprehensive study of the subject, Ronald Knox sees enthusiasm, whether Catholic or Protestant, distinguished chiefly by the enthroning of inspiration and the rejection of reason in religion. The usual concomitants are: a belief that grace is something that must be felt, an emphasis on individual testimony, and a consequent denigration of theology. These characteristics, according to Knox, mark such diverse movements as Jansenism, Quietism, Quakerism, and Evangelicalism. In the mind of the ordinary Christian believer, he writes, "the two principles of reason and revelation are interlocked. . . . It is not so with the convert to enthusiasm. In his mind a sudden *coup d'état* has dethroned the speculative intellect altogether."[9]

It was this very issue that the Anglican Richard Hooker had dealt with in his attack on early Puritanism. Because the Puritans were inclined to think of man's intellect as too weak or depraved to reason about religion, they often regarded faith infused by grace as the only trustworthy monitor. This led to a rejection of theology and a dependence on inspiration. In opposing this emphasis, Hooker insists that reason is also influenced by grace, but what the Holy Spirit directs us to know through the intellect is generally clearer than the testimony asserted to come from within, because the operation of the Spirit in the soul is of a secret and often indiscernible nature. Without the aid of reason, Hooker observes, we cannot even understand Revelation. For the whole purpose of Scripture is to teach theology, which is the science of things divine, and no science can be learned without reason.[10]

Where did Johnson stand on this question? From what has been said earlier, one might surmise that as a lifelong student of theology and as a man of remarkable reasoning powers he would subscribe to Hooker's view. But the *Dictionary* supplies specific evidence of his agreement, as well as an indication of what he thought about the process of conversion. Under his definition of "faithless," he quotes a key sentence from Hooker's defense of reason as opposed to inspiration. The statement reads. "Whatever our hearts be to God and to his truth, believe we, or be we as yet *faithless,* for our conversion or confirmation, the force of natural reason is great."[11] This quotation strongly suggests that Johnson would be unsympathetic to any form of Christianity that rejected reason, or to any type of conversion based on justification by faith alone.

As we have mentioned, Johnson liked several of the Evangelicals, such as John Wesley and his sister Mrs. Hall. But he saw that justification by faith, as well as other teachings, linked the Evangelicals with the Puritans of the previous century. Consequently, in the *Dictionary* he defines "Methodist" as "one of a new kind of puritans lately arisen . . ." Although the term "inner light" had been chiefly associated with the Puritans, Johnson referred to some Methodists as pretending to be endowed with this "principle," which he denounced as "utterly incompatible with social or civil security."[12] A further identification of the two groups with each other is made in his *Life of Francis Cheynel.* In a discussion of the proselytizing activities of this Puritan preacher, Johnson interpolates the satiric comment: "We now observe, that the methodists, where they scatter their opinions, represent themselves, as preaching the gospel to unconverted nations; and enthusiasts of all kinds have been inclined to disguise their particular tenets with pompous appellations, and to imagine themselves the great instruments of salvation."[13]

Despite such unsympathetic comments, shortly before his death a rumor began to circulate to the effect that Johnson had himself been converted to the "particular tenets" of the Evangelical movement. Because I have discussed this report in detail in a separately published article,[14] I shall deal with it here as briefly as possible. The first reference to such a conversion, so far as I have been able to discover, is contained in a letter written by the poet William Cowper, dated May 10, 1784. Cowper was writing to John Newton, one of the leading Evangelical clergymen within the Establishment, and it appears that the poet was commenting on a report received from this correspondent. It further appears that Newton had passed on to Cowper something he had heard from the Moravian clergyman Benjamin Latrobe. Since all three of these men were Evangelicals, they would naturally have in mind a conversion based on justifying faith. Cowper, who had experienced this kind of conversion himself, certainly assumed that Johnson had been similarly inspired. In his letter to Newton he writes, "We rejoice in the account you give us of Dr. Johnson. His conversion will indeed be a singular proof of the omnipotence of grace." The next year, in his poetic "Epitaph on Dr. Johnson," Cowper speaks in similar terms when he alludes to Johnson as a man who crowned a notable career by at last attaining *faith* and thereby salvation.

While it is true that Latrobe knew Johnson in the final years of the latter's life, no evidence has been discovered as to what Latrobe may have told Newton.[15] The only written testimony related to the subject is a statement Latrobe's son, Christian Ignatius, wrote for a religious periodical forty-six years later. Repeating what he could remember after the lapse of several decades, he recalled his father's having said that Johnson had become more humble and pious in the months preceding his death, that he talked much of salvation through the Atonement of Christ, and that he died a true penitent with a sense of peace.

In 1834, a related report appeared in the *Memoirs of the Life and Correspondence of Hannah More,* edited by William Roberts. In this account Johnson is supposed to have expressed a desire at the approach of death to see a clergyman with whom he could discuss his spiritual state. Friends recommended Thomas Winstanley, Reader in Divinity at St. Paul's Cathedral. Johnson asked Hawkins, it was said, to dispatch a letter to him. Although poor health prevented the clergyman from visiting Johnson, in his reply he advised him not to worry about small failings, but to place his whole faith in "the lamb of God." Johnson was impressed by this advice, further correspondence ensued, and through Winstanley's letters and the conversations with Latrobe, it was asserted, Johnson was converted.

Hawkins never mentions Winstanley, and it may be doubted that any correspondence between the two took place. It is true, of course, that Evangelicals like Mrs. Hall and Latrobe visited Johnson. It is also clear that as death approached, his piety became more pronounced than ever. But it should be observed that the allusions to a conversion emanated chiefly among the Evangelicals, to whom conversion would have meant an awakening in some sense related to the doctrine of justifying faith. Furthermore, the Evangelicals, who were well known for their proselytizing activities, would be particularly pleased to be able to claim a great man as one of their flock. This characteristic was noted by a writer (possibly John Gibson Lockhart), following the publication of Roberts' *Memoirs of Hannah More*. After denouncing the report of Johnson's conversion as "a dream, a blunder, or more probably a bungling piece of quackery—a pious fraud," the author comments, "this attempt to persuade us that Dr. Johnson's mind was not made up as to the great fundamental doctrine of the Christian religion until it was forced on him *in extremis* by sectarian or Methodistical zeal, cannot redound to the credit of Mr. Roberts' understanding."[16]

Quite apart from their wishful thinking, however, the Evangelicals may have been led by certain details in the accounts of Johnson's death to believe he had been converted in their sense of the word. In addition to his own reference to a "late conversion," there was the incident that occurred at the making of his will. When John Hawkins asked if he would like to incorporate a statement signifying he was a member of the Established Church, Johnson said, "No!" Instead he seized the pen, and with the practised hand that had always excelled at composing a preface, he wrote a sentence that fittingly expressed his dying sentiments: "I commit to the infinite mercies of Almighty God my soul, polluted with many sins; but purified, I trust, with repentance and the death of Jesus Christ."[17] This reference to the propitiatory sacrifice was but one of many he made in the last weeks. William Windham reports that a few days before his death, "He insisted on the doctrine of an expiatory sacrifice as the condition without which there was no Christianity."[18] James Fordyce, a liberal Presbyterian clergyman who saw him in the closing period, attests that "he earnestly supplicated forgiveness through the merits of his Saviour alone."[19] And, as we have earlier shown, he exhorted Dr. Brocklesby to read Clarke, and when asked why, he replied because "he is fullest on the *propitiatory sacrifice*."

Because a strong personal conviction that Christ has atoned for one's sins was a main tenet of the religious revival, the Evangelicals probably interpreted Johnson's emphasis on this doctrine as a sign that he had been converted in the manner most of them had been. But the propitiatory sacrifice is at the core of all traditional Christianity. What the Evangelicals did was to dramatize its significance. Their converts were usually *awakened* to a sense of its personal implications, causing them to feel liberated from sin and justified by their faith. Johnson was not awakened in this sense. From what we have said earlier, his commitment to a firm belief in the vicarious nature of the sacrifice appears to have developed over a period of years, as the result of study, meditation, and reflection. While his attained acceptance of this doctrine probably gave him a greater measure of hope, he never achieved complete confidence in his salvation. Finally, as we have seen, the person who most influenced his whole-hearted acceptance of this doctrine was not Latrobe or any other Evangelical, but the rationalist Samuel Clarke, who described faith as a moral virtue, "always founded upon reason,"[20] and who was the kind of clergyman the Evangelicals would hardly consider a Christian.

What then did Johnson mean by "conversion" in his

prayer? He meant something quite different from either a mystical or an Evangelical type of conversion. He meant "conversion" in a third and common signification of the term, as it had been used by various Anglican writers. One of these was Bishop Thomas Wilson, a contemporary of Johnson. Wilson comments: "Christians should consider that repentance and conversion are not to be separated. The Spirit of God has joined them together in the text: 'Repent, and be converted, that your sins may be blotted out' and 'Repent, and turn to God, and do works meet for repentance' " (Acts 13:9; 26:20). In this sense, Wilson adds, repentance is a step to conversion, but it must be followed by amendment to be a true repentance; otherwise, "it is only repentance to be repented of."[21] It is interesting to note that Johnson had used the same expression of St. Paul in a conversation with Mrs. Knowles, when he observed that no one can be sure that his obedience has been sufficient "or that his repentance has not been such as to require being repented of."[22] There was nothing sudden or inspirational about the kind of change Wilson describes. Like William Law, and like Johnson himself, he believed that "a Christian's life is *a state of repentance,* in which he must always be getting the mastery over his corruptions, and labouring daily to grow better."[23]

Henry Hammond, the seventeenth-century divine, had much the same idea. As we have noted, in the *Dictionary* Johnson quotes Hammond's statement that repentance is "a change of mind or a conversion from sin to God. Not some one bare act of change, but a lasting durable state of new life which I told you was called also regeneration." Like other Anglican divines, Hammond was sceptical of the efficacy of a deathbed repentance or conversion, because such a change was likely to be too sudden to allow for the necessary "preparatives." These preparatives, he writes, consist of: (1) a sense of sin, produced by "pondering" its offense to God; (2) contrition which is lasting, "not one initial act of sorrow for sin past," and which is based on a love of God, not merely on fear; (3) confession of sin, first to God, and secondly to others, chiefly presbyters; (4) a firm resolution and vow to a new life, accompanied by an abjuring of former evil habits, a resigning of self to the will of God, and the performing of deeds of piety and charity.[24] Such a conversion, issuing as the result of protracted preparations, obviously differs from the inspirational kind, where there might be "initial" sorrow for sin accompanying the sense of justification, but where repentance and amendment would normally have to follow the conversion.

Hammond also explicitly asserts that conversion, as he sees it, is not to be associated with a belief in salvation by faith alone. While the sinner must have faith in God and in his promises, he writes, "faith, in whatever acceptation, is no proper efficient cause of justification." Ultimately man is saved, not by faith or even by repentance, but by Christ's sacrifice, which makes possible God's acceptance of man's inadequate and imperfect obedience and repentance. If a person is truly repentant, Hammond adds, God is reconciled with him. He is then given more grace, and if good use is made of it, justification will follow. But "good use" means the performance of works which are also necessary for salvation. Consequently it is possible for a sinner who truly believes to fail at salvation, if he omits or defers the works needed for justification.[25]

One sentence that Hammond writes in the course of this discussion is particularly signficant to our purpose, for Johnson quotes it in the *Dictionary* as a commentary on "justification." It reads: " 'Tis the consummation of that former act of faith by this latter or, in the words of St. Paul and St. James, the consummation of faith by charity and good works, that God accepteth in Christ to *justification,* and not the bare aptness of faith to bring forth works, if these works, by the fault of a rebellious infidel, will not be brought forth."[26] Because Johnson nowhere, so far as I know, supports a belief in justifying faith, his citation of Hammond's positive denial of the doctrine is important evidence of where he stood. It should be sufficient, in my mind, to refute a recent, unsupported statement that "the doctrine of justification by faith alone is the foundation of the whole edifice of Johnson's religion . . ."[27]

If Johnson meant the same thing by "conversion" as Hammond, namely, a profound spiritual change, effected by true repentance, amendment, and the performance of works, why did he pray, "accept my late conversion, enforce and accept my imperfect repentance?" Had he not for years in his prayers expressed sorrow for sin and asked for pardon? Had he not, besides being repentant, performed notable works of charity? Yes, but religion was no simple formula to Johnson. To one of his scrupulous conscience, to one who had been so deeply and lastingly impressed by the doctrine of Christian perfection, all his earlier endeavors seemed inadequate. As he examined his conscience in the last few years of life, he must have asked himself if he was truly contrite—if his sorrow for sin was not motivated merely by fear, rather than by the love of God. While there would have been comfort in the knowledge that Christ had performed a vicarious sacrifice that atoned for the weak efforts of mankind, his conscience may have been troubled by his "lateness" in being convinced of the extent of Christ's mercy. One thing that particularly disturbed him, as his letters show, was his resistance to the prospect of death and his failure thereby to reconcile himself to the will of God. In that connection he may have recalled Law's statement, "Whenever, therefore, you find yourself disposed to uneasiness or murmuring at anything that is the effect of God's providence over you, you must look upon yourself as denying either the wisdom or the goodness of God. For every complaint necessarily supposes this."[28]

Whatever his particular thoughts, a realization that his remaining time was brief led to an intensification of his piety. As Thomas Tyers observes, "He was all his life preparing himself for death: but particularly in the last stage of his asthma

and dropsy."²⁹ What special preparations he made and the way
he met death will be the concern of the remainder of this chapter.

During his last year or two Johnson asked his friends to pray
for him, and to those who knew him best he wrote candidly
about the state of his health and mind. In April, 1784, he con-
fided to John Taylor, "O, my Friend, the approach of Death
is very dreadful. I am afraid to think on that which I know, I
cannot avoid. It is vain to look round and round, for the help
which cannot be had. Yet we hope and hope, and fancy that
he who has lived to day may live to morrow. But let us learn to
derive our hope only from God."³⁰ Here one may detect a note
of self-admonition—as if the moralist who had written on the
vanity of wishing for long life had caught himself doing just
that; then, recalling his own counsels, he adds the reminder
that what is most important is the theological hope of salvation.

His feelings were determined, to some extent, by his physical
condition, but even more by the caprice of association or by
thinking repentantly about the past. In September, 1784, he
wrote John Ryland that his condition was improved, but
added: "From the retrospect of life when solitude, leisure, ac-
cident, or darkness turn my thoughts upon it, I shrink with
multiplicity of horrour. I look forward with less pain. Behind,
is wickedness and folly, before, is the hope of repentance, the
possibility of amendment, and the final hope of everlasting
mercy." No matter what his mood, in these late letters there is
almost always a note of hope. A month later he again addressed Ryland. Although he now reports being in a poor state
of health, he comments cheerfully, "My mind, however, is
calmer than in the beginning of the year, and I comfort myself with hopes of every kind, neither despairing of ease in this
world, nor of happiness in another."³¹

Thirty-five years earlier, in *The Vanity of Human Wishes,*

he had observed that hope and fear should find their proper objects in prayer. During his final eighteen months, besides engaging in meditation and devotions, he composed a distinct group of prayers—distinct from his others, because they are in the form of Latin verses; and different from his English prayers in that they are the reflections of one specifically engaged in preparing for death. Sir John Hawkins, the first editor to print these pieces, explains that "many were composed in those intervals of ease, which during his last illness he at times experienced, others, and those the greater number, were the employment of his thoughts, when, being retired to rest, the powers of sleep failed him, when the remission of pain became to him positive pleasure, and having no outward objects present to view, his ever-active imagination had liberty to wander through the boundless regions of fancy, and his reason to investigate the most important and sublime truths."[32] The reference to his mind wandering in the regions of fancy may be somewhat misleading. The poems are really the petitions of a humble Christian, asking pardon for his offenses and praying for reconciliation with God.

Despite their importance to an understanding of Johnson's religion, these Latin poems or prayers have, on the whole, been neglected. Apparently no prose translation of all of them has ever been published. Several, however, were translated into verse during the nineteenth century by the Reverend J. Henry. His effort is to be commended, but Johnson's Latin is not easy, and much of his personal tone is lost by attempting to put the compositions into English verse. The following will serve as an example of Henry's translations. The original, which begins with the salutation "Pater benigne," is one of several Latin compositions in which Johnson petitions that he may be sufficiently repentant to gain pardon for his sins.

> Parent benign! pity supreme exprest,
> Relieve, weighed down with many a woe my breast.
> Repentance give, and grant thy statute's power

> May me conduct through each eventful hour;
> With torch of sacred light the wanderer guide,
> And shield him round when many ills betide.
> Pardon to him who pardon asks extend,
> In holy joys of peace may pardon end.
> Thee, freed from sin and by no fear possess'd,
> May I exalt, with pure and tranquil breast.
> A suppliant low, I use a suppliant's art,
> For death of Christ these blessings now impart.[33]

The translation loses the spirit of the original chiefly in the last two lines. Anyone who knows Johnson will detect how alien to him is the clause, "I use a suppliant's art." His general dislike of religious poetry, of which we have already spoken, was based on his belief that verse was a too artful and therefore not a sincere means of addressing or praising the Deity. But one must not be too harsh on his translator. In this instance he ran into difficulty because he chose to translate into English couplets a poem that consisted of eleven lines. As a result he was forced to expand the last line into a couplet by adding material not in the original. Johnson's concluding line reads: "Mihi dona morte haec impetret Christus sua."

In view of Johnson's reservations about religious poetry, one may ask why he himself composed several Latin poems to express his religious feelings. In the first place, he probably did not intend originally that they should be published. Most of those to which a date is assigned were written in the last few years of his life. One of these is the four-line verse composed in June, 1783, on the occasion of his losing the power of speech. In this instance, as he explained to Mrs. Thrale, he wrote in Latin as a means of determining whether or not his mental powers were impaired. This was a matter of great concern with him. He also studied Dutch almost daily during the latter part of 1782 in order to test his mental alertness.[34] The same motive probably led him to compose many prayers in the form of Latin verses during the last few years of his life.

As the modern editors of Johnson's poems indicate, many of

the Latin verses are related to specific collects in the Book of Common Prayer. In the *Dictionary* Johnson defines a collect as "a short comprehensive prayer, used at the sacrament; any short prayer." Thus in form his Latin prayers resemble the liturgical prayers recited at public services. But the analogy between them may be overstressed. The chief resemblance is in the spirit and tone of these petitions. For even when the subject matter is similar, Johnson often adds something of his own. For example, let us compare one of his Latin poems with the collect to which it is related, that of the Twenty-first Sunday after Trinity. The collect reads: "Grant, we beseech thee, merciful Lord, to thy faithful people pardon and peace, that they may be cleansed from all their sins, and serve thee with a quiet mind; through Jesus Christ our Lord." Johnson's poem may be translated as follows: "Almighty Father, from thy undefiled heaven look down upon me, sorrowful and fearful, oppressed by dreadful crimes: Grant pardon and peace to me; grant that with a serene mind I may promptly do all things pleasing to you. Grant, Father, that the payment by which Christ atoned for the transgressions of all be paid for me, too."[35]

Though the two prayers are similar in petitioning for pardon and peace, Johnson's is distinctly his own. Particularly significant is the reference to the Atonement in the last two lines. As we have previously indicated, such references are rare in his English prayers, probably because during most of his life he had believed that Christ's sacrifice was more of an exemplary than a propitiatory nature. The change in his thinking is clearly marked in the last two years of his life. Nowhere does it appear so distinctly as in his Latin verses. Note, for example, how each of the following prayers concludes with an emphatic expression of his new belief that by the death on the Cross, Christ took the burden of sin from mankind.

The following is the translation of a prayer for which we have a specific date, January 18, 1784. "Greatest Father, illumine my breast with pure light, lest a gloomy anxiety afflict me. So foster in me the seeds of virtue, scattered with open hand, that a harvest filled with good may come forth. May joyful hope recur to my mind night and day; may sure faith be kindled in me by holy love. May sure faith forbid me to doubt, may joyful hope forbid me to fear, may holy love forbid me to wish evil to anyone. Grant me, Father, lest the rewards be offered in vain, always to cherish and love your laws. Grant these rewards to me, a sinner, by the blood wherewith, O Christ, you have atoned for peoples and generations."

This petition, with its stress on the vicarious sacrifice, was composed, it should be noted, before Johnson's remarkable recovery from the dropsy. A few days after that event, on February 27, 1784, he wrote another Latin prayer. Although it makes no specific mention of the improvement in his health, the verse is noteworthy for its serenity, for the strong note of hope, and particularly for the reference—the only one, I believe, in his writings—to the Beatific Vision. Translated, it reads: "My mind, why do you lament? A gentler hour will come for you, when you may look, rejoicing, upon the Father in highest majesty; Jesus appeased the divine wrath against the guilty; now there is for culprits repentance instead of punishment."

The serenity that marks this meditation is not always so evident in his other Latin verses. Nevertheless, they differ from his earlier English prayers. Several of the Latin poems, like his petitions in English, are penitential exercises in which he alludes to himself as a sinner, but in them he seldom mentions specific transgressions, and he seems less reluctant to use *"amor"* than he had been to employ the word "love" in relation to the Deity. Furthermore, the cry of anguish so prominent earlier is now muted by a stronger note of hope.

A similar stress on hope for salvation through Christ's sacrifice occurs in Johnson's final English prayer. In a clause immediately preceding the reference to a late conversion, he asks, "Grant, O Lord, that my whole hope and confidence may be in his merits and in thy mercy." Inasmuch as the two petitions are joined, the "lateness" for which he prays forgiveness might, although we cannot be certain of this, refer specifically to the lateness of his acquiring a firm belief in the vicarious nature of the sacrifice. In any event this belief, now strongly held, contributed in the last months of life to his hope that through even an "imperfect repentance" he might attain salvation.

The manner in which Johnson met death is described by various friends who visited him. During this time, two young clergymen, George Strahan and Samuel Hoole, served virtually as his private chaplains. Others who saw him frequently included John Hoole and his wife, the parents of the clergyman; Francesco Sastres, a young Catholic of Italian extraction; John Ryland; Sir John Hawkins; Bennet Langton; William Windham; and various physicians. Several of these wrote accounts of his terminal period. Others passed on information that Boswell was to use in his biography. This body of testimony shows that Johnson was principally concerned with preparations for making a good end. Though never eager to die, he did achieve a degree of resignation. Indeed, if he could have foreseen much earlier the manner in which he would expire, the circumstances we shall now detail might have done much to comfort him.

Surrounded by friends, he had time to put his house in order, to clear accounts, and, as a final act of charity, to use his situation as a warning to others to prepare for their own end. From his old friend Joshua Reynolds he exacted three promises—to forgive him a debt of thirty pounds, to read the Bible, and to forego painting on Sunday.[36] A similar concern for the spiritual state of Dr. Brocklesby prompted him to urge his physician to read Clarke on the propitiatory sacrifice. To Francesco Sastres, his young Catholic friend, he spoke gently, admonishing him to let his moribund state serve as a constant reminder of the brevity of life. He added: "I say nothing of your religion; for if you conscientiously keep it, I have little doubt but you may be saved; if you read the controversy, I think we have the right on our side; but if you do not read it, be not persuaded, from any worldly consideration, to alter the religion in which you were educated: change not, but from the conviction of reason."[37] This scarcely sounds like the voice of an Evangelical convert. The statement *is* in keeping with his remark to Mrs. Knowles on the wisdom of remaining in the church in which one is raised, and with the quotation he borrowed from Hooker, "for our conversion or confirmation, the force of natural reason is great."

Johnson's faculties, the loss of which he had dreaded most of his life, remained acute until the end. His will remained equally strong. When his doctors refused, because they thought it would be dangerous, to lance his swollen legs, Johnson performed this act himself. As a result, he suffered a loss of blood that may have hastened his death by a few hours. Whether it was done in the hope of relieving pain or of prolonging life, this impulsive measure was the deed of a determined but very ill man. He himself had once observed, as we have noted, that every indulgence, except impiety, must be allowed suffering humanity.

In keeping with his piety was another strong manifestation of his will. Several years earlier when his attempts to save Dr. Dodd from the gallows had failed and the forger's death appeared certain, Johnson advised that he should devote the short time that remained to reconciling himself to God. "To this end," he had written, "it will be proper to abstain totally from all liquors, and from other sensual indulgences, that his thoughts may be as clear and calm as his condition will allow."[38] The man who had thus instructed another how to die now followed the same course. When, in answer to his pressing inquiry, Dr. Brocklesby was forced to tell him nothing but a miracle could effect his recovery, Johnson promptly asserted: "Then I will take no more physick, not even my opiates; for I have prayed that I may render up my soul to God unclouded."

His fear of dying, though not completely vanquished, had sufficiently abated to allow him to make his will, to discuss funeral arrangements calmly, and to accept his coming demise with considerable resignation. According to Joshua Reynolds, ". . . he appeared to be quieter and more resigned." He asserted that "he had been a great sinner," but he found consolation in the belief that he had never given a bad example "by his writings nor to his friends."[39] Two weeks before his death he told Hawkins: "I had, very early in my life, the seeds of goodness in me: I had a love of virtue, and a reverence for religion; and these, I trust, have brought forth in me fruits meet for repentance; and, if I have repented as I ought, I am forgiven. I have, at times, entertained a loathing of sin and of myself, particularly at the beginning of this year, when I had the prospect of death before me; and this has not abated when my fears of death have been less; and, at those times, I have had such rays of hope shot into my soul, as have almost persuaded me, that I am in the state of reconciliation with God."[40]

In his sermons he had frequently warned against the danger of dying before there was time to perfect one's repentance. But, having known for nearly two years that his end was near, he had taken advantage of this period to read more in religious works, to meditate, and to pray. As a result, while not certain that he had done enough, he could say, "I think that I have now corrected all bad and vicious habits."[41] But if time had aided him to correct his failings, contrition for past trespasses seemed more important than ever. As he reviewed his life, he particularly dwelt upon the occasions when he had lacked forbearance. James Fordyce reports: "Then it was I heard him condemn, with holy self-abasement, the pride of understanding by which he had often trespassed against the laws of courteous demeanour, and forgotten the fallible condition of his nature. . . . How deep was the contrition which then penetrated his soul, in the remembrance of his sins."[42]

Having had time to meditate, to examine his conscience, and to repent, Johnson was able to take the Viaticum in a devout frame of mind. This solemn event occurred on December 5, eight days before his death. The Reverend George Strahan conducted the services, and several friends joined in taking the Sacrament. For this occasion Johnson composed two final prayers, one in English and the other in Latin. The English prayer is reproduced above on page 183. The Latin prayer may be translated as follows:

Greatest God, to whom the hidden interior of the heart lies open; whom no anxiety, no lust escapes; from whom the subtle craftiness of sinners keeps nothing secret; who, surveying all things, rulest all everywhere; by your divine inspiration cast out from our minds earthly uncleanliness, that there may reign within a holy love. And bring powerful eloquence to sluggish tongues, that your praise may sound continually from every mouth. May Christ be willing to have merited this for us by the blood wherewith he atoned for peoples and all generations.[43]

This prayer, though based on the collect for the Communion service, adds a plea for praising God and a specific allusion to the Atonement. Why, especially since the service read by Strahan contains several appropriate prayers, did Johnson elaborate on the collect? For one thing, December 5 was the Second Sunday in Advent and, as he would have known, the Epistle for that day emphasizes the importance of glorifying God. The reason for his adding the reference to the Atonement seems clear, in view of what has been said on that subject. But a comment of William Law may also be relevant. On the subject of prayer he observes: "It should be under the direction of some form, but not so tied down to it but that it may be free to take such new expressions as its present fervours happen to furnish it with, which sometimes are more affecting, and carry the soul more powerfully to God, than any expressions that were ever used before."[44] Johnson, it would appear, had learned this lesson extremely well.

Similarly, the counsels on perfection were much in John-son's mind in the last two years of life, as he strenuously en-gaged in perfecting his repentance. As Law's pupil, however, he knew spiritual perfection is a goal seldom, if ever, achieved. Consequently he prayed, ". . . enforce and accept my imper-fect repentance." A logician might interpose, if repentance and conversion were so closely related in his mind as we have indicated, then he must have considered his conversion as im-perfect also. Probably he did. In the British Museum there is a manuscript with various jottings made by his friend William Windham. These brief notes, R. W. Ketton-Cremer has sug-gested, were probably set down after a conversation Windham had with Johnson on December 10, 1784, just three days be-fore his death. Among other items the notes include a refer-ence to a sermon by Samuel Clarke and an assertion Johnson presumably made to the effect that there can be no morality without free will. There is also a statement, "Pray my late & imperfect conversion—my imperfect repentance."[45] Because this appears to be the only recorded instance, apart from the prayer of December 5, of Johnson's using "conversion" in rela-tion to his own spiritual state, it may serve as a source of fur-ther speculation. To me, however, the indication that he deemed both his repentance and conversion imperfect seems in complete accord with the character of a man, never pre-sumptuous, and always deeply conscious of the lofty ideal of Christian perfection.

Death—"kind Nature's signal for retreat"—was now at hand. In the many decades that had passed since Johnson first read *A Serious Call to a Devout and Holy Life,* he had experienced profound spiritual conflicts—blaming himself for broken reso-lutions, resolving to amend, but doubting that he was suffi-ciently contrite; loving the world and tugged by the flesh, but at times longing for the ascetic life; frequently swayed by pride, but more often governed by humility; reflecting on and at-tracted by Law's counsels on perfection, but only at the end of life trying strictly to follow them. His long struggle with the world, the flesh, and the devil was now over. "I have taken my viaticum," he said with a note of finality. "I hope I shall arrive safe at the end of my journey, and be accepted at last."[46]

One of the first printed tributes paid to Johnson after his demise was an obituary notice, presumably written by John Ryland, in the *Gentleman's Magazine:* "Dec. 13 A little before seven in the evening, without a pang, though long oppressed with a complication of dreadful maladies, the great and good Dr. Johnson, the pride of English literature, and of human nature. Religion has lost her sincerest votary, and her firmest friend; learning her greatest boast and ornament; Mankind their truest benefactor . . ."[47]

Two other comments are of particular interest, inasmuch as they have never heretofore been printed. Both are related to Johnson's posthumously published *Prayers and Meditations,* which, as we have noted, was harshly criticized. Nevertheless, certain of his friends held the work in high esteem. One of these was Samuel Hoole, the young clergyman who attended Johnson during his last days and shared in ministering to his spiritual needs. Even in his father's *Narrative* of this period, the younger Hoole remains a rather dim figure. Yet there is evidence that Johnson had left his mark on him, as he had on so many other associates. Thirteen years later, in a letter addressed to his father-in-law, Arthur Young, Samuel Hoole comments: "Some have conjectured that there is an intermediate state of partial happiness and suffering. Johnson was of this opinion, as appears from his Prayers and Meditations, in which he entreats both for his wife and Mr. Thrale, that God would give them what is best for them in their present state. If you have not that book, allow me to commend it to you. I read a page of it every day . . ."[48]

The other statement is by Edmond Malone, who had first

met Johnson in 1764. Besides being a member of the Club, he was a distinguished scholar, the editor of Shakespeare and Dryden, and the person from whom Boswell probably received most assistance in writing his *Life of Johnson*. Malone's observations on the *Prayers and Meditations* and on the controversy about that book appear, opposite the title page, in his personal copy. Preceding his own statement are two quotations that Malone inserted from the Psalms as they are given in the Church of England psalter:

Unto thee have I cryed, O Lord, and early shall my prayer come before thee. . . . I am in misery, and like unto him that is at the point to die: *even from my youth up, thy terrours have I suffered with a troubled mind.*

Psalm 88

I wept and chastened myself with fasting, and that was turned to my reproof—I put on sackcloth also, and they jested upon me.

Psalm 69

Then follows Malone's own poignant summation:

The Meditations of this devout and excellent man verified the words of the Psalmist, for all the Scoffers endeavoured to turn them into ridicule; but to no purpose: for they will ever remain an incontestible proof of Johnson's tenderness of heart, piety, and virtue.

E. Malone

I might have concluded at this point with Malone's terse comment, but in a volume about Johnson it seems appropriate that he should have the last word. One of his earliest biographies was a life of Hermann Boerhaave, the eminent Dutch physician and scientist. In addition to being extremely learned, Boerhaave was also remarkably devout. This side of his character Johnson dwells upon with admiration, even going so far as to urge emulation of his noble example. Boerhaave had many virtues, but what particularly impressed his biographer was the physician's constant awareness of his own finite nature and his humility in relation to the Infinite. Because a similar consciousness was basic to Johnson's faith, what he wrote about Boerhaave might well serve as his own epitaph.

His piety, and a religious sense of his dependance on God, was the basis of all his virtues, and the principle of his whole conduct. He was too sensible of his weakness to ascribe any thing to himself, or to conceive that he could subdue passion, or withstand temptation, by his own natural power; he attributed every good thought, and every laudable action, to the father of goodness. . . . He worshipped God as he is in himself, without attempting to inquire into his nature. He desired only to think of God, what God knows of himself. There he stopped, lest, by indulging his own ideas, he should form a deity from his own imagination, and sin by falling down before him. To the will of God he paid an absolute submission, without endeavouring to discover the reason of his determinations; and this he accounted the first and most inviolable duty of a christian. When he heard of a criminal condemned to die, he used to think: Who can tell whether this man is not better than I? or, if I am better, it is not to be ascribed to myself, but to the goodness of God.[49]

APPENDIX · NOTES · INDEX

APPENDIX
The Dating of Johnson's Sermons

The following paragraphs are concerned with a method based on one aspect of style, of assigning Johnson's undated sermons to certain periods of his career. The material is particularly related to the discussion of chronology in Chapter V of this book.

Several years ago, in an objective study of Johnson's writing, Warner Taylor produced convincing evidence of distinctive differences between his earlier and his later prose ("Prose Style of Samuel Johnson," *Studies by Members of the Department of English, University of Wisconsin,* No. 2, 1918, pp. 22–56). In general, as Johnson advanced in years, his style grew simpler. This point is further substantiated in the more comprehensive work of William K. Wimsatt, Jr. (*The Prose Style of Samuel Johnson,* New Haven, 1941). Especially noteworthy is the fact that, in the works studied, the length of Johnson's sentences decreased remarkably as he grew older. For example, in the *Rambler* essays, published between 1750 and 1752, the average length of the sentences is 43.1 words; in the major *Lives of the Poets,* published between 1779 and 1781, the average length is 30.1 words. There is also an indication that Johnson consciously abbreviated his sentences during his later period, for remaining proof-sheets of his *Life of Pope* show he sometimes broke up longer sentences when making corrections, in order to improve the style (F. W. Hilles, "The Making of *The Life of Pope,*" *New Light on Dr. Johnson* [New Haven, 1959], p. 283).

According to Taylor, the pivotal period for the change occurred about 1755. This conclusion is based on evidence that between 1750–52, the time of the *Rambler* essays, and 1758–60, the time of the *Idler* essays, sentence length diminished from an average of 43.1 words to an average of 33.4. Taylor did not include the sermons in his study, but if such a distinct and measurable change is revealed in Johnson's other prose, then the sermons merit a similar scrutiny.

Fortunately we know the time of composition for three of the sermons. The one delivered by Aston was written in 1745, the one on Mrs. Johnson's death, in 1752, and *The Convict's Address,* in 1777. Word-counting is tedious business, but while confined to a New Hampshire farmhouse during a three-day Northeaster, I began a tally of these three sermons. The experiment produced rather striking results. In the Aston sermon the average sentence length is 64 words; in the sermon on Mrs. Johnson's death, 56.4 words; in *The Convict's Address,* 25.8 words. Thus two sermons composed when Johnson was in middle life are characterized by extremely long sentences, somewhat longer even than those in the *Rambler.* On the other hand, in a sermon written in 1777, the average length of the sentences has diminished to less than half, but corresponds rather closely with the 30.1 average of the major *Lives of the Poets.* Hence it would appear that so far as sentence length is concerned, Johnson's sermons reflect the same change that occurred in his other prose.

This test, when applied to the undated sermons, may, I believe, serve to indicate, not the specific year of composition, but the general period in which Johnson wrote them. I favor the opinion that those with an average of more than 45 words to a sentence may be attributed to the period before 1755. Apart from sentence length, the substance of these sermons lends support to this theory. Many of them, like the one written for Aston, were apparently composed for a special occasion or for delivery before a special group. Sermon IV (in the 1825 edition), with an average sentence length of 50.7 words, may have been delivered, as we indicate in Chapter V, before supporters of a charity school at Bath. Sermon XIX, averaging 50.3 words to a sentence, and also dealing with charity, may, as James L. Clifford suggests, be the sermon John Taylor preached in 1745 for the benefit of one hundred twenty children of Tower Ward, London (Introduction to *A Sermon Preached at the Cathedral Church of Saint Paul,* Augustan Reprint Society, No. 50, 1955). Sermon VIII, with an average sentence length of 49 words, is especially concerned with "the dangers which men of learning may incur," a topic, one might infer, intended for a special group of listeners, perhaps a college gathering or an assembly of professional men. Thus these sermons, all having, on the average, a high word count in their sentences, were probably works Johnson was commissioned to write for particular occasions, at a time in his career when, because of poverty, he would have welcomed the opportunity to earn two guineas.

It is difficult, if not impossible, to ascribe sermons having a medium sentence length to a specific time. Although Warner Taylor found the pivotal period for the change from longer to shorter sentences occurring about 1755, there appears to be no such clearly defined pivotal period for the sermons. The most that can be inferred is that those with a remarkably high average in number of words per sentence probably belong to the period before 1755. Those with a particularly short average sentence length, corresponding with the briefer sentences in *The Convict's Address* and in the major *Lives of the Poets,* probably belong to the last ten years or so of Johnson's life. Nevertheless, I am aware that this system should be employed with caution. It seems helpful chiefly as an ancillary means of dating the sermons, to be used in relation to their substance and to whatever other evidence may exist for assigning them to a particular period. In the main, this is the way I have considered the factor of sentence length in my discussion of chronology in Chapter V.

Two further points should be made in connection with the methods I have followed in compiling figures for the average sentence length of particular sermons. First, for the collected sermons I have used the text of the first edition: *Sermons on Different Subjects, Left for Publication by John Taylor* (2 vols.; London, 1788 and 1789). Secondly, because I am principally concerned with style as related to chronology, my figures are based solely on the indicated sentence length. That is, I have considered a sentence as a unit beginning with a capital letter and ending with a period. I have counted all sentences except: (1) entire sentences enclosed in quotation marks, (2) those in enumerative sections in which Johnson lists points he will treat in the remainder of the sermon (omitted because they sometimes include sentence fragments), (3) those in *The Convict's Address* appearing in paragraphs that, according to Boswell, were composed by Dodd.

NOTES

Abbreviations and Short Titles

Boswell   *Boswell's Life of Johnson,* ed. George Birkbeck Hill and L. F. Powell, 6 vols., Oxford, 1934–50.

Diaries   *Samuel Johnson: Diaries, Prayers, and Annals,* ed. E. L. McAdam, Jr., with Donald and Mary Hyde, New Haven, 1958.

ELH   *Journal of English Literary History.*

GM   *Gentleman's Magazine.*

Hawkins   Sir John Hawkins, *The Life of Samuel Johnson, LL.D.,* 2d ed., London, 1787.

JEGP   *Journal of English and Germanic Philology.*

Letters   *The Letters of Samuel Johnson,* ed. R. W. Chapman, 3 vols., Oxford, 1952.

Miscellanies   *Johnsonian Miscellanies,* ed. George Birkbeck Hill, 2 vols., New York, 1897.

MP   *Modern Philology.*

PMLA   *Publications of the Modern Language Association of America.*

Poems   *The Poems of Samuel Johnson,* ed. David Nichol Smith and Edward L. McAdam, Oxford, 1951.

PQ   *Philological Quarterly.*

Thraliana   *Thraliana,* ed. Katharine C. Balderston, 2d ed., 2 vols., Oxford, 1951.

Works   *The Works of Samuel Johnson, LL.D.,* 9 vols., Oxford, 1825.

Introduction

1   "Life of the Author," *A Commentary, with Notes on the Four Evangelists,* by Zachary Pearce (2 vols.; London, 1777), I, xxxvii.

2   Hawkins, p. 601, note.

3   *The Works of Jeremy Bentham,* ed. John Bowring (11 vols.; Edinburgh, 1843), VII, 210.

4   James L. Clifford, *Young Sam Johnson* (New York, 1955), p.

42. While it is not completely certain that Johnson was present when the near-panic occurred, he later made the following comment on his reactions to the closing of St. Mary's Church for repairs: "The church at Lichfield, in which we had a seat, wanted reparation, so I was to go and find a seat in other churches; and having bad eyes, and being awkward about this, I used to go and read in the fields on Sunday. This habit continued till my fourteenth year; and still I find a great reluctance to go to church."—Boswell, I, 67.

5 William Law, *A Serious Call to a Devout and Holy Life,* ed. J. H. Overton (London, 1898), p. 5.

6 Boswell, II, 173.

7 *Miscellanies,* II, 319.

I. Johnson and William Law

1 R. I. and Samuel Wilberforce, *Life of William Wilberforce* (5 vols.; London, 1838), V, 339.

2 Boswell, III, 247-48; IV, 98, 226, 295; V, 351.

3 *Sale Catalogue of Dr. Johnson's Library* (privately printed by A. Edward Newton, 1925).

4 Boswell, I, 68–69.

5 Katharine C. Balderston, "Doctor Johnson and William Law," *PMLA* (Sept., 1960), 382–94; "Dr. Johnson's Use of William Law in the Dictionary," *PQ* (July, 1960), 379–88. Miss Balderston shows many analogies between Law's and Johnson's views, and provides convincing evidence of Law's influence, but I disagree with some of her conclusions. In my opinion, Johnson's sense of charity *was* basically the same as Law's; also, while Johnson never wholeheartedly followed Law's counsels on perfection, I think it erroneous to say: "Law's perfectionism was particularly repugnant to Johnson" (p. 393).

6 William Law, *A Practical Treatise Upon Christian Perfection* (Portsmouth, N.H., 1822), p. 15. For more recent works on Christian perfection, see R. Newton Flew, *The Idea of Perfection in Christian Theology* (Oxford, 1934), and R. Garrigou–La Grange, *Christian Perfection and Contemplation* (London, 1937).

7 *Letters,* I, 83.

8 Boswell, II, 122. Besides the genuine hortatory appeal of *A Serious Call,* I suspect that Johnson was particularly disposed at the time he first examined it to be impressed by such a work.

During the course of his life he read many other persuasives to a devout and holy life, but none seems to have taken such a firm hold on him as Law's book. In his childhood, his mother made him read *The Whole Duty of Man*. He rebelled and said he got little instruction from it, though late in life he returned to it (Boswell, I, 67, 527). Another book with which he was very familiar, as numerous quotations in the *Dictionary* show, was *Causes of the Decay of Piety*. This anonymous work, like *The Whole Duty of Man*, is sometimes attributed to Richard Allestree. Johnson was also familiar with such persuasives to piety as Jeremy Taylor's *Golden Grove* and his *Rules and Exercises of Holy Living and Dying*, *The Imitation of Christ* by Thomas à Kempis, and various exhortations by Richard Baxter.

9   William Law, *A Serious Call to a Devout and Holy Life,* ed. J. H. Overton (London, 1898), p. 6.

10   *Ibid.,* pp. 143–46.

11   *Works,* VI, 72–73.

12   *Diaries,* pp. 56–57.

13   For the Latin text, see *Poems,* p. 205.

14   Boswell, I, 68–69.

15   *Diaries,* p. 26.

16   George Every, *The High Church Party, 1688–1718* (London, 1956), pp. 169 ff.

17   *Practical Treatise,* p. 147.

18   *Miscellanies,* I, 209.

19   *A Demonstration of the Gross and Fundamental Errors of a Late Book* (London, 1769), p. 109 and *passim.* Also *Serious Call,* p. 268, n.4. Law's belief in the Real Presence probably did not conform to the Roman Catholic doctrine of transubstantiation. Many Nonjurors, though rejecting the belief that the Body and Blood of Christ are corporeally present in the Eucharist, held that, by the power of the Holy Spirit, the elements were mysteriously transformed in the communicant into the Body and Blood. C. W. Dugmore, *Eucharistic Doctrine in England from Hooker to Waterland* (London, 1942), pp. 144–45, 163–67.

20   *Practical Treatise,* pp. 273, 280; *Serious Call,* p. 256.

21   *Serious Call,* pp. 156 ff.

22   *Ibid.,* p. 153.

23   In his prayers Johnson almost always employs "Holy Spirit" in preference to "Holy Ghost." In his sermons he uses both terms with about the same frequency. Curiously he does not list "Holy

Spirit" in his *Dictionary,* though he has definitions for the Third Person of the Trinity under both "Ghost" and "Holy Ghost."

24 *Diaries,* p. 43.

25 *Practical Treatise,* pp. 19, 186, 197–98.

26 Robert Nelson, *A Companion for the Festivals and Fasts of the Church of England* (London, 1807), pp. 499 ff. Jeremy Taylor, like William Law, recommends a daily examination of conscience in *The Golden Grove.* In a section labeled "Agenda" he also gives advice on early rising, fasting, and meditation. Though the substance is similar to Law's, Taylor's short precepts lack the hortatory note of *A Serious Call.* Among other popular manuals of piety was *A Companion to the Altar,* which, though published anonymously, is attributed to William Vickers. This little volume appeared in numerous editions during the eighteenth century. It is of particular interest inasmuch as one section is entitled "Prayers and Meditations Preparative to a Sacramental Preparation." Besides having a title similar to that given to Johnson's private book of devotions, this part of the volume contains a series of questions to assist the penitent in an examination of conscience.

27 *Serious Call,* pp. 284 ff.

28 *Ibid.,* p. 293.

29 Hawkins, p. 563.

30 Johnson's stress on using one's talents is discussed in a penetrating article by E. A. Bloom, "Johnson's Divided Self," *University of Toronto Quarterly,* XXXI (Oct., 1961), 42–52.

31 *Miscellanies,* I, 456.

II. *Johnson and Samuel Clarke*

1 *Sale Catalogue of Dr. Johnson's Library* (privately printed by A. Edward Newton, 1925).

2 "Anecdotes by William Seward," *Miscellanies,* II, 305.

3 Aleyn L. Reade, *Johnsonian Gleanings* (11 vols.; London, 1939), IX, 99.

4 *GM,* LVIII (Jan., 1788), 39.

5 Leslie Stephen, *History of English Thought in the Eighteenth Century* (2 vols.; New York, 1949), I, 129.

6 Roland N. Stromberg, *Religious Liberalism in Eighteenth-Century England.* (Oxford, 1954), pp. 44–45.

7 George Every, *The High Church Party, 1688–1718* (London, 1956), p. 154.

8   Boswell, III, 248, n. 2; Norman Sykes, *From Sheldon to Secker* (Cambridge, 1959), p. 166.

9   Stephen, *History of English Thought,* I, 119, 129.

10   Mark Pattison, "Religious Thought in England," *Essays* (2 vols.; Oxford, 1889), II, 55–56.

11   Clarke's sermon, "Of Faith in God." Clarke's sermons were published in numerous editions. Today even the largest American libraries are likely to have only broken sets, with volumes from different editions. For the most part I have consulted *Sermons,* 3d edition, corrected (10 vols.; London, 1732), but I have also drawn material from other editions. Because the numbering of the sermons and the pagination differ according to the set, when quoting Clarke I refer merely to the particular sermon by title.

12   First sermon entitled "Of the Unity of God."

13   *Discourses Concerning the Unchangeable Obligation of Natural Religion and the Truth and Certainty of Christian Revelation* (6th ed.; London, 1724), p. 39; see also James E. Le Rossignol, *The Ethical Philosophy of Samuel Clarke* (Leipzig, 1892).

14   Basil Willey, *The Eighteenth Century Background* (London, 1949), pp. 59–60.

15   *Discourses,* p. 43.

16   Stephen, *History of English Thought,* I, 124, 129.

17   Quoted by Stromberg, *Religious Liberalism in Eighteenth-Century England,* p. 10.

18   Ernest C. Mossner, *The Life of David Hume* (Austin, Texas, 1954), p. 597.

19   Boswell, IV, 416, n. 2.

20   Richard Cumberland, *A Treatise of the Laws of Nature,* trans. John Maxwell (London, 1727), p. 189.

21   *Discourses,* p. 29.

22   *Miscellanies,* II, 305.

23   Boswell, IV, 31, n. 1.

24   Boswell, III, 248.

25   "Of the Duty of Prayer" and the second sermon on "Of the Catholic Church of Christ."

26   The first of three sermons entitled "Of the Grace of God."

27   For further comparisons of Johnson and Clarke on the Eucharist, see Chapter V.

28   "Dr. Johnson as a Churchman," *Church Quarterly Review,* CLVI (Oct.–Dec., 1955), 376.

29   "Narrative of John Hoole," *Miscellanies,* II, 156.

III. The Atonement

1   William Law, *A Serious Call to a Devout and Holy Life,* ed. J. H. Overton (London, 1898), p. 196.
2   *Selected Mystical Writings of William Law,* ed. Stephen Hobhouse (London, 1938), pp. 297–98.
3   John Wesley, "An Extract of a Letter to the Reverend Mr. Law," *Works* (32 vols.; Bristol, 1773), XIX, 182 ff. See also J. B. Green, *John Wesley and William Law* (London, 1945).
4   Boswell, I, 68, n. 3; V, 89; *Miscellanies,* II, 297.
5   *Boswell's Journal of a Tour to the Hebrides,* ed. Frederick A. Pottle and Charles H. Bennett (New York, 1936), pp. 63–64. In a context in which Johnson appears to be rejecting the idea of a vicarious atonement, it seems strange that he should say Christ's sacrifice "might operate even in favour of those who never heard of it," but he may have been referring to Abraham and other Old Testament patriarchs, born before Christ.
6   Boswell's exegesis is not completely satisfactory, since his image of "a sun placed to show light to men" can hardly be applicable to those who never heard of the sacrifice. He seemed to realize this himself, for he commented further: "There is, however, more in it than merely giving light—'a light to lighten the Gentiles.' I must think of it at leisure and with attention."
7   V. J. Brook, "The Atonement in Reformation Theology," *The Atonement in History and in Life,* ed. L. W. Grensted (New York, 1929), p. 238.
8   Boswell, IV, 124–25.
9   *Diaries,* pp. 258–60.
10 Boswell, V, 88, n. 2.
11 *Christian Observer,* XXVIII (Jan.–March, 1828), 32, 178.
12 *Christian Observer,* XXVII (Oct., 1827), 587–91.
13 Samuel Clarke, "How Christ Has Given Us the Victory Over Death" and "The Necessity of Holiness," *Sermons* (3d ed.; 10 vols.; London, 1732).
14 *Miscellanies,* II, 123.
15 *Diaries,* pp. 105, 122, 129, 132, 155.
16 Boswell, IV, 286, n. 3.
17 *Thraliana,* I, 183.
18 *Memoirs of the Life and Correspondence of Hannah More,* ed. William Roberts (2 vols.; New York, 1837), I, 222.
19 Boswell, IV, 416.

IV. Repentance

1 *Doctrine in the Church of England: The Report of the Commission on Christian Doctrine Appointed by the Archbishops of Canterbury and York in 1922* (London, 1957), pp. 184–98.
2 E. J. Mahoney, *Sin and Repentance* (London, 1928), pp. 43 ff.; Gordon J. Spykman, *Attrition and Contrition at the Council of Trent* (Kampen, 1955), pp. 228 ff.
3 *Doctrine in the Church of England*, p. 25.
4 J. Goodman, *The Penitent Pardon'd* (London, 1700), p. 218.
5 Henry Hammond, *A Practical Catechism* (London, 1655), p. 71.
6 William Nicholson, *An Exposition of the Catechism of the Church of England* (Oxford, 1842), pp. 173, 192 ff.
7 Gilbert Burnet, *An Exposition of the XXXIX Articles of the Church of England* (Oxford, 1814), p. 366.
8 *Ibid.*, p. 378.
9 Jeremy Taylor, "The Doctrine and Practice of Repentance," *Works* (15 vols.; London, 1828), IX, 239–40.
10 Hammond, *A Practical Catechism*, pp. 77–79.
11 Boswell, IV, 373; *Miscellanies*, II, 427.
12 Katharine C. Balderston, "Johnson's Vile Melancholy," *The Age of Johnson, Essays Presented to Chauncey Brewster Tinker* (New Haven, 1949). For evidence of Johnson's strong sexual drives and for a well-balanced discussion of his sense of guilt about them, see James L. Clifford, *Young Sam Johnson* (New York, 1955), pp. 312–17.
13 Boswell, III, 294–95.
14 Sermon, "Of the Necessity of Holiness," *Sermons* (3d ed.; 10 vols.; London, 1732).
15 Laetitia Hawkins, *Memoirs, Anecdotes, Facts, and Opinions* (2 vols.; London, 1824), I, 188.
16 W. B. C. Watkins, *Perilous Balance* (Princeton, 1939), p. 55.
17 *Thraliana*, I, 191.
18 Sermon XIII.
19 Goodman, *The Penitent Pardon'd*, p. 247; Hammond, *A Practical Catechism*, pp. 72 ff.; Burnet, *An Exposition of the XXXIX Articles*, p. 379; Daniel Waterland, *Sermons* (2 vols.; London, 1747), I, 429.
20 *GM*, LIII (March, 1783), 227–28.
21 Hammond, *A Practical Catechism*, pp. 72–74.

22 *The Convict's Address to His Unhappy Brethren,* (2d ed.; London, 1777), pp. 15–16.
23 In my opinion, based on a test of sentence length, Sermon II was written much earlier than *The Convict's Address.* See the Appendix.
24 *The Convict's Address,* p. 9.
25 Boswell, IV, 212.
26 *Diaries,* pp. 368–69.

V. *Johnson's Sermons*

1 Thomas Taylor, *A Life of John Taylor* (London, [1910]), p. 18.
2 *Letters,* III, 171; *Monthly Review,* LXXX (Dec., 1788), 528–30.
3 Boswell, III, 506–7; Laetitia Hawkins, *Memoirs, Anecdotes, Facts, and Opinions* (2 vols.; London, 1824), I, 163.
4 A discussion of Sermon XXI, which Hagstrum doubts is by Johnson, appears later in this chapter. James Gray believes that certain other sermons represent a degree of collaboration, in which Johnson supplied the superstructure and argument for a framework at least partly suggested by Taylor. James Gray, "Dr. Johnson and the King of Ashbourne," *University of Tortonto Quarterly,* XXIII (April, 1954), 242–54.
5 *Letters,* II, 400.
6 Boswell, III, 506–7; V, 67.
7 Boswell, III, 142.
8 Boswell, V, 483–84. There is also at the Yale University Library a manuscript sermon which may, at least in part, be Johnson's composition. Like Sermon XXIV in the *Works,* it is concerned with the reciprocal obligations of governors and those governed. For this point and for various other observations in this chapter I am indebted to Jean Hagstrum, "The Sermons of Samuel Johnson," Unpublished dissertation, Yale University, 1941.
9 *The New Bath Guide* (Bath, 1789), p. 39.
10 Jean Hagstrum, "The Sermons of Samuel Johnson," *MP,* XL (Feb., 1943), 255–66. In his unpublished dissertation (p. 51) Hagstrum argues, as seems likely, that the biblical texts on which the sermons were based may be related to the celebration of particular feast or fast days, or to certain Sundays in the calendar of the Established Church. For instance, the text of Sermon VIII, "Be not wise in your own conceits" (Rom.

12:16), appears in the Epistle for the Third Sunday after the Epiphany.

11   *GM*, XLVII (Sept., 1774), 450.

12   Katharine C. Balderston, "Doctor Johnson and William Law," *PMLA*, LXXV (Sept., 1960), 382–94.

13   *The Christian Morals* (3d ed.; London, 1761), p. 32.

14   *The Imitation of Christ*, ed. Edward J. Klein (New York, 1943), Bk. I, Ch. xiv.

15   See above, note 12.

16   The present owner of Malone's copy of *Prayers and Meditations* is W. R. Batty, Esq., of Southport, Lancashire, who has kindly allowed me to transcribe the notations and to use them in this volume.

17   To this transcript of Johnson's notes Malone adds the following comment: "See two excellent prayers, one to be used at the holy table, and the other at departure or at home; both founded on the foregoing notations:—pp. 206, 207, ante. In another prayer, p. 212, he has shortly summed up the great ends of the Eucharist: 'Let the commemoration of the sufferings and death of thy son, which I am now by thy favour once more permitted to make: fill me with *faith, hope* and *charity*.' " (The page references are to the text of the first edition of *Prayers and Meditations*.)

18   Numbered VIII, IX, X, XI, in Volume III of the 1756 edition of Clarke's *Sermons* (8 vols.; London).

19   *Sermons* (1756 ed.), Vol. III.

20   "The Sermons of Samuel Johnson," *MP*, XL, 260. It may be noted, however, that one passage in Sermon XXI seems to echo a clause in one of the *Rambler* essays. *Cf. Rambler* 149: "No depravity of the mind has been more frequently or more justly censured than ingratitude . . ." and Sermon XXI (*Works*, IX, 486): "Ingratitude among men hath in every age, and every region of the earth, been an object of general detestation, and universally accounted a glaring indication of depravity of heart."

21   *Papers Written by Dr. Johnson and Dr. Dodd in 1777*, ed. R. W. Chapman (Oxford, 1926), p. 17, The comment appears on a separate scrap, possibly in the hand of Edmund Allen, who served as an intermediary between Johnson and Dodd. It is captioned, "Wrote by Dr. J. as P.S. to Dr. Dodd's Convict's Address."

VI. *Johnson's Sense of Charity*

1 Boswell, III, 333.
2 That the charitable impulse was not lacking in the preceding centuries has been demonstrated in two important studies by W. K. Jordan: *Philanthropy in England, 1480–1660* (London, 1959) and *The Charities of London, 1480–1660* (London, 1960). In these works it is shown that many individuals, especially among the class of merchant princes, gave considerable sums for the relief of the poor, the endowment of schools, and other charitable purposes. During the Tudor and Stuart periods, however, individual benefactions were commonly made in the form of legacies, without public solicitation. What was relatively new in the eighteenth century, as Johnson indicates, was the development of organized charities that made public appeals on behalf of particular institutions and to which even those of moderate means contributed.
3 See, for instance, W. S. Lewis, *Private Charity in England, 1747–1757* (New Haven, 1938).
4 Boswell, III, 401.
5 Cecil A. Moore, "Shaftesbury and the Ethical Poets," *Backgrounds of English Literature* (Minneapolis, 1953), and Robert Voitle, "Shaftesbury's Moral Sense," *Studies in Philology,* LII (Jan., 1958), 17–38.
6 R. S. Crane, "Suggestions Toward a Genealogy of the 'Man of Feeling,'" *ELH,* I (Dec., 1934), 205–30. In this article, though Crane is acutely aware of the complex strands of benevolence, he is chiefly concerned with tracing its origins before Shaftesbury.
7 Cited by Moore, "Shaftesbury and the Ethical Poets," *Backgrounds of English Literature,* p. 51. It should be noted that "benevolence" meant different things to different people. To Boswell it was sometimes the equivalent of "affability." In his *Journal* he says both he and Bennet Langton complained that Johnson "was deficient in active benevolence; for instance, we could not mention anyone whom he had introduced to another." —*Boswell for the Defense,* ed. W. K. Wimsatt and F. A. Pottle (London, 1960), p. 132.
8 *Miscellanies,* I, 441.
9 Boswell, V, 211; I, 443; V, 211, n. 3; III, 48.
10 Robert Voitle, *Samuel Johnson the Moralist* (Cambridge, Mass.,

1961), p. 21. This book deals with much of the material discussed in the current chapter, though often from a different point of view, and with different conclusions reached. While the author sees religion as a factor in Johnson's "altruism," in my opinion he gives too much credit to Richard Cumberland for shaping Johnson's sense of charity, and not enough to Christian tradition or to William Law.

11 William Law, *A Serious Call to a Devout and Holy Life,* ed. J. H. Overton (London, 1898), p. 243. Samuel Clarke discussed charity both as a Christian virtue and as a native impulse in man. See his two sermons, "Of the Virtue of Charity" and "The Great Duty of Universal Love and Charity."

12 R. A. Knox, *Enthusiasm* (Oxford, 1957), pp. 580, 590.

13 M. Dorothy George, *England in Transition* (London, 1931) pp. 213 ff.

14 Boswell, II, 390 and 130.

15 Boswell, IV, 3.

16 Boswell, II, 119.

17 *Miscellanies,* I, 219; II 251 and 168–69.

18 *Miscellanies,* I, 204, II, 393.

19 Boswell, II, 250–51; V, 373.

20 Hawkins, p. 400.

21 Boswell, III, 124–25.

22 Henry Hervey Aston, *A Sermon Preached at the Cathedral Church of Saint Paul* (1745) [attributed to Samuel Johnson].

23 *Works,* VI, 148–49.

24 *Miscellanies,* II, 370.

25 Maurice J. Quinlan, "Dr. Franklin Meets Dr. Johnson," *New Light on Dr. Johnson,* ed. F. W. Hilles (New Haven, 1959).

26 For discussions of philanthropy in the eighteenth century, see Benjamin K. Gray, *A History of English Philanthropy* (London, 1905); John Hutchins, *Jonas Hanway, 1712–1786* (London, 1940); Betsy Rodgers, *Cloak of Charity* (London, [1949]).

27 Boswell, III, Appendix D.

28 Hawkins, p. 413.

29 Hawkins, pp. 400, 408.

30 *The Percy Letters,* ed. David N. Smith and Cleanth Brooks (Baton Rouge, La., 1946), pp. 84–86 (Correspondence of Thomas Percy and Richard Farmer).

31 *Portraits by Sir Joshua Reynolds,* ed. Frederick W. Hilles (London, 1952), p. 74.

32 Herman W. Liebert, "Reflections on Samuel Johnson," *JEGP,* XLVII (Jan., 1948), 80–88.
33 Boswell, IV, 280–81.
34 Boswell, III, 271.
35 Hawkins, p. 601, note.

VII. *The Fear of God and the Love of God*

1   Boswell, III, 178.
2   *Letters,* III, 241.
3   Boswell, III, 498.
4   Boswell, III, 153.
5   William Agutter, *On the Difference between the Deaths of the Righteous and the Wicked, Illustrated in the Instance of Dr. Samuel Johnson and David Hume, Esq.* (London, 1800).
6   Boswell, I, 75; II, 79; III, 394.
7   *Private Papers of James Boswell from Malahide Castle,* ed. Geoffrey Scott and F. A. Pottle (18 vols.; Mount Vernon, N.Y., 1928–34), XVIII, 117.
8   *Ibid.,* XVI, 199–200; XIV, 201.
9   Boswell, II, 126; IV, 329.
10 John Taylor, *A Letter to Samuel Johnson, LL.D. On the Subject of a Future State* (London, 1787).
11 R. W. Chapman, "Dr. Johnson and Dr. Taylor," *Review of English Studies,* II (July, 1926), 338–39. Jean Hagstrum shows that Taylor employed many phrases that appear in various sermons by Johnson; since these were not published until after Taylor's death, the clergyman must have plagiarized from the manuscript sermons in his possession. "The Sermons of Samuel Johnson," *MP,* XL (Feb., 1943), 258.
12 Anna Seward, who disliked Johnson, attacked his religious character after his death in a series of letters contributed to the *Gentleman's Magazine* under the signature *Benvolio.* See Maurice J. Quinlan, "The Reaction to Dr. Johnson's *Prayers and Mediations,*" *JEGP,* LII (April, 1953), 125–39.
13 *Miscellanies,* I, 439.
14 *The Plays of William Shakespeare,* ed. Samuel Johnson and George Steevens (10 vols.; London, 1778), II, 82–83. See also Elizabeth Pope, "Shakespeare on Hell," *Shakespeare Quarterly,* I (1950), 162–64, and T. W. Baldwin, "Commentary on Dr. Pope's 'Shakespeare on Hell,' " *ibid.,* 296.
15 *Boswell's Journal of a Tour to the Hebrides,* ed. Frederick A.

Pottle and Charles H. Bennett (New York, 1936), p. 155.
16 Boswell, III, 295–96.
17 Boswell, III, 153.
18 Ernest C. Mossner, *The Life of David Hume* (Austin, Texas, 1954), p. 287.
19 Preface, *Androcles and the Lion.*
20 Johnson's fear of death is treated with understanding in two articles particularly: Jean H. Hagstrum, "On Dr. Johnson's Fear of Death," *ELH*, XIV (Dec., 1947), 308–19; Philip Williams, "Samuel Johnson's Central Tension: Faith and the Fear of Death," *Tòhoku Gàkuin Daigaku Ronshū (Journal of Literary Studies*, North Japan College, Sendai), Nos. 33–34 (Sept., 1958), pp. 1–35.
21 William Law, *A Serious Call to a Devout and Holy Life* (London, 1898), p. 151.
22 For a discussion of the relation of Johnson's reading to the selections in the *Dictionary*, see W. K. Wimsatt, *Philosophic Words* (New Haven, 1949), Chapter 2.
23 Boswell, III, 339.
24 *Diaries*, pp. 64, 76, 227, 265.
25 *Works*, VII, 213–14.
26 William Law, *A Practical Treatise Upon Christian Perfection* (Portsmouth, N.H., 1822), pp. 186 ff. Cf. Thomas Aquinas, *The Summa Contra Gentiles*, Bk. IV, Ch. xxi. Although Johnson seldom, if ever, quotes St. Thomas, he owned his works (*Sale Catalogue*).
27 *Diaries*, pp. 138, 228.
28 *Diaries*, p. 300.
29 *Serious Call*, pp. 242–48.
30 *Diaries*, pp. 302, 418.
31 It is not easy to select a few books from the many on mysticism, but the reader may find the following particularly worthy of attention. For a brief and clear exposition, with extracts from medieval mystics, Dom Cuthbert Butler, *Western Mysticism* (London, 1960); for a survey with an extensive bibliography appended, Evelyn Underhill, *Mysticism* (London, 1960); for comparisons of Eastern and Western mysticism by a distinguished author, Aldous Huxley, *The Perennial Philosophy* (New York, 1945); for a sympathetic treatment of the subject by a scientist, Raynor C. Johnson, *The Watcher on the Hills* (New York, 1959).
32 *Works*, VI, 287.

33 *Diaries,* pp. 258–60.
34 *The Convict's Address to His Unhappy Brethren* (2d ed.; London, 1777), p. 13.

VIII. *Johnson as a Church of England Man*

1 Boswell, I, 405.
2 *Boswell's London Journal,* ed. Frederick A. Pottle (New York, 1950), p. 283.
3 Boswell, II, 150–51.
4 Boswell, II, 104.
5 Boswell, II, 40, 254.
6 *Of the Laws of Ecclesiastical Polity,* Bk. V, Ch. xxii, in *Works of Richard Hooker,* ed. John Keble (3 vols.; Oxford, 1845).
7 Boswell, IV, 293.
8 L. S. Thornton, *Richard Hooker* (London, 1924), p. 100.
9 *Ecclesiastical Polity,* Bk. III, Ch. i, Sec. 2.
10 *Ibid.,* Bk. I, Chs. ii and iii; Thornton, *Richard Hooker,* pp. 26 ff.
11 The rumor of Johnson's coming under Evangelical influence will be discussed in the final chapter.
12 Boswell, II, 458.
13 Quoted by R. Newton Flew, *The Idea of Perfection in Christian Theology* (Oxford, 1934), p. 312.
14 *Works,* IX, 61.
15 *Letters of Anna Seward* (6 vols.; Edinburgh, 1811), I, 392.
16 *Works,* VI, 420.
17 Robert Anderson, *The Life of Samuel Johnson* (London, 1795), pp. 29–30.
18 *Ibid.,* pp. 267–77.
19 Boswell, V, 21.
20 *GM,* LXVIII (July, 1798), 630.
21 *Boswell's Journal of a Tour to the Hebrides,* ed. Frederick A. Pottle and Charles H. Bennett (New York, 1936), p. 41.
22 *Diaries,* p. 231; *The French Journals of Mrs. Thrale and Dr. Johnson,* ed. Moses Tyson and Henry Guppy (Manchester, 1932), p. 148.
23 Sermon III.
24 James M. Osborn, "Johnson and the Contrary Converts," *New Light on Dr. Johnson,* ed. F. W. Hilles (New Haven, 1959).
25 Boswell, II, 105; IV, 289.

26 *Miscellanies,* II, 176.
27 Joseph Mawby, "Anecdotes of Hesiod Cooke," *GM,* LXI (Supplement, 1791), 1184.
28 Boswell, I, 476.
29 *Works,* VII, 405.
30 *Works,* V, 438.
31 Boswell, IV, 289.
32 Boswell, III, 407.
33 Boswell, II, 104–5.
34 Maurice J. Quinlan, "The Reaction to Dr. Johnson's *Prayers and Meditations," JEGP,* LII (April, 1953), 125–39.
35 Andrew G. Hoover, "Boswell's First London Visit," *Virginia Quarterly,* XXIX (Spring, 1953), 242–56.
36 Boswell, II, 105–6; IV, 289.
37 Boswell, IV, 329. The term "doctrines above reason" was used in the seventeenth century by Hooker, Robert Boyle, Thomas Browne, and other writers.
38 Boswell, II, 104–5.
39 Archibald Campbell, *The Doctrine of the Middle State* (London, 1721), Preface.
40 Boswell, V, 356; *Diaries,* pp. 289, 304. According to Hawkins (p. 543), Johnson got his idea of the middle state from the Nonjuror Thomas Brett; but Brett repudiates the Catholic idea of purgatory. See *Tradition Necessary to Explain and Interpret Holy Scriptures* (London, 1718), p. 69.
41 *French Journals,* p. 156.
42 Boswell, V, 71, 88.
43 C. W. Dugmore, *Eucharistic Doctrine in England from Hooker to Waterland* (London, 1942), pp. 145 ff.; *Doctrine in the Church of England: The Report of the Commission on Christian Doctrine Appointed by the Archbishops of Canterbury and York in 1922* (London, 1957), pp. 159–82.
44 Boswell, I, 444.
45 Boswell, III, 299. Mrs. Knowles later objected to Boswell's report of this conversation. Her own account, supplied by an anonymous writer, appears in the *Gentleman's Magazine* for June, 1791 (LXI, 500–502), and was reprinted as a separate publication entitled *Dialogue Between Mrs. Knowles and Dr. Johnson* (London, 1805). In this version Mrs. Knowles succeeds in outarguing Johnson. Boswell alludes to this disagree-

ment in his *Life* (III, 299, n. 2), where he asserts he could neither recollect nor find in his own records any part of the exchange that Mrs. Knowles protested had taken place between herself and Johnson. Both Boswell's *Journal* and his manuscript copy of the *Life of Johnson* are now at Yale, and through the courtesy of the editors of the Boswell Papers I have been able to check the pertinent portions of these manuscripts. They show that Boswell's printed account of what took place on the evening of April 15, 1778, closely corresponds with his preliminary records. Because the *Journal* for this date contains a highly detailed report of the conversations, Boswell was able to transfer his notes to the *Life* without making substantial changes. There is no evidence that he altered or omitted anything of significance that appeared in his original manuscript of the discussion that took place between Mrs. Knowles and Johnson.

46 Sermon XVI.

IX. *End of the Journey*

1 *Letters,* III, 15, 18, 61.
2 *Letters,* III, 34.
3 Hawkins, p. 564; Boswell, IV, 271–72; *Diaries,* p. 368. For two interpretations in which Johnson's temporary recovery from the dropsy is seen as marking a turning point in his religious life, see: Chester F. Chapin, "Samuel Johnson's 'Wonderful' Experience," and Donald J. Greene, "Dr. Johnson's 'Late Conversion': A Reconsideration," both in *Johnsonian Studies,* ed. Magdi Wahba (Cairo, 1962).
4 *Miscellanies,* II, 156.
5 *Diaries,* pp. 417–18.
6 Boswell, III, 295.
7 Evelyn Underhill, *Mysticism* (London, 1960), p. 179.
8 William James, *The Varieties of Religious Experience* (New York, 1960), p. 184 and *passim.* Wesley himself was disturbed by the claims some of his followers made to achieving Christian perfection. Though he preached this doctrine, he never professed to having personally attained perfection. See L. Tyerman, *The Life and Times of the Reverend John Wesley* (3 vols.; London, 1870), I, 462–63.
9 Ronald Knox, *Enthusiasm* (Oxford, 1957), p. 586 and *passim.*
10 *Of the Laws of Ecclesiastical Polity,* Bk. III, Ch. viii, in

Works of Richard Hooker, ed. John Keble (3 vols.; Oxford, 1845).
11 *Cf. Ecclesiastical Polity,* Bk. III, Ch. viii, Sec. 3.
12 Boswell, II, 126.
13 *Works,* VI, 417.
14 Maurice J. Quinlan, "The Rumor of Dr. Johnson's Conversion," *Review of Religion,* XII (March, 1948), 243–61. For a disagreement with my contentions, see Greene, "Dr. Johnson's 'Late Conversion': A Reconsideration," *Johnsonian Studies.* Greene, who fails to distinguish among different kinds of conversions, sees Johnson's "conversion" as identical with that the Evangelicals preached. He goes further than they, however, in pinpointing Johnson's conversion, or the beginning of it, as happening on February 20, 1784, the day he received temporary relief from the dropsy. In this connection Green infers much from the fact that Johnson had several weeks earlier ordered from a bookseller Richard Baxter's *Call to the Unconverted.* Johnson had frequently before this time praised Baxter's *Works.* But Baxter, though a Puritan, combined various Christian views. According to a writer for Hastings' *Encyclopedia of Religion and Ethics* (II, 440), "He lays the greatest stress on the necessity of repentance for justification, and, indeed, seems to aim at combining Roman and Reformed doctrines."
15 It would be interesting to know just what Latrobe may have told Newton, for, characteristic of the emphasis many Evangelicals placed on illumination, Latrobe expressed doubt that Wesley was ever genuinely converted. Ronald Knox, *Enthusiasm,* p. 436.
16 *Quarterly Review,* LII (Nov., 1834), p. 431.
17 "Narrative by John Hoole," *Miscellanies,* II, 149. In the will itself, as reproduced by Boswell (IV, 402, n. 2), the sentence reads: "I bequeath to God, a soul polluted with many sins, but I hope purified by Jesus Christ."
18 *Miscellanies,* II, 387.
19 James Fordyce, "On the Death of Samuel Johnson," *Addresses to the Deity* (Boston, 1813), p. 187.
20 Clarke, "Of the Faith of Abraham," *Sermons* (3d ed.; 10 vols.; London, 1732).
21 Thomas Wilson, "The Mistakes of Christians Concerning Repentance," *Sermons* (4 vols.; Bath, 1796), III, 200–202.

22 Boswell, III, 295.
23 Wilson, "The Mistakes of Christians Concerning Repentance," *Sermons,* III, 295.
24 Henry Hammond, *A Practical Catechism* (London, 1655), pp. 56 ff.
25 *Ibid.,* pp. 42, 78–82.
26 *Cf. ibid.,* p. 44.
27 Greene, "Dr. Johnson's 'Late Conversion': A Reconsideration," *Johnsonian Studies,* pp. 74–75. While this author quotes from Hammond, he neglects to note that Hammond was opposed to the doctrine of justification by faith alone and fails to see that Hammond's belief in conversion through repentance differed from the Evangelical type.
28 William Law, *A Serious Call to a Devout and Holy Life,* ed. J. H. Overton (London, 1898), p. 274. As J. H. Overton, the editor of this work, points out, at the time he wrote *A Serious Call,* Law's emphasis on the importance of reason to religion would have been disapproved by the Evangelical school. See p. 203, n. 1.
29 *Miscellanies,* II, 336.
30 *Letters,* III, 152.
31 *Letters,* III, 214, 233.
32 "Advertisement," *Works of Samuel Johnson* (11 vols.; London, 1787), I, ix.
33 J. Henry, *Translations of the First Satire of Juvenal and Johnson's Latin Poems* (Belfast, 1869), p. 14.
34 Boswell, IV, 21, n. 3.
35 The Latin originals of this and the following translations are printed in *Poems,* p. 207 (V and VII), and p. 208.
36 I shall not specifically document information taken from the account of Johnson's death in Boswell, IV, 394–421.
37 *Miscellanies,* II, 151–52.
38 *Papers Written by Dr. Johnson and Dr. Dodd in 1777,* ed. R. W. Chapman (Oxford, 1926), pp. 14–15.
39 *Portraits By Sir Joshua Reynolds,* ed. Frederick W. Hilles (London, 1952), pp. 79–80.
40 Hawkins, p. 583.
41 *Miscellanies,* II, 156.
42 James Fordyce, "Devotional Reflections on the Death of the late Dr. Samuel Johnson," *Universal Magazine,* LXXVII (Sept., 1785), 147.

43 *Cf. Poems,* p. 232.
44 *Serious Call,* p. 151.
45 R. W. Ketton-Cremer, *The Early Life and Diaries of William Windham* (London, 1930), pp. 303–4.
46 *Miscellanies,* II, 155.
47 *GM,* LIV (Dec., 1784), 927.
48 British Museum, Add. MSS. 35, 127, f. 424. Arthur Young apparently did not take Hoole's advice until many years later. By 1806, when he did read Johnson's *Prayers and Meditations,* he had become an ardent Evangelical. His response seems rather typical. He writes: "His religion seems to have been against the very grain of his soul, and all the tendencies of his mind to have arisen from his understanding only. . . . 'Tis well his mind was morbid, for he seems to me (from this work) never to have been converted."—*Autobiography of Arthur Young,* ed. M. Betham-Edwards (London, 1898), pp. 421–22.
49 *Works,* VI, 290–91.

INDEX

Aberdeen, 51

Adams, Dr. William, Master of Pembroke College, 34

Agutter, Rev. William: sermon on death of SJ and Hume, 129

Allestree, Richard, 215 *n8*

Ambrose, Saint, 4

Amendment: emphasis on in Church of England, 66–69. *See also* Johnson: Beliefs, Characteristics

Anderson, Robert: accused SJ of Calvinistic leanings in his *Life of Johnson*, 162–63

Anselm, Saint, 4

Aquinas, Saint Thomas: his works owned by SJ, 4, 12; Hooker drew upon, 154–55; mentioned, 108–9

Ashbourne, 94, 126, 132, 182

Associates of Dr. Bray, 117–18

Aston, Henry Hervey: SJ wrote sermon for, 87

Athanasius, Saint, 4

Atonement (Christ's); teachings of Church of England, 46–47; as vicarious sacrifice, 47; as exemplary sacrifice, 47; Law favored exemplary interpretation, 47–49; Wesley objected to Law's view, 49; SJ's views, 50–59; SJ discussed with Boswell, 51–52, 54–55; Clarke's views on, 60–65. *See also* Johnson: Beliefs, Characteristics

Atterbury, Francis, Bishop of Rochester: 4, 109, 160

Attrition: in Roman Catholic Church, 70; SJ's view, 70–71

Augustine, Saint, 4, 12

Balderston, Katharine C.: influence of William Law on SJ's *Dictionary*, 5; SJ may have invited physical punishment, 76; mentioned, 91

Barber, Francis, 119, 120–21

Bath: charity school for which SJ may have written Sermon IV, 87

Baxter, Richard, 4, 158

Benedictines: SJ visited monastery, 164–65; wish to return to, 166

Benevolence: popularity of term, 102; economic reasons for, 103; related to philosophical optimism,

103–5; its broad impact, 104–5; contrasted with charity, 105, 108, 110

Bentham, Jeremy: view of SJ, ix–x

Blair, Dr. Hugh, 3, 143

Boerhaave, Hermann: SJ's biography of, 145, 205; death of, 146; religion of, 205-6

Boethius, *De Consolatione Philosophiae*, 4

Book of Common Prayer: prayer of general confession, 20–21; petition for forgiveness, 67–68; mentioned 46, 54, 58

Boothby, Brooke, Jr., 132

Boswell, James: as biographer, xiii, 123–24, 169, 227–28; on SJ's indebtedness to Law, 5, 13; visited dying Hume, 33–34; conversed with SJ on the Atonement, 51–52, 54–55, 59; interviewed Dr. Brocklesby, 64–65; emphasized SJ's fear of death, 127–28; his own preoccupation with death, 128–30; curiosity about Evangelicals, 128–29; conversion to Roman Catholicism, 169; mentioned or quoted, xi, 3, 34, 37, 56, 60, 86, 106, 116, 120, 121, 123, 127, 131, 134, 143, 150, 157, 159, 163, 164, 166, 167, 171, 173, 183, 199

Boyle, Robert: Clarke delivered Boyle Lectures, 28; SJ quoted in *Dictionary*, 35

Bristol, 117

British Lying-In Hospital, 118

Brocklesby, Dr. Richard: SJ urged him to read Clarke on propitiatory sacrifice, 27, 65, 190, 192; on SJ's death, 64–65; mentioned, 126, 132, 133, 182, 200

Browne, Sir Thomas: SJ edited his *Christian Morals,* 91; on self-delusion, 91; SJ defended his Christianity, 151; mentioned, 126

Burnet, Gilbert, Bishop of Salisbury: favored views of Protestant Reformers on repentance, 69; opposed Roman Catholic belief in attrition, 70; mentioned, 81

Burney, Fanny, 126

233